THE
PLOT TO KILL
THE POPE

THE
PLOT TO KILL
THE POPE

Paul B. Henze

Charles Scribner's Sons • New York

Copyright © 1983 Paul Henze

Library of Congress Cataloging in Publication Data

Henze, Paul B., 1924–
   The plot to kill the Pope.

   Includes bibliographical references and index.
   1. John Paul II, Pope, 1920–   —Assassination
attempt, 1981.   I. Title
BX1378.5.H46   1983   364.1'524'0945634   83-20018
ISBN 0-684-18060-X

1 3 5 7 9 11 13 15 17 19   F/C   20 18 16 14 12 10 8 6 4 2

Printed in the United States of America.

CONTENTS

ACKNOWLEDGEMENTS

Many individuals and organizations gave me help in the investigations and research which made this book possible. I am grateful to the *Reader's Digest* for setting me to work on the subject in 1981, to NBC for the opportunity to serve as consultant in preparation of the White Paper originally produced in September 1982, to the *Christian Science Monitor* for requesting a series of articles in the winter of 1982/3 and to several other broadcasting organizations, newspapers and magazines for stimulating interviews, discussions and consultation. Participation in conferences and seminars of the European American Institute for Security Research, the Turkish Political and Social Studies Foundation, the Turati Foundation in Rome, the Rand Corporation, the Baltic American Freedom League and the European Conference on Human Rights and Self-Determination helped me to advance my analysis. Talks—followed by lively question periods—at the State Department's Open Forum, at the Washington Institute of Foreign Affairs and at the Kennan Institute of Advanced Russian Studies were valuable exercises in preparation for writing this book. I thank all the people involved in arranging these occasions.

I am indebted to the Turkish government for many kinds of help in the course of several visits to that country, to the Italian authorities as well, and to American and local officers of the US Information Agency for facilitating my researches in Turkey and Italy by arranging meetings and setting up discussion sessions with journalists and professors. The Voice of America has given me several opportunities to discuss the progress of my research in programs aired in many languages.

References in the notes demonstrate how important the high quality research reports of Radio Free Europe/Radio Liberty have been as sources of data on topics as varied as internal tensions in the Italian Communist Party and persistence of religion in the Ukraine. The Staff of *Milliyet* in Istanbul has provided much useful information both from files and personal recollections. Dozens of individuals on both sides of the Atlantic provided ideas, facts, background information, encouragement, constructive criticism and assistance of other kinds. I should like to single out a few of them for special thanks: Alex Alexiev, Zbigniew Brzezinski, Leyla Çambel, Şükrü Elekdag, Mükerrem Hiç, Donald Jameson, Leopold Labedz, Jan Nowak, Anthony Potter, Kenneth Tomlinson, Kaya Toperi, Albert Wohlstetter and Aydin and Nilüfer Yalçin.

The steady and cheerful help of several members of my family was also essential to completion of this book. My wife Martha, my son John, my daughter Mary and my son-in-law Roger Pierson performed indispensable services as critics of substance and style and as 'word processors' in preparing the final text.

Moscow and Sofia will undoubtedly label this book a CIA-slander against communism. The CIA had nothing to do with it. Neither did the State Department. No agency of the US government counseled either for or against my writing it and no US or any other government's officials bear responsibility for any judgements or hypotheses expressed in it. No individual or organization subsidized it. I have not sought or used classified information.

Portions of Chapter 2 appeared in an article in *Encounter* in May 1983. An adaptation of Chapter 6 is scheduled for appearance in the *Wilson Quarterly*. Most of Chapter 9 will appear in the *Washington Quarterly* in September 1983. I am grateful to these publications for their interest in the subject.

Paul B. Henze
Washington, DC July 1983

INTRODUCTION—FACING REALITY

The plot against the Polish Pope, John Paul II, was not a casual intrigue undertaken for the amusement of the plotters. It was not the work of smugglers creating a diversion or criminals looking for notoriety. Mehmet Ali Agca, who came within inches of killing the Pontiff on 13 May 1981, was not a crank or a demented loner. Demented loners can become assassins, as the attack on President Reagan by John W. Hinckley on 30 March 1981 demonstrates. But Agca was no Hinckley. He was not mentally deranged. If he had been, he would not have been selected for the key role in this most serious international conspiracy. He was no loner either, though he was told to claim he was and he occasionally appeared to be. It nevertheless became apparent early in his interrogation in Rome that he was carrying out a *plot* to kill the Pope. That is beyond debate. Even the Russians admit it and did from the start. But they maintain that the American government was behind it.

Conspiracy requires motives. Agca is a Turk but there are no credible Turkish grounds for killing a Polish Pope. Moscow's frantic efforts to put the blame on the CIA began almost as soon as the shooting had taken place, well before substantial suspicion began to be directed towards the Kremlin. They have continued ever since. Shrill Russian denials, slander against Italian judges, allegations of US government complicity and a steady flow of disinformation from Eastern Europe all heighten the impression of Soviet guilt. So do the abusive attacks on the Pope which appeared in the Soviet provincial press long before the shooting took place in Rome. The Soviet Union stands alone among concerned governments in never having encouraged any objective investigation or independent assessment of the plot.

John Paul II is an anathema to the old men who rule from the Kremlin. There are three interlocking reasons for their fear of him: (1) he is a Pole; (2) he is head of the Roman Catholic Church; and (3) he is a tireless advocate of freedom of the human spirit and the right of the individual human being to choose his course in life. This is a poisonous combination for the Soviet rulers. The problem is not only that it undermines their control over Poland. Ultimately it threatens their power over their own people. Stalin's crude jibe about the 'Pope's divisions' has come back to haunt his successors.

It will be years, perhaps decades, before we have a *full* picture of how this plot was developed and put into motion, but we have already learned much more than I thought likely when I started on the investigations reported in this book. When the *Reader's Digest* asked me to make an initial assessment of the case in May 1981, it was clear that Agca was not what his sponsors wanted him to appear to be. I did not expect so many loose ends to have been left to be exposed. I did hope that Agca would decide to talk. When he did, the importance of a direct Bulgarian connection in Italy was revealed. Sergei Antonov, the Bulgarian airline representative arrested in Rome on 25 November 1982, may nevertheless turn out to be a less central figure in the case than has been assumed. There is no reason to think that he had much to do with the conception of the plot or the early phase of Agca's travels. He was in all likelihood following orders from higher authority when he began dealing directly with Agca in the winter of 1980/1. He may not even have been the top man in the team that dealt with Agca in Rome. Their job was to see that this high-priority scheme stayed on track and achieved its purpose.

I do not pretend in this book to give all the answers about the plot. New facts are bound to be discovered. Much more is already known from interrogations and investigations in Italy than has been publicly revealed. Agca undoubtedly has more to tell us—but he may well have been kept in the dark by his sponsors or they may have deceived him—so there are likely to be unusual twists and turns. New defectors may shed light on the background of the plot. A knowledgeable Russian defector is almost certain to turn up one of these days. There may be more Bulgarian defectors. We may find that Russians or Bulgarians were dealing with Agca in Turkey in 1979 when he committed his first major assassination of a Turkish newspaper editor. A reinvestigation of Agca which is now under way in his own country is also going to produce new information. We cannot even be sure that Agca was the only man chosen to try to kill the Pope. Perhaps there were other Agcas held in reserve. What we do not know about this plot could justify *not* writing a book at the present time.

I decided to do so nevertheless because a great deal is now known and it is a good idea to bring it together and provide a framework within which further developments can be understood. The purpose of this book is to sum up all the main facts, circumstantial and inferential evidence and relevant background and then to pinpoint the main questions on which we need more information, as investigation and research continue.

THE
PLOT TO KILL
THE POPE

SECTION ONE
The Crime and Its Aftermath

I have divided the book into three sections. A simple chronological approach becomes hopelessly complex as the story unfolds. One cannot get into it very far before it becomes apparent that the plot to kill the Polish Pope was braided together from many strands. Few people involved in it knew them all. Some were not what they seemed to be. As investigation has continued, there has been distortion, misinformation and misunderstanding as well as enlightenment. So even to begin to reconstruct what seems to have happened a great deal of background is needed. This case is unusual also because the trial and conviction of the would-be assassin served only as the first step in the process of exposing the plot. Pursuit of the plot has continued for more than two years, but the end is not yet in sight.

The first section of the book, which follows, recounts what happened in the wake of the attack in St Peter's Square on 13 May 1981: Mehmet Ali Agca's interrogation and trial; and reactions, both Western and Eastern European, to his crime. This section also reports my trip to Agca's home town in south-eastern Turkey, Malatya, to interview his family and search for traces of his life as he was growing up.

In Section Two, I give some of the international background that is needed for an understanding of the political and historical context of the plot. Finally, in Section Three, I examine the evolution of the assassin and of the plot in the light of all we have learned to date. After analyzing Eastern European, and some Western reaction to all this, I conclude by discussing what we still have to learn and how the story is likely to unfold further.

1
THE SHOOTING AND THE TRIAL

Shots in St Peter's Square

It was a sunny afternoon in late spring. The rich golds, tans and earthy reds of Rome's buildings reflected the warm light, the fountains of the Eternal City sparkled. The vast expanse of St Peter's Square, with the immense dome of the Popes' church rising above it, was thronged with pilgrims, spectators and tourists from all over the world. John Paul II, the Polish Pope, the first Slav to occupy the Throne of St Peter, was making one of his famous public appearances—smiling, waving, blessing the multitude that had assembled to greet him.

Well into his third year as Pope, this energetic man, born Karol Wojtyla in Wadowice, Poland, on 18 May 1920, had already established himself as the most dynamic, most traveled, most assertive leader of the Roman Catholic Church in modern times. Standing in his white robe in a slow moving white jeep and communicating with the crowd in several languages in a relaxed manner, John Paul II seemed completely at ease, confident of the love, respect and admiration of the crowd. He was obviously enjoying himself. These Wednesday afternoon appearances, always photographed and seen by millions of TV viewers, had become an integral feature of the Polish Pope's exercise of his ministry. He said he drew strength from the people who assembled on these occasions. Among them were busloads of pilgrims from his native Poland: workers, priests, nuns, schoolgirls.

In a violent age like ours, there had of course been worry about the Pope standing with little protection in an open vehicle. Journalists had written of the danger from fanatics or cranks. Churchmen had expressed their apprehensions, statesmen their fears. Occasionally there was allusion to the fact that the Kremlin found the Polish Pope an awkward problem. But the appearances in the square had gone on unchanged. John Paul II said he trusted in God. There had been nothing known publicly in advance to make this particular day in Rome, 13 May 1981, different from any other.

3

Then the joy of a perfect May afternoon was broken by shots. The Pope slumped, grimacing. Attendants rushed to support him. People screamed and shouted. Within half a minute sounds of jubilation changed to the noise of panic and confusion. A mass of bystanders surged in around the jeep. The man who had fired the shots was swept up in this mass movement. He tried to run. People helped two plainclothesmen catch and handcuff him. Those with cameras photographed frenziedly. In some of their pictures other men dashing away were captured on film, mostly as blurs. Soon a way was opened for the jeep to speed away to find first aid for the bleeding Pope. Two tourists had also been wounded by stray shots and were helped away. Terror had struck in one of the world's holiest places . . .

The Rush to Judgment

Within minutes reporters began to flash the ghastly news to all corners of a shocked world. Though in the excitement the would-be assassin was first described as an Armenian, it soon became clear that he was a Turk. He was Mehmet Ali Agca, a fugitive from justice in his own country where he had been sentenced to death for killing Abdi Ipekçi, the widely respected editor of the Istanbul daily newspaper *Milliyet*, on 1 February 1979. Caught nearly five months later, interrogated and put on trial, he had escaped from one of Turkey's highest security prisons the night of 23 November 1979. For eighteen months he had been the subject of Interpol alerts. Turkish security authorities had searched for him at home and abroad, throughout Europe and the Middle East. Now he had turned up in Rome, trying to kill the Polish Pope. Why? Was he a loner? If not, who was behind him?

Newspapers searched their files and press bureaus made priority queries to Istanbul and Ankara. An extraordinary episode was soon recalled. Agca's escape from Kartal-Maltepe prison near Istanbul had occurred less than four days before John Paul II's long-scheduled arrival on 27 November 1979 on his historic visit to Turkey. The day after his escape, Agca had called the offices of *Milliyet* to advise the newspaper of a letter he said he had deposited in a mailbox across the street. It was found exactly where he said it would be. Published immediately, it declared:

Western imperialists, who fear that Turkey may establish a new Political, Military and Economic Force in the Middle East with brotherly Islamic countries, have rushed at a sensitive time to send Crusader Commander John Paul to Turkey under the mask of a religious leader. If this ill-timed and pointless visit is not cancelled, I will definitely shoot the pope. This is the only reason I escaped from prison. Besides, US and *Israeli* responsibility for the repression in Mecca should be raised. Otherwise please don't exaggerate my quiet, bloodless and simple escape.

Here now in Rome was the same terrorist carrying out the grim threat he had made a year and a half before!

Turks had been embarrassed by Agca's escape and the threatening letter, but the only practical effect of it at the time was to cause the government to tighten already elaborate security arrangements for the papal visit. It went off without incident. There was widespread appreciation in Turkey, in fact, of the Pope's visit as a brave and friendly act at a time when the country was being torn by a mounting wave of irrational terrorism. But this tended to be forgotten in the initial journalistic rush to judgment in May 1981.

Agca's political background had never been clarified during the five months he was under interrogation for the Ipekçi murder in Turkey in the summer and fall of 1979. Turkish leftists had claimed he was a rightist, a 'Gray Wolf' follower of Alparslan Türkeş's National Action Party. All rightists, including Türkeş, condemned the Ipekçi murder and disclaimed responsibility or sympathy for Agca. Agca himself maintained he belonged to no political party or grouping. He insisted he was acting on his own as a terrorist serving some abstract higher cause. There was a good deal of circumstantial evidence of organizational support but its source remained obscure. After his escape, given the political confusion that existed in Turkey then, clarification of the case was not a high priority.

So in the wake of the shooting in St Peter's Square it is not surprising that most Western commentators saw the case in simple terms; a Turkish 'Gray Wolf', no doubt a fanatical Muslim, had threatened the Pope when he came to Istanbul in 1979; now he had carried out his threat. Georgie Ann Geyer, a reporter with a good deal of experience in the Middle East, jumped immediately to this conclusion:

Agca is a cold-eyed fanatic—a Turkish ultra-nationalist and religious zealot who hates the West and Christianity and sought the most effective way to attack them. (*Washington Star*, 15 May 1981)

Joe Kraft pontificated on a grander scale a few days later:

> At the root of this terrorist attempt against the Pope is a turbulent Islamic society, pregnant with nasty surprises. The lesson is that those who look to the Moslem world as a sure supplier of oil or a steady ally against Moscow do so at their peril. (*Washington Post*, 19 May 1981)

As he was taken to police headquarters for interrogation, Agca shouted in broken English to reporters that he was sorry he had wounded two tourists but not sorry he had shot the Pope. He claimed the Pope was 'leader of a Crusade against my religion' and declared, 'I hold him responsible for the reaction of the West toward Islam.' But his Islamic fervor quickly waned. During the 75 hours of initial interrogation to which he was subjected, he claimed no religious motive for his action. He showed no signs of religious devotion. Religion had never been claimed or alleged as a factor in the Ipekçi murder. But it was a period when, in the wake of Khomeini's coming to power in Iran, Europeans and Americans were preoccupied with Muslim fanaticism. It was seen as a mysterious force, unfathomable to the Western mind, capable of monstrous evil.

Nevertheless, those familiar with Turkey found an Islamic explanation of the attack on the Pope incongruous. They knew that the right side of the Turkish political spectrum had been sharply divided between a religious-oriented party and a nationalist party which glorified the pre-Islamic, Central Asian past of the Turks. A left-leaning Turkish Cypriot journalist pointed this out the day after Agca's attack:

> Despite the religious references in the alleged threatening letter from Agca, his identification with the ultra-rightist party does not suggest that he is connected with the religious fundamentalists in Turkey. (Metin Munir in the *Washington Post*, 14 May 1981)

Agca, as had proven to be the case when he was first arrested in Turkey for the murder of Abdi Ipekçi, was not going to be easy to categorize or to explain. Or easy to interrogate. He began talking in Rome soon after he was taken into custody. He seemed to enjoy the process. He readily confessed to the shooting. What he said then about his motivation he summed up in a few dramatic sentences during his trial two months earlier:

I acted alone. I did not want to talk to anyone about my plan to kill the Pope. I acted independently, in the name of truth above ideologies. I do not belong to any organization. International terrorism as I conceive it is not concerned with ideology. It needs no idea. It needs a gun.

It was a good line, calculated to appeal to apologists of violence and rationalizers of terrorism who had been vocal in the 1970s. But these were already a declining breed by the beginning of the 1980s. Agca might still have appeared credible if it had not been for much of the rest of what he had to say. His own allegations and 'admissions' undermined his claim to be a non-ideological loner and raised suspicions of sponsorship. As for the press—if he was not religious, perhaps he was simply a reactionary, a fascist. The *New York Times* headlined a full-page story to which ten of its reporters contributed 'Trail of Mehmet Ali Agca: 6 Years of Neo-Fascist Ties' (25 May 1981).

Agca meanwhile regaled his Italian interrogators with stories of other assassinations he had allegedly planned. He had supposedly gone to England to shoot the king but abandoned the scheme when he discovered that the king was a queen because 'We Turks don't shoot women' . . . Things like this made no sense. There was no evidence he had been in England. Agca did not seem to have his heart in his tales. He was too rational, too proud to be able to make himself appear deranged. For a while it seemed that he was inclined to say the least about the countries where he had spent the most time on the run: Germany, Austria, Switzerland, Italy. But he was not consistent, for he admitted very early spending time in Bulgaria, staying at the Hotel Vitosha, receiving the passport there in the name of Faruk Özgün which he carried when he was arrested in Rome. A Turk who worked in Munich, Ömer Mersan, had delivered it to him, he said. During the first 24 hours after his arrest he also claimed ties to George Habbash's Popular Front for the Liberation of Palestine and mentioned training with Palestinians in Lebanon.

As soon as this information got out, alarm signals went up. Palestinian apologist Reverend Hilarion Capucci went to the Gemelli Hospital in Rome, where the Pope was in intensive care, and held a press conference on 15 May to tell reporters that Agca was lying when he claimed sponsorship by a Palestinian organization:

What he did had nothing to do with Islam. This Turk is a criminal of the far right.

How could the Reverend Capucci be so sure? He offered no explanation and reporters did not press him. But Palestinian desire to put distance between the PLO and Agca was understandable. Only two months before, on 13 March 1981, Yasser Arafat's right-hand man, 'foreign minister' Farouk Khaddoumi, had been received by the Papal Secretary of State, Cardinal Casaroli. The Vatican has never recognized Israel and has consistently adhered to the position that Jerusalem should be an international city. Thus the PLO, as such, would have no motive for abetting the assassination of the Pope. But the fact that Turkish terrorists had for years been trained by Palestinians was well known. Why not Agca too? Evidence had come to light in his interrogation in Turkey in 1979, but the Turkish government of that time did not pursue the issue.

Looking back on all of this two years later, we can see several conflicting strains of cover-story imperfectly braided together right here at the beginning. Agca's sponsors must have drilled him first in one version, then in another, as plans for him changed direction. He may have been under instruction to appear mentally unbalanced, but the charade did not work. Nothing Agca said about himself and no simple conclusions others reached about him during this early phase of the case fitted together in a coherent pattern.

A Rightist?

Most Western reporters were ready to classify Agca as a rightist, with or without religious motivation. In Turkey, where the shooting in Rome generated an enormous burst of attention in the press, Agca was not credible as a religious fundamentalist, but there was a strong tendency to see him as an ultra-nationalist. Thus much of the reporting out of Turkey during the first days following the shooting in Rome bolstered the Western tendency to classify Agca as a fascist. The explanation was tenable, however, only on a superficial level. It kept breaking down in the face of detail. There was the note, for example, which Agca had left behind in his room in the Pensione Isa the afternoon he set out for St Peter's Square. This note must have been intended to be found and read after the deed had been successfully accomplished. In it Agca claimed he had attacked the Pope for the sake of freedom in Afghanistan and El Salvador! It was hard to square this note with a rightist or fascist view of the world. Or with Agca's tales of other planned assassinations. Whose freedom in Afghanistan and El Salvador?

Though Afghanistan had not been a major concern of Pope John Paul II, he was identified with real freedom there. There was a good deal of evidence that Afghans and Poles, both resisting Soviet coercion in different ways, were sympathetic to each other's struggles. In the summer of 1980 I had asked a prominent Polish writer visiting the West whether people in Poland were interested in Afghanistan. He replied:

> You would be astonished how many Catholic Poles are praying in church every day for the success of the Muslim freedom fighters in Afghanistan!

It was illogical for a Turk to see freedom in Afghanistan in terms of Russian domination—unless he were an extreme leftist or Soviet agent. Turkey and Afghanistan have a long record of mutual friend-ship. Many Afghan officers were trained in Turkish military academies and Afghan students came to Turkish universities. Prac-tically all Turks, whatever their political or religious affiliation, were alarmed by the Soviet invasion of Afghanistan. Agca's statement was especially illogical for a Turk who was alleged to be a rightist.

Agca's reference to El Salvador had an even more peculiar ring. It was as far from Turkish concerns as any issue in today's world. Rightist opinion in Turkey was oblivious to El Salvador and leftists had other axes to grind. The notion of an allegedly fanatic Muslim Turk killing the Pope to advance the freedom of El Salvador was ludicrous.

How then was Agca to be explained? Shooting the Pope to advance freedom in Afghanistan and El Salvador made no sense. Some com-mentators still preferred to interpret Agca's statement, as well as the declarations he was making to his interrogators, as evidence of con-fusion in Agca's mind, if not genuine mental derangement. Arnold Hottinger of the *Neue Zürcher Zeitung*, deeply knowledgeable of the Arab world, analyzed the statement Agca left in his room in Rome as revealing 'strong anti-Western and "Islamic"-based feelings of hate' which predispose terrorists to accept propaganda allegations spread, among others, by Moscow as truths:

> These are propaganda myths which in Europe are usually regarded

as leftist rather than rightist. They are nevertheless characteristic
. . . of many half-educated people in the Near East and they are
found also among extreme rightist activists in Turkey. The real
force behind them is hatred of the West . . .Whether an activist
who holds these ideas moves to the 'fascists' of the extreme right or
to the extremists of the left depends mostly on his family situation
and his relationships with friends. (*Neue Zürcher Zeitung*, 17/18
May 1981)

An Eastern Connection?

Zdzislaw Rurarz, Poland's ambassador in Tokyo who defected when
the Polish military took over the country in December 1981, commented that all Poles had immediately assumed when Agca shot the
Pope that the Soviet Union was the ultimate instigator of the act. This
kind of conclusion comes easily to a people among whom the memory
of Soviet atrocities such as the Katyn Forest massacre is still alive.
Most Western journalists shied away from such uncomfortable speculation in the immediate wake of the Rome shooting, but the *Christian
Science Monitor* reported on 17 May that a story was circulating in
Rome that Agca had been acting on behalf of Qaddafy who, during
his late April visit to Moscow, had offered to help the Russians cope
with Poland by arranging to have the Pope assassinated so that he
could not carry out his vow to return to his homeland to support his
countrymen if Soviet armies invaded.

Qaddafy had ended his visit to Moscow two weeks before the attack
on the Pope with a joint communiqué in which Libya and the USSR
rejected 'attempts by imperialist circles to equate international terrorism with the liberation struggle of peoples'. The phraseology was
politically neutral—no distinction was made between right and left.
There was even a certain similarity to some of what Agca had said.
Agca told his Italian interrogators he had gone to Tunisia at the end of
November 1980. He claimed to have stayed for two weeks at a resort
hotel in Hamamet. Libya borders Tunisia on the east. Did he go into
Libya?

This question can still not be answered, but it is less important than
it seemed in May 1981. The information Agca kept providing about
his travels during the year before he shot the Pope soon fell into a
pattern that made it possible to sort fantasy from fact. Police in
several countries checked hotel records and journalists interviewed

hotel keepers and others who had contact with him. The notion that a scheme to kill John Paul II could have been concocted as late as the end of April 1981, with Qaddafy offering to do the Russians a favor in Moscow, evaporated in the face of evidence that the plot to shoot the Pope had much deeper roots. Agca had been supported by an efficient and extensive organizational structure from the time he escaped from prison in Turkey in November 1979. There could be no doubt of that.

During his travels around Europe he used every form of public transportation, never failed to pay hotel bills, seems never to have gone hungry, never asked for charity, never even pretended to be interested in a job. He had ready cash to pay in advance for a 'holiday' flight to Majorca. He made frequent international telephone calls. Employees of hotels where he stayed recalled the good quality of his clothes. There was no evidence that he had ever robbed for funds. There was also no evidence of bank accounts, safe-deposit boxes or official money transfers in any of the aliases he had used. A highly professional clandestine support organization would avoid all these.

The conclusion was inescapable: Agca was no loner. He had sponsors who valued him. Who could they be? Turkish rightists? Türkeş's National Action Party had been suspended in Turkey after the military leadership took control to stop terrorism on 12 September 1980. The same action was taken against Erbakan's National Salvation Party, the religious fundamentalists. Leaders of both these parties were jailed. Türkeş's party, however, retained an extensive organization abroad, primarily among Turkish workers in Germany. It was also influential in the Turkish Federation, an ostensibly non-political organization for co-ordinating cultural, welfare and religious activities among Turks in Germany. Many scraps of evidence linked Agca to Turkish rightists in Germany.

The Turkish government, anxious to recapture Agca, had received reports from its security agents of his appearance in various German cities during the fall and winter of 1980/1. The Turkish Embassy in Bonn had sent diplomatic notes to the German Foreign Ministry requesting priority investigation of many of these reports. German authorities did not give them high priority and Agca was always long gone by the time police arrived to check out places where he had reportedly been seen. A case could be made that Agca had been sheltered and prepared for action against the Pope inside a Gray Wolf network in Germany.

Musa Serdar Çelebi, a 28-year-old Istanbul University law graduate, who headed the Turkish Federation main office in Frankfurt, was interviewed by media organizations in the days immediately following the Rome shooting. He strongly condemned the attack, denied knowing Agca and, when asked to explain his possible motivation, characterized him as an 'international terrorist' operating outside conventional ideologies. As in the shooting of Abdi Ipekçi in Turkey in 1979, no Turkish rightist political figure claimed responsibility for Agca or professed sympathy for his act.

Journalists who continued to write about the case showed an increasing inclination to explore contradictions in Agca's background and behavior though others, such as Joe Harsch, rejected all suspicion of an Eastern European connection. He wrote in the *Christian Science Monitor* on 2 June 1981:

> There can be no serious suggestion that the deed was motivated from Moscow or the man trained by Moscow or its agents.

Hugh Sidey took a contrary view. In a syndicated column, 'Playing an Assassin like a Fish' (*Washington Star*, 14 June 1981), he postulated a KGB plot, having its origin in Kremlin frustration over the growing influence of the Pope in Poland and the rise of Solidarity. The plan to kill the Pope was developed, Sidey suggested, as a means of avoiding military invasion and the possibility that Polish military units would fight the Russians. A Turk who could be made to appear to be a rightist was ideal as an assassin. Under death sentence in his own country, he could be promised help in escaping or rescue:

> The KGB . . . of course, really planned to kill Agca if he escaped from St Peter's Square or when he got out of prison. However it worked out, Agca was far from the Kremlin, his convoluted trail forming an impenetrable skein, or as they say in the Department of Wet Affairs, disappearing like water into sand . . .

Sidey concluded his hypothetical reconstruction of the plot with some prescient words of caution:

> Anyone who fully believed this tale would be foolish. Anyone who claimed such a thing did not happen would be just as foolish.

East European Reactions

The first East European country to react to the shooting in St Peter's Square on 13 May 1981 was, not surprisingly, Poland. Warsaw TV interrupted its program at 6:25 to announce:

> At 17:21 hours in St Peter's Square Pope John Paul II was wounded by two pistol shots. The Holy Father has been taken to the Gemelli Clinic. He is in the intensive care unit. Vatican police have detained the assassin. It is stated that he does not speak Italian but his nationality has not yet been established. Throngs of Romans are hurrying to St Peter's Square, where prayers for the Holy Father are being said. The Italian President, Alessandro Pertini, has gone to the hospital where the Pope is . . .

Warsaw Radio made a similar announcement 17 minutes later. During the next hour and a half statements condemning the attack by Prime Minister Kania, President Jablonski and Armed Forces Commander Jaruzelski were broadcast and a lengthy statement by the Polish episcopate was read by a priest. At 10:05 in the evening Polish TV broadcast a 50-minute special program on the assassination attempt, including correspondents' reports from Rome and dispatches from Warsaw, Wadowice (the Pope's birthplace), Krakow and Gdansk on prayers being offered for his recovery and on general public indignation. A mass for the Pope and for Poland's primate, Cardinal Wyszynski, himself mortally ill, was announced for the following morning in St John's Basilica, Warsaw, and masses were scheduled in numerous other locations. All public entertainments on 14 May were cancelled.

The Polish press on 14 May was filled with news of the attack. A commentary by Teresa Brodzka in the Warsaw daily, *Zycie Warszawy*, was typical of the reaction of most Poles:

> Destiny has put us to a hard test . . . believers and non-believers, all Poles. The tragic news . . . fell like a blow on every Polish home. Yesterday we were linked by a helpless pain, anxiety, a sense of danger. And also anger. Helpless because it is a response to the brutal laws which govern the world of politics. . . It is unbelievable, but true, that someone was found who dared to raise his hand against a man whose words matched his deeds so accurately, against a man who wants to change the world. Unbelievable

that someone could be found who decided that for such a man there could be no place in this world.

Meanwhile Moscow Radio broadcast a brief report of the assassination attempt at 9 p.m. local time, a little over an hour and a half after it occurred. *Pravda* carried a 15-line dispatch on the shooting the next morning. There was no special TV coverage. Leonid Brezhnev sent a message of condolence to the Pope which was printed in *Pravda* on 15 May. It was remarkable for its brevity:

> I am deeply upset by the criminal attack carried out against you. I wish you a rapid and complete recovery.

From 15 May onward Soviet media gave the story a good deal of attention—spurred no doubt by realization that Soviet citizens (especially those in Catholic areas in the western part of the country) would be listening to Western broadcasts as well as broadcasts from Poland. While the basic tone of Soviet reporting was formally sympathetic toward the Pope and the attack on him was straightforwardly condemned, treatment of Agca was harsh and oversimplified. He was characterized as an 'ultra-rightist terrorist' (Moscow Radio, 15 May), as 'having close links with extreme rightist terrorist organizations' (TASS, 16 May) and 'a member of a banned pro-Fascist party' (*Izvestia*, 15 May).

On 17 May TASS reported from Rome that many organs of the Italian press had concluded that the Pope was a victim of 'a broad international neo-Fascist plot' and went on to claim that it had been established that during his time in Italy Agca had met with representatives of local rightist terrorist organizations. Though investigation of the plot against John Paul II was continuing, TASS concluded, it was already possible to reach a basic conclusion: the attack had been a provocation of neo-Fascists on the international plane. On 18 May the KGB-supported Soviet press agency, Novosti, carried a statement by Soviet Muslims condemning 'the criminal act'.

None of the contradictory information about Agca's background and travels that preoccupied the Western press during this period was reported in Moscow. The fact he had spent time in Bulgaria went unnoted. 'Just who is Mehmet Ali Agca?' asked the Moscow weekly *Nedelya* on 17 May. 'He is 23, born in Turkey, joined the rightist pro-fascist party which had as its aim the establishment of a fascist dictatorship in the country . . . ' This account concluded by calling attention to Agca's November 1979 letter.

For Moscow it was all cut and dried very early, much more so than for even those Western reporters who were inclined to accept an explanation not very different from that which the Soviet leadership wanted their people—and the world—to believe. General allegations of an international neo-fascist plot were not enough, however. They needed to be fleshed out. The journal *Nauka i Religia* ('*Science & Religion*', a bi-monthly appearing in Moscow) featured an article by Yosif Grigulevich, a writer who had long preoccupied himself with papal affairs, in which he postulated a conspiracy to 'denigrate all leftist forces', possibly involving the secret Italian masonic lodge, 'P-2, working hand in hand with the CIA'. The murder of the Pope, he claimed, 'would fully meet with the aspirations of ultraconservative clerical circles in Italy'.[1]

Soon Soviet propagandists were laying responsibility for the attack on the United States. With time, they were able to contrive elaborate, interlocking theories. *Sovetskaya Rossia* and *Komsomolskaya Pravda*, large circulation national newspapers, featured articles on 31 May which drew on a rich mixture of themes that went back to the notorious fake US Army Field Manual which had originally surfaced in Turkey in 1975. The basic purpose of this forgery, one of the most elaborate the Kremlin has ever produced, was to 'prove' that the United States builds up rightist political parties and terrorist organizations as a matter of policy in order to pressure governments allied with it to do its bidding.[2]

This, according to the author of the article in *Sovetskaya Rossia*, is how terrorism developed in Turkey and, of course, the CIA was the prime agency responsible for the effort:

The American secret service supplied the Turkish terrorists not only with training, but with weapons. On the majority of the pistols, bombs and explosive devices which have been confiscated it is not difficult to make out the familiar stamp: 'Made in USA'.

But the United States is not alone—there are 'local Maoists' too:

They also rob banks, wreak vengeance on genuine patriots and democrats. The only difference lies in the fact that their masters are on the other side of the ocean—Peking.

Meanwhile, Novosti had also been experiencing a burst of creativity. It set one of its most imaginative writers, Vladimir Katin, to work on a dispatch which first went out over its foreign wire on 27 May 1981. The basic purpose was identical to that of the *Sovetskaya Rossia* article, but the argumentation was more specific. Entitled 'The Attack on the Pope—Not the Action of a Loner but a Plot by Extreme Rightist, Neo-fascist Forces', this story implied, without ever quite saying so directly, that the attack had been launched because the American ambassador to the Vatican, William Wilson, had had an unsatisfactory meeting with the Pope on 13 March when Palestinian issues were discussed. 'The Pope emphasized the fact that . . . peace cannot be guaranteed with the help of arms but only through negotiations,' Katin wrote; and continued:

> this opinion . . . is diametrically opposed to the political stand taken by the White House. Moreover, John Paul II added that the situation in El Salvador should be resolved in a peaceful manner— i.e. through special negotiations—but in fact Washington is against this theory.

Katin went on to claim that Washington had been irritated by the meeting the same day between Cardinal Casaroli and PLO 'foreign minister' Khaddoumi as well as a visit to the Vatican by a leftist Salvadorean leader. He concluded by declaring:

> All these things put together represent the unmistakable political background against which the episode of the assassination attempt on the head of the Catholic Church stands out.

This Novosti piece attracted little attention at the time, but it was soon used in Italian translation in the June issue of the monthly magazine the Soviet Embassy in Rome distributes, *URSS Oggi*. This eventually led to protests by both the American and Italian governments and a disclaimer by the Soviet press attaché in Rome who maintained that it did not represent the official view of the Soviet government.[3]

Thus, less than three weeks after Agca's attack on the Pope, at a time when no Western leader or government had even voiced tentative suspicion of Kremlin involvement (and the US government had been particularly cautious), and at a time too when the Western press, by and large, was still inclined to regard the attack as the work of Turkish rightists in league perhaps with mysterious fundamentalist

Islamic forces, leading Soviet media outlets had begun heaping blame on the United States.

The line has never changed. There was no mystery about the plot for Kremlin propagandists, no additional facts to be gathered, no background to be examined. Agca's personality and political linkages did not interest them. They knew: the CIA was behind it. Even when disinformation began to circulate, it merely embroidered these same themes.[4] Did this insistence on a crude, rigid explanation of the plot betray a guilty conscience from the very beginning? Was it merely accidental that El Salvador kept coming up in Soviet commentaries—just as Agca had talked of it in the note he left behind in the Pensione Isa?

The Trial

While the Pope, whose large intestine had been pierced by one of Agca's bullets, experienced a long and difficult recovery and was not able to resume normal duties until the end of the summer, Agca's interrogation continued and preparations for the trial began. Security experts came from Turkey, sat in on the interrogation sessions, but were not permitted to ask questions of Agca themselves. This annoyed and puzzled them, because they were eager to help and confident that they would be able to get more information out of Agca than the Italians were obtaining. One of them summed up his reactions after returning to Turkey:

Agca in his activities makes a plan, a program, very early. He draws support from the fact that he has made careful preparations. To break Agca it is necessary to overcome this wall of will. The Italian police have not got beyond it. Each society has characteristics different from another. If well trained Turkish policemen had interrogated Agca and pressed him to talk, the curtain of fog that lay behind his planning would have been lifted. Agca's weak sides were known to the Turkish police. For example, they could have stressed questions relating to his mother and sister. Agca was very apprehensive about drawing them into this affair . . . He is ashamed of the embarrassment he has caused them and this should be driven home to him. He was devoted to his family. He dosen't want to throw dust on them. It's like doctors giving acupuncture—you have to know the exact spot to penetrate.

The Italians didn't know this with Agca.[5]

The Turkish government wanted to have Agca back for completion of the legal proceedings that had been under way when he escaped from prison in November 1979 and to learn more about the organizational network that had supported him in Turkey. His Turkish trial had been resumed early in 1980 and he was sentenced to death for the Ipekçi murder *in absentia* by an Istanbul military court on 28 April 1980. Turkish and Italian interests conflicted.

While individual Turkish security officers resented being excluded from active preparations for the trial in Italy, the Turkish government did not press Italy to accept more help than Italian courts felt they needed. The question of eventual extradition to Turkey could not be dealt with until after Agca had been tried for attacking the Pope. Both countries soon realized that it was best to shelve the issue entirely, for Italy has a law forbidding extradition of a criminal to a country with the death penalty. Turkey has a mandatory death penalty for premeditated murder. There was also the danger that the trial process could be complicated by a plea of insanity or by other legal stratagems on Agca's part.

The experience Italian security and judicial authorities had gained in pursuing spectacular cases, such as the murder of former Prime Minister Aldo Moro, was good preparation for coping with Agca. Practical decisions on how to handle the case were taken quickly and implemented systematically. Agca would be tried on the simple charge of having attempted to kill the Vatican Head of State and wounding bystanders. Only witnesses relevant to this charge would testify. Questions of motive, sponsorship and possible accessories to the crime would not be posed in such a way as to make these issues part of the trial. They would be deferred for further investigation and later action.

All Agca's Turkish activities and the possibility that he had committed at least one other murder in Germany late in 1980 would for the time being be ignored. Thus the trial would be brief. The likelihood that Agca's sponsors could communicate with him and confound the process would be minimized. Agca could be sentenced and isolated in maximum security facilities and dealt with further in whatever manner would be justified by additional information gathered on him. Confined under life sentence in an inaccessible, well-guarded prison, he would also be as safe as he could be made in Italy from danger of assassination or rescue.

The Italians did not forget that Agca had been rescued in Turkey in 1979. Some aspects of his behavior under interrogation in Rome aroused suspicion that he had been promised rescue if caught after killing the Pope, but there was at least as good a reason to suspect that his sponsors' plan had been to kill him. Either way, he needed to be well guarded in prison. Ultimate solution of the mystery of his sponsorship depended on keeping him imprisoned and keeping him alive, no matter how unco-operative he seemed to be. This was a further reason for trying him quickly and keeping the trial short. Agca remained in Rome's Rebibbia Prison while the trial was prepared.

The trial opened on Monday morning, 20 July 1981, in the Palace of Justice in Rome with a specialist in Islamic law, Judge Severino Santiapichi, presiding, assisted by a six-man jury. First, a summary of the interrogation was read. It included several interesting points: Agca characterized himself as an international terrorist determined to help terrorists of every color and to make no distinction between right and left terrorism. He disavowed any sympathy, however, with 'neo-fascist crimes' such as the attacks in 1980 on the Oktoberfest in Munich and on the Bologna railway station. He insisted that he had decided on his own to attack the Pope but that he had not wanted to kill him. He maintained that if he had aimed to kill he would have used all his ammunition instead of firing only two or three shots.

The summary also provided a detailed listing of his travels to the extent they were then known. He claimed he had extorted money to cover travel expenses. He maintained he had obtained his pistol in Bulgaria. He insisted that he had never visited Libya but admitted spending 35-40 days in a Palestinian camp near Beirut where he had been trained in weapons handling and document falsification. The summary did not attempt to reconcile contradictions and gaps in Agca's confessions, of which there were many.

Agca's court-appointed defense lawyer, Piero d'Ovidio, challenged the competence of the court to deal with a crime committed in Vatican territory. The court ruled that the 1929 Lateran Treaty was applicable. It gave Italy police power over Vatican territory and obligated Italy to treat an attempt on the life of a pope in the same manner, subject to the same punishment, as an attack on the Italian head of state. On hearing this ruling, Agca revoked his defense lawyer's mandate to represent him and delivered a short speech in firm, clear Turkish:

I absolutely do not accept the jurisdiction of the Italian court. On

13 May I found myself within the Vatican State and this was when I
shot the head of the Vatican State . . .

Agca's confession did not constitute a formal guilty plea under
Italian legal procedures, but it had the same effect. Agca claimed that
he had been held in prison under inhuman conditions, tortured and
threatened with death. He arrogantly appealed to the Vatican to act
as an independent state and concluded with a refusal to co-operate in
the trial—'Ali Agca will continue to resist, as he did yesterday, today
and tomorrow!' he shouted. He vowed to go on hunger strike in five
months, on 20 December 1981, unless the trial were shifted to the
Vatican. When the judge asked him whether he would answer questions in court, he replied, 'I will not answer. I do not recognize this
court. The trial is finished, thank you.'

What advice or thought process had led Agca to take this particular
tack is still not known. Most likely he was playing for time. His setting
of the unusually long deadline for going on hunger strike—five
months later—may have been a signal to his sponsors that he would
talk if not rescued by that time. Whatever motives or logic behind his
conduct in court, the net effect of Agca's stance during his trial was to
help the Italian authorities achieve the clean, quick conclusion they
wanted.

Agca was sentenced to life imprisonment on 22 July 1981. The next
day, in Rebibbia Prison, he advised his lawyer that he did not want to
exercise his right of appeal. Did he have other expectations? Or was
he simply at a loss to know what to do?

There was criticism in the wake of the trial that it had been too
brief. Some observers maintained that it had deliberately avoided
raising broader questions about Agca's background and sponsorship
because a bargain had been struck between Italian politicians and the
Vatican. There were even hints that pressures from the East had
played a role. In the light of what happened subsequently, such
complaints seem ill-founded. It soon became apparent that they were
premature, for the Italian judicial process had not yet run its course.
A major trial in Italy is concluded with a formal written verdict made
public by the court. Judge Santiapichi's 50-page verdict was issued on
25 September. It stated unequivocally that Agca had been acting as
part of a conspiracy when he attacked the Pope. Written with literary
flair and a sense of drama, the document declared:

The threatening figure of Mehmet Ali Agca suddenly appeared

among the crowd to execute, with almost bureaucratic coolness, a task entrusted to him by others in a plot obscured by hatred . . . But we have to admit . . . that evidence collected so far has not permitted us to uncover the identity or the motives of the conspirators . . . The plan had one immediate objective, the killing of the Pope, but was also aimed at promoting . . .terrorism and creating the conditions for the destruction of established social order . . .

End and Beginning

The first phase of the process dealing with Agca's crime was completed with publication of the verdict four months and twelve days after the shooting had occurred. Compared with judicial proceedings in other similar cases, this was fast action, especially in Italy, a country that has too often been accused of chronic inability to do anything in good time. John W. Hinckley, who shot President Reagan on 30 March 1981, had not even been brought to trial a year later. Agca's first interrogation and trial in Turkey had been under way for five months when he escaped and was not brought to a conclusion, minus Agca, until five months after that. All trials in Italy do not go as fast as Agca's did either. The Dozier kidnappers, the Moro kidnappers and most Red Brigades cases have taken years. There had to be a rationale behind the speedy handling of the Agca case. Though it has not yet been acknowledged publicly, we can discern what it was. The *end* of the trial, the conviction of Agca, was merely the *beginning* of the investigation of the plot which led to his action against the Pope.

The Pope had formally forgiven Agca immediately after the shooting. After the trial word began to come out from Vatican circles that the church hierarchy had a very clear idea who had been behind the attack. The implication was always that it had been instigated by Moscow. But what were the channels through which Agca had been selected, trained, supported and guided? Was it PLO, Qaddafy, Turkish rightists or East Europeans? Or all of them? If prime responsibility lay in Eastern Europe, then which East Europeans? Did the Italian Red Brigades have a role? Or was it, after all, simply a wild scheme that had been concocted by smugglers or cranks seeking notoriety?

There was plenty yet to be investigated and no dearth of leads to follow. Looking back, we have also to assume that at least an inner circle among Italian security and judicial officials had information that justified more specific suspicions. We know now that Agca, when apprehended, had several notes on him. One said, '13th, 17th, 20th at the latest'. These were the dates when the Pope would make public appearances in mid-May. The note reveals urgency. Another note was a list of telephone numbers. All of these were subsequently traced to *Bulgarian* apartments or offices in Rome. They provided prime evidence that Agca was in contact with Bulgarian officials in Italy. We know now, in addition, that Italian suspicions of Bulgarian connections with other aspects of subversion in Italy were growing. How long it took Italian security to trace these numbers we do not know. Unless they were overlooked, it is hard to believe that the tracing process could have been very time-consuming. But nothing was said of them at the time. No hint of their existence was leaked to journalists at a time when many other tidbits of information were. This must have been deliberate. It did not necessarily spring from a desire to spare the Bulgarians embarrassment, though there may have been differences among Italian security officials on this issue.

The fact that such evidence existed must have influenced Judge Santiapichi to suspect a plot. He knew Agca was no loner in Rome. Agca did not act on his own inspiration, as he tried to insist.

By reserving the Bulgarian telephone numbers for later investigation, the Italians avoided having evidence of a specific East European connection raised at a time when (a) Agca was still being uncooperative and adhering to his story that he had had no outside inspiration and (b) when there was no other hard evidence of a Bulgarian connection. Opening this issue at an early stage might have complicated the trial, generated serious East European pressures and delayed accomplishment of the basic initial goal: getting Agca convicted and incarcerated.

The important thing was that firm groundwork was laid for what followed. Many things were clear to those who were not inclined simply to ignore the significance of the attack or to wish away evidence of an East European link: Agca had sponsors and had operated with the benefit of extensive organizational support. He was not mentally unbalanced—quite the contrary, he had an unusually agile and alert mind. He had been instructed to put up a complex cover story, but he appeared to have been told to say different things at different times, with the result that there was a self-destructive illogic to his story as a whole.

Moscow media reaction demonstrated that the Kremlin was desperately eager to see Agca accepted as an ultra-rightist, implementing some kind of international plot that Soviet propagandists were unable to define convincingly. Their efforts to lay the scheme on the doorstep of the United States were dismissed by some as merely bad habit. To others these shrill accusations aroused suspicions of an urge to wash the blood off their own hands.

2
THE ASSASSIN'S TRAIL

Arrival in Malatya

The sun had just set, bringing to an end a cool, bright autumn day
when I stepped off the bus near the central square of Malatya on 12
October 1981 and set out to search for a hotel. I had come to probe
into Mehmet Ali Agca's background in his home town. The next day I
would go to see the assassin's family, visit his schools and see what
traces I could find of his life before he was recruited into terrorism.[1]

A friendly passenger on the bus had recommended the Hotel
Sinan. People were helpful in setting me on the right street toward it.
As I made my way through the early evening crowds, past stands piled
high with eggplant, peppers, melons, grapes and huge purple figs, I
noted that Malatya seemed a much more pleasant town than press
stories at the time Agca shot the Pope gave to believe.

The huge main square, dominated by an enormous statue of
Malatya's most famous citizen, second president of the Turkish
Republic, Ismet Inönü, has a modern underground shopping mall at
its center. Bookshops around the square were filled with browsers
and people buying newspapers and magazines. Little boys slapped
their shoeshine boxes to gain attention and young men offered
roasted chestnuts and ears of golden corn from charcoal grills. The
evening prayer call sounded from a mosque in the still bustling market
area. Malatya looked like an agreeable place to spend a few days.

The Hotel Sinan had a small room at the equivalent of less than $5
per day and the desk clerk directed me to the Emniyet Lokantasi, a
short walk away for dinner. Did I like Malatya? I said it looked
pleasant. Why had I come—was I an engineer? An archaeologist? I
said I was traveling and had never seen this part of Turkey before.
Where had I been? In most parts of the country over a period of
nearly 30 years. 'We are happy you have come to see our city,' the
clerk concluded:

We think it is a fine city and we are proud of it and we like to have visitors—but not the kind of journalists who came rushing in here when Mehmet Ali Agca shot the Pope. They wrote terrible things about Malatya. Agca was not a typical *Malatyali*. He left here and fell into bad hands. He must have been mad—or Communists paid him to do what he did.

I did not tell him I had come to look into Agca too.

I slept well my first night in Malatya. The odor of wood smoke laced the chill night air coming in my window. Sounds of traffic did not wake me until daybreak. My first call was to the governor's office—'Come over immediately; welcome to Malatya!' his assistant said. I walked to the spacious provincial government building that forms the north side of Inönü Square. Even at 8:30 in the morning the governor's waiting room was crowded with men and women with papers to sign and petitions to present. Government in the provinces in Turkey is still a very personal process. An obliging aide showed me into Mr Aydin Özakin's spacious office. 'The Foreign Ministry telephoned about you from Ankara. We are pleased to have you,' he said, and we settled down to talk over hot tea and dried apricots stuffed with almonds—'Our best local product,' the governor reminded me. I explained that I wanted to see Malatya and get a good understanding of Mehmet Ali Agca's roots here.

'The Best City in the East'

In between phone calls to alert officials to be ready for me, the governor, a native of Izmir, talked about Malatya. He had recently been transferred from Muş and was already an enthusiast of his new province. 'Malatya is the best city in the east,' he declared and continued:

> It has enormous potential. Population growth is slowing. It is our policy to keep people in the villages by bringing water and electricity to them, improving schools and helping them earn more from agriculture.

Mehmet Ali Agca was an aberration, a young man from Malatya gone hopelessly wrong and the governor had not thought much about him. He had no pet theories to lay before me, but he had a clear understanding of the context out of which Agca had emerged:

> We still have enormous numbers of young people entering the labor force. We export labor now at a higher rate than most Turkish provinces. We have 15,000 in Germany. Saudi Arabia and Libya are recruiting workers here now. But our people don't like to go to those countries—they don't like the climate and social conditions are too backward. If we don't create jobs for our young people, in five or ten years we will have a repeat of what we had before 12 September 1980. Communists will pour in money again and rile everybody up to destroy our society and our democratic system.

Genealogy of the Agcas

After leaving the governor's office, I was driven to provincial security headquarters on the edge of the city. The security director, a husky, blue-eyed man in his late 30s, had a brief on the Agca family ready for me and stacks of files on his desk. In 1979, after Agca was arrested for the Ipekçi shooting, security had traced the family back to the great-grandfather. They had always been simple people, Turks not Kurds, of no particular distinction. They had lived in the Kayseri area, worked as herders and part-time as laborers. The father's father had emigrated eastward to Hekimhan, a country town north of Malatya. Mehmet Ali's father, Ahmet, had been his only son. There were no other close relatives on the father's side.

The security people had picked up gossip that the mother's family had originally been *çingene*—gypsy, nomadic. They were now marginal agriculturalists and laborers. There were several brothers and sisters. Müzeyyen Agca had married late for a Turkish country girl—well into her 20s—and the story was told that her husband, who was said by this time to have had a reputation for rough living and drinking, had been persuaded to take her because she had a doubtful reputation. The security people did not take this very seriously. While Ahmet and Müzayyen Agca lived in Hekimhan, the security director observed, they seem to have been very ordinary, law-abiding citizens. Mehmet Ali had started school there and had been an outstanding student.

The Agcas moved to Malatya so that the father could get steadier work and give the children a better life. The mother still had relatives around Hekimhan. She was reported to have a sister living in

Charleroi in Belgium, married to a Turkish worker there, who occasionally sent her money. There were vague reports, apparently never confirmed, of a brother working in Switzerland. The security brief concluded with the observation:

> There is no evidence of religious sectarianism in the family. There was no evidence found of links with Alevi (Shi'ite) activity or with Armenian interests.

Malatya once had a substantial Armenian population. Thirty to fifty Armenian families, I was told, remain now, largely assimilated. In some, only the older generation has stayed. The children have gone to Istanbul or emigrated. In Malatya there was no reflection of Armenian terrorist activity abroad. Mehmet Ali Agca, growing up there, was unlikely to have had any meaningful Armenian contacts or cause for prejudice. It was peculiar that he had been rumored to be an Armenian when caught in Rome. He was reported to have written a poem, when in junior high school, against Armenians, and had been the subject of a brief police investigation at the time. But nothing had been kept about this in Malatya security records. He had no reputation as a troublemaker or leader of student agitation during clashes a few years before. He was on no membership lists of political parties or youth groups. There was no indication that he had been active in religious organizations. The security director summed it up after I had looked over his material, drunk tea and was ready to depart: his headquarters had found no evidence that Mehmet Ali Agca had been linked to extremists of any kind: religious or secular.

A Cool Welcome

The next step was to visit the Agca family itself. I was accompanied by a driver and two young men who had escorted other journalists to visit them, knew the way well and were known to the family. Their manner was easy-going and they seem to have developed considerable rapport with the mother, sister and brother. I had a strange feeling of having fallen into a surrealistic drama as I came face to face with the family of this would-be papal assassin. Only two weeks before I had tried to think myself into Agca's mind as he made his way around Rome. Here I was now driving into a modest area of small mud-brick and stone houses on the outskirts of Malatya—a settlement exactly like those on the edges of all Turkish cities, not as extensive or lively as some, not as downtrodden as many.

I had visited areas like this hundreds of times before in all parts of Turkey, spent time talking to the people who live in them. They are almost never depressed or alienated people. Usually less than a generation from the countryside, they are busy improving their lives. Several members of a family usually work, everyone of school age goes to school, people seek out all the opportunities the city offers. However meager their circumstances may appear to the outsider who judges them from the vantage point of his own affluence, the great majority of such people who live in Turkish *gecekondular* (dwelling areas 'put up over night') see themselves as improving their chances in life.[2] Would the Agca family fit the pattern?

Arriving at the simple whitewashed house and walking from the muddy street through a gate and along a short path to its main entrance, I was greeted by the mother, Müzeyyen Agca, with shrieks of protest:

Another journalist! I have seen enough of journalists. They are all the same. They ask me the same things over and over. They have no understanding for my pain and the misery I have had to endure because of this son whom I want to forget. Why should I repeat what I have already said dozens of times? What good does it do anyone? I have nothing to say.

She stood at her door, motionless, looking at the ground. She kept her white scarf pulled across her nose and mouth, showing only her pale, lined forehead and acutely crossed brown eyes. Wisps of graying hair were visible at the edge of her scarf. She was dressed in the long skirt and sweater of a peasant woman and looked thin, strained, fragile. She was about as far from living up to the promise of her name—Müzeyyen, an uncommon, old-fashioned Arabic one meaning 'Decorated', 'Embellished'—as could be imagined.

In spite of her shouting at me, which violated all the tenets of traditional Turkish hospitality, I found myself feeling profoundly sorry for this woman. What a nightmare she had lived for nearly 2½ years! A son who had once been the best proof that she had won out over the vicissitudes of a raw life had gained fame as one of the most spectacular criminals of the era. Investigators and journalists, TV cameramen, the idly curious had come to keep her wounds open. Would they never heal?

Müzeyyen Agca made a motion as if to walk back into her house, then hesitated and motioned to us to sit down on benches under a vine which shaded a small porch but now, with yellowing leaves, let the fall sunlight through. She had not expected me to know Turkish; apparently no other foreign journalists who had come to talk to her had. And the young men with me had the habit of repeating everything I said, as if they were interpreting when they were not. As she realized I was speaking her own language, her curiosity was aroused. I explained I had come as an *araştirmaci* (researcher), not as a *gazeteci* (newspaperman). I was not looking for news stories. I was doing basic research on her son and was studying the whole theme of terrorism in Turkey. I assured her I did not want to embarrass or injure the family with anything I wrote. I told her I had recently been in Italy and had visited the Vatican . . . That triggered a quick turn in the conversation.

You have been in Italy? What have you heard of my son? Why aren't the Italians letting the letters he is writing be sent? I want to know how he is, what he is thinking. Why do they deny me this small consolation? Why don't they send his letters? What harm can that do to anyone? Can't you tell the Italians to let his letters go?

I confirmed that I had been told in Italy that he was writing letters but they were not being sent. I said I had urged they be sent. They might help everyone understand why he had attacked the Pope and who had put him up to doing it . . .

How is the Pope?—she asked with a deep sense of concern. I admire him greatly and I have prayed for him. How many days did he spend in hospital? How serious were his wounds? I hope he has made a complete recovery. It was a terrible thing my son did to this man. I cannot understand it.

I told her everything I had heard in Italy indicated that the Pope had recovered well. 'I hope he has a long life,' she added; 'he is a good man.' The scarf had come off her face, revealing her drawn features, sunken cheeks, tense mouth. She looked as if she ate little, lived in a state of perpetual strain.

The Sister

The daughter, Fatma, emerged from the house and stood beside her mother. She looked wary and a bit haggard, older than 20, but it was also apparent that she was basically an attractive girl: taller than her mother, with dark brown hair and fine features, blue-green eyes, a good feminine voice. She spoke cultivated, carefully enunciated Turkish without the peasant harshness in the mother's voice. She had finished high school last year. She liked school. Her favorite subjects were history and literature. What was she doing now? 'Living at home, keeping house,' she replied with an air of resignation. Probably no one would want to hire Fatma Agca, the sister of a killer . . . I did not press the question of work. She would have no alternative but to remain at home and pass the days with her tense, sad mother. She would not be regarded as very marriageable either. Only a man who could not find a wife easily would marry the sister of a killer . . . Mehmet Ali had put his family under a crushing burden. This is what was depressing about the Agca household, rather than the conditions in which Mehmet Ali had grown up in a time when there was hope of a better future. I shifted the conversation to the subject in which I was most interested: the eldest son and brother.

The mother, now relatively relaxed, was willing to talk about him, eager in fact. It was clear that much of her thought still revolved around him, in spite of her protestations that she wished to forget him. She was contradictory, of course; at times irrational. Tension, frustration and despair welled up over and over again in great outbursts of shouting, and wailing when I pressed questions that she found awkward.

In respect to her eldest son's infancy and childhood, she confirmed what had already been published in the Turkish press in May and June: he had suffered from a mild form of epilepsy, a condition termed *sara* in rural Turkey: spells of fainting and rigid unconsciousness. After about the age of ten, Mehmet Ali outgrew these. He had no medical treatment. His mother attributes the nervousness, short-temper and impatience which he often displayed as a teenager to the effects of this condition.

Her husband seems to have been a man greatly affected by stress, who alternated between brooding moods and outbursts of energy, excitement, anger and turned to drink which undermined his health. She did not want to talk about him. She recounted with sadness and pride how she had kept the family together after she lost her husband

and raised three young children between three and eight on a meager pension of less than $100 per month with help from relatives and neighbors, and from Mehmet Ali after he was old enough to work:

> He was a good son—she recalled with a surge of pride. He helped us whenever he could. He never wasted money. As soon as he was able to earn, he went to work, selling water in the railroad station, helping out on construction sites, carrying sand, earning money for his clothes and buying things he needed for school and books.

The mother whispered to Fatma who went out the gate and returned a few minutes later with a small package. Inside the house sounds were heard in the kitchen. I could see through a window that the house had both refrigerator and TV—not necessarily exceptional among Turkish *gecekondu* families these days. Shortly Fatma emerged with a tray holding cups of steaming, fragrant Turkish coffee. The ice had been broken. The rituals of traditional hospitality were now being observed.

'School was his Life'

'Mehmet Ali liked school then?' I asked.

> From the beginning it was his life. He was always studious, serious. He read everything that came into his hands. He would stay up until three in the morning reading.

'What were his favorite subjects?'

> History and literature. He liked reading Turkish history and historical novels. He wrote poetry from the time he was 10 or 11. He even wrote a novel when he was 13.

his mother volunteered. 'What was it about?' I could scarcely conceal my excitement. Here perhaps was a document that would shed light on Agca's early thinking processes. 'I am not sure,' she replied; 'it was something historical.' 'Where is it?' I pressed hopefully:

> I burned it—I burned all of his papers when the Abdi Ipekçi business developed. I didn't want anything in the house to remind

me of a son who had disgraced it. I wanted to forget that he had lived here.

'Do you still have any of the books he read?' I was hopeful that these at least might reveal what influences had come to bear on him as he was growing up. 'I burned them too,' the mother insisted. I asked Fatma whether she remembered any titles. 'I was younger and wasn't interested in books then, but I know that later he kept reading history and economics.' The mother became impatient and began shouting:

What does it matter what he read? The effect of it all is lost now. He didn't learn what he should have from it. He fell into the hands of an organization and disgraced us all.

The poor woman fell into wailing and moaning, visibly embarrassing Fatma, who had been ready to discuss her brother with greater openness.

I shifted the subject, asking Fatma: 'Who were Mehmet Ali's friends?'

He didn't have any close friends. There are none around now. When he was in high school, his closest friends were all teachers. They gave him things to read and he spent a lot of time with them.

I asked Fatma if she could remember any of their names. She insisted she could not: 'I was a girl and I wasn't interested in the things he was interested in.' Having taken hold of herself again, the mother added:

Mehmet Ali did not waste his time in idleness. He was not interested in sports or girls and did not wander around the streets just to pass the time. He worked whenever he could. He was a very good boy. First he was going to be a teacher, but later he wanted to get a higher education. He loved me and the whole family very much and always showed me great respect. He would not push me aside. 'I will never be able to forget what you have gone without, what you have done for my sake,' he would say. When he went to the university in Ankara, he came home summers and went to work as soon as he could find a job.

Here was a new fact. Mehmet Ali had gone two years to the University of Ankara before transferring to Istanbul. Somehow the published accounts of his life had missed this information.

To Ankara and Beyond

Mehmet Ali Agca took the university entrance examination in his last high school year (1975-6) and had done well, qualifying for the History and Geography Faculty of the University of Ankara, which he entered in the fall of 1976. During his final year at high school in Malatya he told his brother Adnan, 'I won't be a teacher for TL 10,000 a month [then equivalent to about $250] I will find a way to earn a lot more money in this system.'

In 1976 Turkey had more than 300,000 students at universities and other higher institutes. In nationwide competitive examinations each year, approximately one out of seven students succeeds, but many do not get high enough scores to choose the university and faculty they wish. While one in four candidates in Istanbul passes the examinations, in the provinces, especially in the east, only one out of 15 or 20 succeeds. Mehmet Ali Agca was among the top students in Malatya. His ambition drove him to take the examination again two years later (a common practice among Turkish university students) and he was then able to qualify for his first choice: economics at the University of Istanbul.

But his transfer to Istanbul, when he had already been drawn into terrorism, seemed to me less interesting than the fact he had spent two years in Ankara. In the capital he could have come into contact with recruiters representing every extremist faction, both of the right and the left. He would have been accessible to Soviet and East European intelligence operatives working out of their overstaffed embassies, information centers and trade missions. From Ankara he could have been sent for training to a PLO camp. I kept these thoughts to myself and tried to follow up on them by attempting to learn something from his mother and sister about his travels during this period.

They knew he came home from Ankara in the summers; they claimed to know nothing else. Turkish security officials were suspicious that Agca might have gone to Lebanon as early as the summer of 1976, but had no proof. He would have gone in alias. He might also have gone during the fall or winter of either year he was in Ankara. Perhaps he went more than once. Discipline at universities in Turkey was lax during this period, especially so at Ankara. Students came and went as they pleased. Classes were often suspended for long periods

because of turbulence and clashes. Increasing numbers of Turks were
being trained in PLO camps in the late 1970s.

In Rome Agca confessed to PLO training and then denied it. The
Italians concluded in the summary of his interrogation presented at
the beginning of his trial that his original confession was more valid
than the retraction. The story he told in Rome fits other descriptions:
everyone using false identities, both students and teachers; lessons in
weaponry, tactics, document forgery. During the first phase of his
interrogation in Rome he claimed to be acting on behalf of George
Habbash . . . But if his mother and sister had any light to shed on this
mysterious part of his life—which was obviously less related to theirs
after he left Malatya for Ankara—they could not be persuaded to
reveal it.

I asked Müzeyyen Agca about her son's religious orientation. 'He
was not religious,' she replied without a moment's hesitation. 'He had
no interest in religion and went to the mosque only a few times on
religious holidays.' We talked about what he had planned to do with
his life. They did not seem to know. Did he ever show an interest in
getting into politics? They were emphatic that he had not even had
strong opinions about parties. This was a rather exceptional kind of
attitude for a young Turk of the mid-1970s, when every aspect of life
took on political coloration. Most high school and university students
had then felt compelled to profess party preferences, even if they
were very shallowly based.

Suddenly the mother interjected the comment, 'You know, my son
did not kill Abdi Ipekçi.' 'How do you know?' I asked.

> He told me. He told me when we visited him in prison—this was the
> last time I saw him—in the fall of 1979. We all went to Istanbul to
> see him—Fatma, Adnan and myself. He said to me, 'Mother, I did
> not kill Abdi Ipekçi. I was made the scapegoat for others who did it.
> They set me up for it.'

'You believe your son?' I asked the mother again. 'Yes, I believe
him . . . ' Her voice trailed off. There was no point pressing her
further.[3] 'When,' I continued, 'did you last see him before his arrest?'
'When he came home in February 1979. He stayed some time. It was
between terms at the university. Then he went back to study.' Fatma
began to speak, but then hesitated and fell silent. 'Did he come back
to Malatya after he escaped from prison in November 1979?' They
both insisted that he had not. There had been no letters from him, no

word passed through anyone else. Until he shot the Pope, they had no idea where he was. The mother sighed, wiped her eyes, stared at me in silence for what seemed like several minutes, then declared:

> The organization he fell into took possession of him. They got him out of prison and prepared him to attack the Pope.

As a simple summary, this seemed to be as close to the truth as anyone had come. We talked a bit longer but nothing of great significance was said. I asked about the second son. He was at school. It was the same school Mehmet Ali had attended in junior high school. Now the building was divided in two and housed a senior high school too. He would be home in the afternoon. I thanked them for their hospitality and wished them well. It was no casual wish.

I walked back to the street feeling depressed and angered by the tragedy which Mehmet Ali Agca's crimes had brought upon this bedraggled, depressed and agitated woman, old before her time. She never had much reason for high expectations in life. Without education, marrying late and badly, she had had more than her share of pain and strain. But she had been blessed with three good-looking and intelligent children, and she worked hard to give them opportunities in life of which she and her husband could never have dreamed. The pace of economic and social development has been so fast in this part of the world that the son of marginal parents living in poverty can take advantage of the opportunities a modern state creates to bring himself to the highest levels of academic accomplishment—and on to the doors which such accomplishment opens for him.

Mehmet Ali Agca went awry, but there seemed to be nothing in his heritage or in the circumstances of his upbringing which made this inevitable. He was not victimized by religious fanaticism—there was none in his life. He did not suffer from minority status. Poverty and lowly origin did not deprive him of opportunity. He was gifted with first-class intelligence and he used it to good effect, passing tough national competitive university entrance examinations twice and being accepted at two of his country's best universities. Agca's misfortune was that in spite of his intelligence and drive, he fell into the hands of elements who exploited him for utterly destructive purposes.

The Brother

My visit with the Agca family was not finished. There turned out to be a more positive side: the younger son, Adnan, 18. We overtook him at about 2:30 on his way home from school. Newspaper photographs of him after the attack in Rome had given the impression of a crude, unattractive young man and he had been described by Erhan Akyildiz, the *Milliyet* reporter who had done a series of articles on Agca and his family background in late May 1981, as

> with a broad forehead, sunken cheeked, protruding cheekbones, continually open-mouthed. At first glance looking 30, but only 18.

A clean shaven, neatly combed, dark-haired young man wearing a well pressed suit with a white shirt and tie jumped into the jeep when we pulled up beside him.[4] He was obviously familiar with the driver from the security headquarters who had been assigned to me and, after brief explanations of who I was and what I was doing, talked readily. He was articulate, quick, bright-eyed, not open-mouthed. I started by talking about him rather than his older brother. Did he enjoy school? Very much. What were his favorite subjects? History and English. What did he like least? Mathematics. Was he getting good grades? Yes, even in mathematics he was well above passing. What were his best grades? In English and literature. He was working very hard on English: 'I want to master the language and I am reading extra books on my own.' He showed me a text he was carrying. What had he done during the summer? He had worked on a construction project and had enough money to buy his clothes for the year and the extra books with which to study on his own and prepare for the university entrance examinations. What did he want to do? To get a higher education: 'I'm not sure what I want to specialize in, but I am determined to go to the university so that I can help my family.'

Looking sufficiently like his older brother to be recognizable, but with less of the harshness and coldness about the eyes, he seemed nevertheless to be almost a duplicate of him. Mehmet Ali Agca might well have responded in much the same way to similar questions five years ago. It was time to talk of the brother.

Adnan said most of the things that had already been reported in press stories. He did not seem to resent saying them again—in straightforward and matter-of-fact fashion. He recalled the name of the student dormitory where Mehmet Ali had stayed during his time in Ankara—Beşevler—but he said he knew very little about his brother's life there. There was too much difference in their ages. He had not gone to Ankara to visit him, but he had been in the capital on his own and was impressed with it. I asked him to give me his judgement where his brother had gone wrong—what was the organization that had got hold of him? Whose interest did he think he was serving?

> I don't know—Adnan replied. I can't understand my brother. What he did was stupid and he was intelligent and should have known it. But I don't think about that now. I am not going to let my brother spoil my life. I want to live my own life and I am going to live it for the good of my family and my country. I am not going to let my life be darkened by the shadow of my brother.

We had pulled up in front of the Agca house. The mother came out and stood at the jeep window as we continued the conversation. Adnan was explaining the work he was doing on his own at home to prepare for university entrance exams. He lamented the lack of opportunities to practice English. I talked to him a bit in English and he answered intelligently in carefully formed sentences with fair pronunciation. The mother broke into the conversation. He told her not to interrupt. Fatma appeared in the background. I asked Adnan to write down his address so that I could send him some books that might be helpful in his studies. He thanked me and shook hands before alighting. I wished him success in his studies and examinations. Saying a second good-bye to the tense old mother and to Fatma standing quietly on the side, I felt more hope for them. Perhaps this second son could compensate for the tragedy which the first brought upon them. Like them, he must have endured a great deal of strain during the past 2½ years, embarrassment with his schoolmates, shame in being identified as a murderer's brother. But he seemed to have stood it well, to have matured quickly as a result. His determination to make something of his life was impressive.

The Schools

I went on to visit the schools Mehmet Ali Agca had attended. The Yeşiltepe junior high school, easy walking distance from the Agca house, stands at the edge of the settled area. It was built a decade and a half ago to accommodate more students than it now has. The area has been growing slowly. Population pressure has not been heavy and the school was not overtaxed. Students, both boys and girls—the latter all in blue skirts and white blouses with only their sweaters showing more color and individuality, were playing volleyball in the play-yard. The principal confirmed that Agca had been among the school's best students in his day.

The senior high school to which Mehmet Ali went is close to the center of the city. A teacher-training high school then, with boarding students from smaller towns in the province, it has been turned into a vocational high school serving only the city and has a totally different teaching staff. Well constructed in landscaped grounds with trees and flowerbeds, the school consisted of several buildings, including a large separate sports hall, unusual in Turkish high schools. Well dressed students were walking, sitting, standing in groups around the grounds—immaculately well behaved, as they all are now since the takeover by the military. We found a man who was part of the service staff and had worked here for ten years—the only person left from the time when Agca was a student here:

I did not know Mehmet Ali Agca—he said. Of course I must have seen him, but he did not call much attention to himself as a student and did not play a role in student politics. Besides he was a day-student from the city, so he did not live at the school. He went home when classes were over. It was the students who came in from the surrounding areas and lived in the dormitories who were caught in agitation. There were periods when we had constant fighting and the school could not operate at all. If they lived here, they couldn't escape it. Some of the teachers encouraged the students. It was a miserable situation. I am glad those times are over. Our students are learning now. In those years of terrorism, they couldn't learn if they wanted to.

I was reminded of what Agca had written in his confession on 30 June 1979, shortly after he was captured and charged with the murder of Abdi Ipekçi:

I continuously went around by myself. I went to the movies, to games, to the theater . . . When there was time I went to libraries. In this way I took advantage of what was interesting in my surroundings. In spite of the fact that there were fights among Alevis and Sunnis in the district in which I lived in Malatya, I did not take sides and even though I was a Sunni, I had many Alevi friends.

Agca's accomplice who drove the escape car in the Ipekçi murder, a fellow native of Malatya, Yavuz Çaylan, gave a similar description of Malatya in his own confession to the police:

> While I was at the Turan Emeksiz high school in Malatya, there were rightist and leftist groups. There was also the Alevi-Sunni question. From involvements in this question, right-left questions became apparent. I was a Sunni. Because Alevis were generally leftists, the Sunnis rightists, and because my friends were also Sunnis, I inclined to the view of the right. In school these issues became hardened.

Çaylan attended Yeşiltepe junior high school at the same time as Agca, but he went to a different high school in another part of the city. It was an academic multi-purpose high school. It has not been established whether they were close friends or remained in contact during high school. It is very common in Turkey for students from the same city or province to form friendship groups and room together in universities. They often develop ties they did not have in their home area.

I went back and asked the security people about Çaylan. They had investigated him at the time he was tried as an accessory of Agca but they did not have evidence to link him with Agca during their high school years. Nor had they uncovered links between either of them and the Turkish terrorist, Teslim Töre. 'That would not be proof there was none,' one of them volunteered. 'The police and security officials had so much to do during those times that they couldn't keep up with everything.' Another recalled the period of intense violence Malatya had gone through in 1976:

> Elementary school students were caught carrying dynamite in bookbags. They were being used by radical students and teachers as couriers. Leftists and rightists fought each other in several parts of the city. Our mayor, Hamit Fendoglu, was a non-party man who tried to keep things under control. On 18 April 1978 he was blown up, and his daughter-in-law and two grandchildren were killed when a package bomb sent to him in the mail exploded. Violent demonstrations broke out. Four people were killed and dozens

wounded. Several buildings were set on fire. It was one of the worst outbreaks of violence in Turkey up to that time.

'Who sent the package bomb to the mayor?' I asked.

We still don't know—he replied. The right blamed the left and the left blamed the right. Both sides used it as an excuse to attack the other. That's the way things went in Turkey in those times. It was much worse in Kahramanmaraş later that year. The people who were supporting terrorism were trying to rip our country apart.

What Agca Was Not

I stayed two more days in Malatya, visiting all sections of the city. I got up early each day to have breakfast in one of the soup restaurants where workers order a big bowl of chicken, tomato or sheep's foot soup and half a loaf of bread, follow up with a glass of tea and are then ready to face the day. I talked with tradesmen in the bazaars, bookshop owners, businessmen, archaeologists at the museum. I took a taxi out to visit the ruins of Eski—old—Malatya, look at its dilapidated caravansary and admire the blue tilework of the thirteenth-century Seljuk mosque. On the way back I stopped at the tomb of the son of Battal-Gazi, an early Muslim hero. It was a striking green structure on a hilltop, surrounded by other graves, and evidently a place of pilgrimage. Back in the city, I walked through pleasant modern residential areas of houses in gardens interspersed with apartment buildings as well as districts with what in the nineteenth century had been elegant town houses of merchants, now falling into decay. They were inhabited by families recently in from the countryside. I heard Kurdish spoken in some of these areas, but the predominant language everywhere in Malatya was Turkish. Political slogans on walls and buildings had been painted over.

Everything was peaceful. Everyone had praise for the order and stability Turkey's military leaders had brought to the country. Many reminisced about the time of terrorism, giving dramatic personal accounts of their experiences. But nobody knew much about Mehmet Ali Agca, or wanted to talk about him. People resented the fact he had given the city a bad name. No one tried to justify his attack on the Pope on religious grounds. Views were like those of a devout Muslim taxi driver I had met in Kars in June:

I admire John Paul. I respect his religion. We have high regard for
him both as a religious leader and as a Pole. We know what the
Poles are going through. It is much worse than what we have
experienced. No honest Turk could want to kill this man. Agca was
mad, or a tool of the Communists, or both.

My last morning, before catching the 11 o'clock bus for the 700 km
ride to Ankara, I stopped to say goodbye to Governor Özakin. I told
him about my visit to the family and the schools and thanked him for
the help his security officials had given. 'What do you conclude about
Agca?' he asked. 'Nothing in this city or in his early life here provides
an explanation of his attack on the Pope,' I answered, 'or clarifies his
shooting of Abdi Ipekçi either. His mother seems to be right: an
organization took hold of him and turned him into a killer. The task is
to uncover that organization.'

'I wish you good luck in your further research,' the governor
replied, 'but I also wanted you to know there is much more to Malatya
than Mehmet Ali Agca.' He gave me a quick explanation of a pile of
folders and charts on his desk which he was going to use to brief Prime
Minister Ulusu, due to arrive the next day. I wished this energetic
man success in his efforts to speed up economic development, and
rushed off to the bus station.

During the twelve hours it took to reach Ankara over the same
route Agca had often taken I had plenty of time to reflect on my visit
to his home town. I felt most sure about what he was *not*. He was *not* a
Muslim fanatic, *not* a rabid rightist, *not* anti-modern, *not* a hater of
the outer world, *not* obviously sick, *not* mentally deranged. I was still
far from sure what he was, who had motivated and directed him.
Malatya did not explain Agca as the murderer of Abdi Ipekçi or as the
would-be assassin of Pope John Paul II, or as the presumed killer of
perhaps three or four other men as well. Nothing he learned in
Malatya, no example set for him there in his first 18 years could have
made him want to spend a year and half on a roundabout route to
Rome to try to eliminate the head of the Roman Catholic Church.
Catholics—all Christians, even Armenians—seemed as far from the
concerns of Malatya as Buddhists. Nor could Malatya explain the
resources and support which sustained Agca in his terrorist exploits.
He drew no money, no sustenance from his home town. He would be
better off if he had never left it . . .

SECTION TWO
The Background of Terror

If Mehmet Ali Agca's own background does not easily explain his involvement in the plot against the Pope perhaps more will emerge from the international context. This section of the book, therefore, examines the international background of terror which had developed during the 1970s. For it is clear that however this plot was sustained, it was initially linked to the network of terrorist activity which had become so widely cast over the previous decade.

The focus must first be on Turkey and Italy. Not only did they provide the source and the location of the assassination attempt, they were also plagued by terrorism during the 1970s.

This section also considers the background to Soviet involvement in the plot. In particular, it traces the long history of the use of terror as an instrument of internal control and foreign policy in Imperial Russia and the Soviet Union. It also explains the relationship between Bulgaria and the Soviet Union and how the KGB has long used East European intelligence services as subcontractors in its more sordid adventures. Perhaps most importantly in presenting the evidence for Soviet involvement, this section reviews Soviet–Polish relations since the Russian Revolution. It is in the context of the mistrust and suspicion which permeate relations between these countries that an explanation of the plot can be found. Karl Marx, no friend of Russian imperialism, underscored the importance of Poland to Russia when he observed in 1854:

Russia may lose the Crimea, the Caucasus, Finland, St Petersburg, and all such appendages; but as long as her body, with Moscow for its heart, and fortified Poland for its swordarm, is untouched, she need not give an iota.[1]

3
TERRORISM AND SOVIET SUBVERSION IN TURKEY

Out of the Ashes

The graceful Bosporus Bridge in Istanbul, completed in 1973 to celebrate the 50th anniversary of the founding of the Turkish Republic, links Europe and Asia. So does Turkey. The country is a bridge between East and West, the only Islamic member of NATO, the only successful parliamentary democracy in the Muslim world. But Islam is not a state religion in Turkey. Turkey has other unique characteristics. It is a developing country, but it was never a colony. The modern republic was forged out of the ruined Turkish core of the Ottoman Empire which, as an ally of Germany was defeated in World War I. If World War I had worked out as the Allied Powers had originally intended, the Russian Empire would have been awarded Constantinople and the Straits and much of the rest of Asia Minor would have been divided up among Greece, Italy and France, leaving a large Armenia in the east. Instead, it was the Russian Empire which fell into disarray before Ottoman power collapsed. Mustafa Kemal (later Atatürk), who had dealt the Allies a bitter defeat at Gallipoli, rallied the Turks of Anatolia to rebirth as a new nation during the years 1919 to 1922.

It is hard to find other twentieth-century leaders to compare to Atatürk in the grandeur of his vision for his country and the practicality of his methods of achieving it. He lived only 15 years after the founding of his republic, but he left it a legacy that has gained value ever since. His most distinguished biographer, Lord Kinross, summed up his achievements in the final paragraph of his monumental biography, *Atatürk, Rebirth of a Nation:*

What Atatürk left to the Turkey he had freed was strong foundations and a clear objective for her future growth. He gave her not merely durable institutions but a national idea, rooted in patriotism, nourished by a new self-respect, and promising fruitful rewards for her energies. He created, by his deed and words, a

45

personal myth to feed the imagination of a people given to worship heroes. He infused them with a belief in the values of Western democracy . . . All that he gave them survives as a living force in the Turkey of today.[1]

Russian Ambitions

The Russian and Ottoman empires fought 13 wars in their last 250 years of existence, with the Turks almost always the losers. The Crimean War, when England and France came to their aid and Russia was soundly defeated was an exception. But the process went on, as if inexorable, and the Ottoman Empire again suffered territorial losses to the Russians in 1878. Was it surprising that in the early twentieth century enlightened Europeans thought it foreordained that the Russian flag would eventually fly over Constantinople, the city medieval Russia had known as Tsargrad?

Atatürk established the capital of the new Turkey in Ankara, in the Anatolian heartland, because he wanted the republic to be freed of the burden of the Ottoman past, but he loved the old city on the Bosporus and appreciated its cultural, commercial and strategic value. No foreign power, least of all Russia, would be permitted a foothold astride the Turkish Straits. The Russians knew they would have to bide their time. Soviet–Turkish co-operation in the 1920s is one of the earliest examples of Soviet foreign policy pragmatism. Atatürk banned communism. Lenin told the first Soviet ambassador to Ankara not to dabble with the small group of Turkish communists who had gone underground or abroad. The Soviets gave Turkey modest economic aid in the 1920s and 1930s.

But memories were long and traditional aspirations had not been abandoned. When the Nazi–Soviet Pact was being negotiated in 1939, Molotov was frank with Ribbentrop about Soviet territorial aspirations in 'the region south of Batum and Baku'. In 1945 Stalin confronted Turkey, which had just become a full-fledged ally of the anti-Axis powers—i.e. of the USSR as well—with brutal demands for cession of territory in the east and establishment of Soviet bases in the Straits. Soviet agents heated up the Armenian issue, provoking riots in Istanbul, and tried to set up an independent Kurdistan in territory occupied by Soviet armies parallel to the Turkish border in Iran. Turks reacted with the toughness that has always been typical of them in a crunch. They rejected Stalin's demands and strengthened ties to the West. The Truman Doctrine brought Turkey and Greece into the American defense perimeter in 1947. Greece was more vulnerable to subversion during this period than Turkey. The vicious Greek Civil War during the years 1944 to 1949 underscored Soviet ambitions in the region.[2] Both countries became members of NATO in 1952.

Democratic Development

All this history is relevant to what began to happen in Turkey a decade and a half later. Relevant too is the fact that Turkey evolved into a full-fledged multi-party democracy during the years between 1946 and 1950 when free elections brought Adnan Menderes' Democrat Party to power, ousting Ismet Inönü's Republican People's Party (RPP), founded by Atatürk and the governing party since his death. During the 1950s Turkey experienced an unprecedented burst of economic, social and political development. The countryside was energized, cities grew, and industry developed rapidly. But Menderes displayed autocratic tendencies which alarmed military officers who saw themselves as guardians of Atatürk's reforms. A group of colonels set his government aside in an almost bloodless coup in May 1960. People (including some Turks) who argue that violence comes naturally to Turks have to explain why there was no bloodshed and very little civil disorder during this period, in contrast to political crisis periods in the late 1960s and 1970s. The Soviets were not yet spending heavily to encourage subversion, though they had started a clandestine radio station, *Bizim Radyo* ('Our Radio') in 1958 which broadcast communist propaganda to Turkey from Romania and East Germany. This was the same year Mehmet Ali Agca was born in Hekimhan, north of Malatya.

The 1960s were a heady period. Far from instituting an oppressive regime after they ousted Menderes, the Turkish military created a more liberal political system and a more open society. Professors helped draw up a new constitution (adopted by a narrow margin in a popular referendum in 1961) which provided for proportional representation and a two-chamber parliament to replace the previous single-chamber Grand National Assembly. When elections were held in October 1961, no party received a majority. The pattern was set for the better part of the next 20 years—coalition governments, intense rivalry between politicians, numerous splinter parties. Socialism, which had been officially regarded as tantamount to communism in the 1950s, was now recognized as a legitimate political philosophy. The Marxist Turkish Labor Party (TLP) was formed and played a major rhetorical (though minor political) role on the Turkish scene until 1968. Students and labor organized too, as did many professional groups. Journalism and book publishing expanded rapidly. Among intellectuals ultra-liberal ideas became chic. The economy boomed. Urbanization and modernization of the countryside accelerated. Excess manpower was drained off to Germany and elsewhere in Europe, where Turkish laborers found jobs that paid well.

Turkey sent soldiers to fight in Korea and maintained the largest standing armed forces in NATO after the United States. It welcomed American missiles. This bothered Kremlin leaders who were shipping arms to new friends in the Arab world and sought opportunities to fan Greek–Turkish tensions over Cyprus. But it was not only Turkey's loyalty to NATO which caused Moscow discomfort. It was the very success of the country as a free democracy, growing economically at a rate of 6–7 per cent a year. The Muslim peoples of the Soviet Union were beginning to increase rapidly and were becoming more conscious of their history. They are overwhelmingly Turkic. Even though the Turkish Republic has never claimed to represent fellow Turks in the USSR, a successful, prosperous Turkey serves as an example of an alternative political system which Kremlin leaders fear might appeal to Tatars, Azeris and Uzbeks.

Prelude to Terrorism

By the mid-1960s Turkey had become a much higher priority for political attention from the USSR—both overt and covert—than it had been for nearly 20 years. I will confine my analysis here to the covert side of the spectrum. A KGB officer who defected in 1967, Vladimir Sakharov, has told how the Soviet Embassy in Ankara began in the early 1960s to recruit agents, train them in the USSR and Syria and then return them to Turkey to build subversive networks among intellectuals, students and labor organizers.[3]

Soviet disinformation operations can invariably be taken as a measure of larger aims. In July 1966 a maverick Turkish senator, Haydar Tunçkanat, made public a collection of forged documents designed to demonstrate that the United States was plotting to purge certain Turkish military officers unfriendly to the Justice Party, then in power with Süleyman Demirel as prime minister. The case these 'documents' made for outrageous and arrogant American meddling in Turkish internal affairs fell on receptive ears among some Turkish intellectuals, journalists and even a few military officers who had been affected by cumulative strains in the alliance relationship exacerbated by the 1964 Johnson letter warning the Turks against military intervention in Cyprus.[4] Denials by both the US and Turkish governments did not fully succeed in discrediting Tunçkanat, who lent himself to Soviet purposes again in 1969 by publishing a book filled with allegations of American duplicity in dealing with Turkey. In the 1970s forgeries were publicized both through leftist journals and the mass-circulation press. A newspaper called *Yeni Ortam* for a time served as an outlet for sophisticated interpretations of Moscow propaganda themes.

Clandestine communist radio stations repeated and embroidered all this disinformation. A new station, the 'Voice of the Turkish Communist Party', began broadcasting from East Germany in 1968. It was aimed at the large and still growing Turkish worker community in West Germany and elsewhere in Europe. Turks in Europe were more accessible to Soviet agents than in Turkey itself. Organization of a political and operational infrastructure among Turks in Germany began in the 1960s. It has served ever since as an essential support element for Soviet subversion in Turkey, channeling funds and weapons and providing false documentation, operational services and asylum. A later chapter will show how this network was utilized to shelter Agca while the plot against the Pope was being developed.

From 1968 onward, university campuses in Turkey were disturbed by almost continual commotion among students. Anti-American propaganda and demonstrations against American installations increased. But, as in the late Menderes period, there was still no political violence resulting in deaths in Turkey between 1961 and 1969. What, then, was the source of the unprecedented violence that suddenly erupted, brought higher education to a halt and soon turned into a wave of terrorism that forced military intervention in 1971?

On the surface, it appeared to be primarily an intellectual phenomenon and in part an imitative one. Turkish professors and students and admiring journalists wanted to keep up with their European and American counterparts who were doing the same things at this time. Peasants and workers were little affected. Industrialists and tradesmen were indifferent and not yet sufficiently aroused to take organized measures to protect their interests.

The Turkish Labor Party played an important role in the development and training of militant groups in the mid-1960s, but its leadership was not amenable to the kind of manipulation Soviet agents now needed to advance the destabilization process to the point where blood would be shed and martyrs created. Mehmet Ali Aybar, head of the TLP, took a strong stand against the Soviet invasion of Czechoslovakia in August 1968. His party lost 13 of the 15 seats it held in parliament in elections the next year and he stepped down as leader. Militants who had previously worked inside the TLP left it and set up new extremist organizations: DEVGENÇ (the revolutionary students federation) appeared on the scene, followed quickly by Turk Halk Kurtuluş Ordusu (THKO) [Turkish People's Liberation Army]. Such groups proliferated.[5]

The First Wave of Terrorism

Violence spread. 1970 was a difficult year. Anti-Western propaganda poured out in many forms. Sources of financial support were obscure. Arms flowed into the country from unidentified points of origin. Soon students, or young people purporting to be students, were forming armed bands that provoked skirmishes with police and threatened US military installations and personnel. There was commotion in many parts of the country but the north and west, with the largest cities, most of the universities and the most accessible US and NATO facilities, were hardest hit. Violence proved to have an enormous potential for exacerbating divisiveness among competing politicians, but political recriminations in the early 1970s were only a mild foretaste of what would happen by the end of the decade.

On 4 March 1971 five THKO members kidnapped four American airmen and demanded ransom. When a party of Turkish police accidentally visited the hiding place, the terrorists panicked and fled and the kidnapped airmen walked out unharmed. This incident marked the beginning of the end of the first wave of terrorist action in Turkey. On 12 March 1971 the military leadership asked Prime Minister Demirel to step aside to make way for an above-party government that could restore public order. Martial law was declared on 28 April 1971 in key urban provinces and those along the Syrian border. The THKO struck back by kidnapping the Israeli consul-general in Istanbul on 17 May and killing him five days later. This brutal episode provided concrete evidence of Palestinian support for Turkish terrorism.

During the next few months 4,000 terrorist suspects were apprehended. Leftist newspapers were closed, publishing houses producing Marxist literature had their licenses revoked and some civil liberties were suspended. Arrests, investigations and trials continued for the next two years. This period of restoration of order was punctuated in March 1972 by the worst terrorist incident of the period when one Canadian and two British technicians were kidnapped from a remote NATO listening post on the Black Sea by a group of terrorists who had escaped from prison. The hostages and nine terrorists were all killed in the course of a Turkish army commando assault on a hiding place in a mountain village. There was further violence, including an aircraft hijacking to Bulgaria when THKO members tried to free three of the kidnappers of the American airmen. Two had already been shot resisting arrest. The remaining three were hanged on 6 May 1972.[6]

A final, unsuccessful hijacking was attempted by terrorists in October 1972. This marked the end of the first terrorist assault on the Turkish republic. With leaders dead and imprisoned, arms caches confiscated and support structure disrupted, the terrorist movement was temporarily crippled. Interrogation of terrorists and their supporters produced a large body of information on direct Bulgarian, Syrian and Palestinian support for terrorism and more circumstantial evidence of Soviet, East German and other East European involvement.[7] The government suspended university autonomy, took the state radio and TV network under direct control and set up a special court and detention system. Restrictions were directed equally at all forms of extremism, both right and left, but the major impact was on the left because rightist activity, except for some religious revivalism which had no relationship to the larger pattern of terrorist destabilization at this period, was of minor consequence.

What, from the viewpoint of those sponsoring it, had been accomplished by terrorism and subversion in Turkey in the late 1960s and early 1970s? Two major martyrs, Deniz Gezmiş and Mahir Çayan (the former executed after trial in 1972 and the latter killed in connection with the British–Canadian hostage incident the same year), and a couple of dozen lesser ones, had been created to be exploited in subsequent mythology. Cadres had been developed for future use. The two Soviet-sponsored clandestine radios and various publications glorified this period during the following decade. The first wave of terrorism had little impact on the Turkish economy, which continued to expand until 1975. Turkey's relations with her NATO allies were probably, on balance, strengthened rather than weakened by terrorism. The basic pro-Western attitudes of the great majority of the population remained unchanged. The wide and deep commitment of most Turks to democracy and the Atatürk reforms was not undermined by terrorism.

Still, in some subtle ways, the self-confidence of the country had been jolted. In Europe and America there was worry that Turkey might be a country so beset by political and social strain that it would become an unreliable ally in the future. Many Turkish intellectuals explained terrorism as a manifestation of the weaknesses, contradictions and imperfections of Turkish society. The Soviets in their propaganda encouraged this kind of interpretation because it took attention away from their own subversive input into what had been happening.

Mehmet Ali Agca was 15 by the time the first wave of terrorism was over. He was already a voracious reader. We know nothing about the impact these dramatic events had on his mind. Malatya was not much affected by them.

Breathing Spell

During the summer of 1973, with security restored throughout the country, political parties were permitted to resume activity and elections were held in October. The 1961 constitution was not replaced. Once again elections produced no majority. Bülent Ecevit's Republican People's Party (RPP) (he had maneuvered the aging Inönü out of the leadership in 1972) got the most votes, one-third of those cast. The RPP, founded by Atatürk to promote his reforms, had always been the chosen party of the military and modernizing elite. Traditional RPP supporters were cool toward Ecevit's enthusiasm for European-style social democracy. In provincial centers such as Malatya, an RPP stronghold because of favorite-son Inönü's popularity, the turn toward socialism caused political confusion that a few years later made it easier for terrorists to agitate the population.

There was already a good deal of political disarray in Ankara in the winter of 1973/4 as coalition negotiations dragged on with a caretaker government in charge. Ecevit finally formed a shaky and incongruous government with Necmettin Erbakan's conservative religious National Salvation Party (NSP) in February 1974. One of the few concrete moves of the Ecevit–Erbakan government before it was overwhelmed by, and eventually fell in the wake of, the Cyprus crisis of mid-1974 was the sweeping amnesty of 25 May which freed practically all the terrorists sentenced during the period 1970 to 1973. Erbakan accepted the amnesty only with great reluctance. Ecevit argued that leniency would cause the terrorists to repent. He hoped, too, that they would become supporters of his program for gradual introduction of moderate socialism. With the same combination of naïve humanitarian good intentions and political opportunism, Ecevit opened the way for ruin of the booming economy by raising the minimum wage but neglecting to increase oil prices and ignoring the burgeoning costs to the treasury of skyrocketing agricultural subsidies and unprofitable state economic enterprises.

In easier times Ecevit's optimism might have generated enough momentum to overcome Turkey's growing problems. He overestimated his political strength in the wake of the Cyprus intervention, resigned to rid himself of Erbakan and precipitated a government crisis that lasted nearly seven months before his arch-rival, seasoned politician Süleyman Demirel, who had not enjoyed office since 1971, returned to power. Demirel, too, had to form a precarious coalition with three small parties. It was a wonder that it held together for more than two years. These included Erbakan's NSP as well as Colonel Alparslan Türkeş's National Action Party (NAP), a radical-nationalist, strongly anti-communist grouping which glorified the ancient Central Asian past of the Turks more than it did Islam and used the gray wolf as one of its symbols. Termed fascist by most leftists, this party's militant youth groups officially known as Ülkücüler (Idealists) and popularly as Gray Wolves, came to be a prominent feature of the terrorist scene in the late 1970s.

Until mid-1975 it seemed that Ecevit's gamble in letting the terrorists out of jail might be paying off. Turkey's main preoccupation during this period was the arms embargo which the US Congress, at the behest of the Greek lobby, voted to punish the Turks for exercising their treaty rights to intervene in Cyprus. Allegedly voted to encourage settlement in Cyprus, the arms embargo reduced to nil what little chance there was that the governments in Athens and Ankara might compose their differences over Cyprus and other sources of strain. It was an enormous boon to the Russians who needed to do very little overtly to encourage rancor between Greece and Turkey and Greeks and Turks in Cyprus. The US Congress did it for them.[8]

But the Soviets did not content themselves with good luck alone.

That was only a starting point. It was a period when Soviet investment in subversion and encouragement of terrorism in many parts of the world was on the rise. Turkey, in spite of the failure of the first great terrorist assault, remained high on Moscow's priority list. In fact, in the wake of information that came to light after the military took power again in Turkey on 12 September 1980, it appears likely that the Soviet Union may have invested more in destabilizing Turkey in the late 1970s than it had spent on any single country since Vietnam.

As in the 1960s, a major disinformation campaign was the harbinger of rougher times to follow. Turkey was the direct target of one of the most ambitious forgeries Soviet disinformation workshops have ever produced: the fabricated US Army Field Manual. It was first publicized in the small leftist Ankara newspaper *Bariş (Peace)* in March 1975. This bogus version of a genuine field manual (FM-30-31B) subsequently appeared in more than 20 other countries. It is a direct descendant of the forged documents and book surfaced by Senator Tunçkanat in the late 1960s.[9] The forgery is designed to nourish suspicions that the United States interferes in the internal affairs of its allies by establishing and manipulating extremist organizations to frighten governments it wishes to coerce into adopting harsher internal security measures than they would otherwise be inclined to favor. It prescribes tactics designed to undermine and discredit politicians who are found insufficiently subservient to US and NATO interests.

The fake field manual was only the most prominent feature of a campaign of forgery and disinformation that continued in Turkey during the entire latter half of the 1970s. It included fabricated reports of American support for NAP leader Türkeş as well as other extremist groups, training for terrorists, allegations of CIA plots as well as conspiratorial plans to be implemented by US military aid officers. Turkey's press, competitive and sensationalist under the best of circumstances, was rampantly free again after the restoration of parliamentary government in 1974. Journalists could be found who would print stories East European agents wanted to appear. Resentments created by the congressional arms embargo encouraged anti-Americanism. It is surprising that communist-inspired disinformation did not have more impact on public opinion than it did. Traditional anti-Russian attitudes were hard to overcome. But disinformation can have a long 'shelf life'. Most of that spread in the 1970s has reappeared in Soviet and Bulgarian polemics on the plot against the Pope.

A Tidal Wave of Terrorism

The Soviets drew lessons from the first terrorist wave and applied them in the second, which began in late 1975 but at first gained momentum slowly. This time terrorists were much more generously supplied with arms and money. The aim was not simply to disrupt Turkey's relations with her NATO allies, but to destabilize Turkish society, undermine the economy, destroy the democratic system and discredit Turkey as a country worth having as an ally or treating as a serious economic partner. To do all this it was necessary to turn Turks against each other and undermine their confidence in themselves.

Rightists played little role in the first wave of terrorism, but by the late 1970s some rightists seemed to be as generously supported with money and arms as the left. Qaddafy seems to have been the source of some of the money rightists received, but there were many channels, including funds allegedly supplied by Turkish workers in Germany. Arms smuggled in from Bulgaria and Syria sometimes went to rightists and leftists indiscriminately. Terrorist fugitives were sheltered in both countries and trained by the PLO. Students were no longer the primary element in terrorism, though universities were continually disrupted by left/right clashes and commotion soon spread to high schools and eventually even to elementary schools. Serious teaching practically ceased. Leadership came in large part from experienced and hardened veterans of the earlier period, including many who had been amnestied in 1974. Some had gone for PLO training soon after release. Urban unemployed and small town youths were drawn into violent partisan struggles which provided new recruits for both sides. The 'organization' which Agca's mother had accused of taking her son was spreading its net.

The radical labor federation DISK became steadily more politicized. It was largely responsible for organizing a huge May Day rally in Taksim Square, Istanbul, in 1977 which led to the deaths of 36 people in a panicking stampede following the firing of shots by unidentified agitators. Demirel's uneasy coalition came to an end soon after elections were held in June 1977. Ecevit proclaimed victory but, as always, there was no majority in parliament and he was unable to form a government. Demirel returned to power with his two rightist partners, Erbakan and Türkeş. The economy declined and Demirel's government fell at the end of the year. Ecevit put a new government together in the first week of 1978.

Ecevit declared terrorism would be brought to a halt. He found it hard to believe that the terrorists he had amnestied four years before could be so ungrateful as to continue their campaign against him. Dabbling occasionally with mild neutralism, Ecevit also found it hard to believe that the Soviets could want to undermine his government. Nevertheless during the first month he was in power—January 1978—Turkey suffered 51 killed, 444 wounded, 129 bombings and 20 terrorist robberies. In 1977 political *killings* had totaled 231; in 1978 they reached 832 and in 1979 passed 1,200.

The Carter Administration persuaded the US Congress to lift the arms embargo against Turkey in August 1978. It was not a moment too soon. Turkey's neighbor to the east, Iran, was nearing political collapse. Before the end of the year that country would dissolve into chaos and all American military presence in Iran would be eliminated. Reopening of US intelligence-gathering bases in Turkey, which Demirel had reluctantly closed in 1975, was a high priority.

It was already too late for the lifting of the arms embargo to have any major effect on the Turkish domestic political scene, though temporarily it strengthened Ecevit against the assertive left wing of the RPP. But neither Demirel nor Ecevit was master of his own political situation. To govern, Demirel had to compromise with Türkeş who gained strength while the religious extremist, Erbakan, declined.[10] Thus both leaders were driven to take tactical political positions more extreme than they personally favored. Worse still, they found it impossible to co-operate in anything and reviled each other publicly with increasing bitterness. On one occasion Ecevit likened Demirel to Idi Amin and on another to Adolf Hitler. Demirel repeatedly cast aspersions on Ecevit's mental stability.

Meanwhile the police and armed forces became targets of violence that had no rationale but disruption of normal life. Leftists set up 'liberated areas' in working-class districts of Istanbul. Some professed Maoism, some anarchism. Moscow still maintains that China was encouraging such groups, but there is no evidence whatsoever of Chinese involvement in terrorism in Turkey. 'Liberated areas' became distribution points for arms and explosives. There were several carefully planned killings of American military personnel. Politicians hurled charges of complicity in terrorism at each other. Rival leftist and rightist police unions had a debilitating effect on police and security forces.

The leftist teachers' union, TÖBDER, was one of the main instruments for management of terrorism throughout the country. When the national security headquarters obtained the telephone bills for the national headquarters of TÖBDER, which allegedly had only the dues of its members for operating expenses, it discovered that they averaged four times higher per month than its own telephone expenses!

Sectarian Violence Unbounded

During the first 50 years of the Turkish republic Sunnis and Shi'ites (called *Alevis* in Turkey) had managed to get along tolerably well. In the 1970s, leftists cultivated *Alevis* and ethnic minorities such as Kurds. Thus religious sectarianism soon became a cause of acute civil strife and tensions built up in Kurdish areas as all elements of the population became fearful of others. The most serious outbreak of civil strife up to that time occurred at Kahramanmaraş in the southeastern part of the country in late December 1978. The ghastly drama of this situation is well described in an official Turkish publication issued in 1982:

22 December 1978—A cold winter day . . . a funeral for two schoolteachers murdered the day before was to take place. The city was tense. Many inhabitants stayed home. Classes were suspended at most of the schools; shops and worksites closed down. Black clouds hung over the city. Something was going to happen. Insidious hands, waiting to apply their plans of treason . . . Shots were heard. Disorder and confusion. Voices rose from crowds taking part in the funeral. Armed groups, others with rocks and sticks in their hands, began to destroy and burn down shops. More shots were heard . . . 33 people are killed, over 300 people wounded, while more than 500 houses and shops were destroyed during this first day of the incidents.

Security forces prove to be incapable of preventing incidents. Gendarmerie troops from Gaziantep and airborne troops from Kayseri are deployed to the area. Jet fighters carry out deterrent flights over the city. Great groups of civil servants take shelter at the provincial headquarters, together with their dependents. But incidents continue to spread all over the city despite a curfew. In Ankara the Council of Ministers is in emergency session. The main opposition leader accuses the government of 'being inactive amidst a sea of blood'.

Groups trying to capture the provincial headquarters carry out raids on houses in the vicinity, ruthlessly murdering mothers, fathers, even babies.

23 December. Incidents continue. Casualties mount. Military troops try to take control and prevent clashes. A police station at the marketplace is burned, a gendarme shot. The number of arrests reaches 100; 200 detained.

24 December. Bloodshed goes on. Corpses are uncovered under debris and in dwellings. Casualties total 98. People take shelter in tents at a military camp. Despite curfew, persons with masks on their faces march in the streets shouting slogans such as 'independent Turkey', 'Moslem Turkey' . . . Terrorist groups continue to start fires in buildings. Ambulances are stopped. The number of wounded exceeds 1,000.

25 December. Disorder spreads to other cities with 11 people killed during marches and rallies. Over 200 schools in Istanbul on strike. Secondary schools, colleges and universities close in Ankara.

26 December. Martial law in 13 provinces declared by Council of Ministers and approved in joint parliamentary session by 537 votes. Balance sheet in Kahramanmaraş: 109 dead, 176 seriously wounded, more than 1,000 others wounded; more than 500 shops and houses destroyed.[11]

Intensified Destabilization

If Turkey's generals had been eager to take over the government, they had ample reason after an outbreak such as this. Instead they stood aside, hoping politicians could muster the will to make the parliamentary process work to produce more decisive leadership. Enforcement of martial law brought a modest decline in sectarian violence. But only five weeks after the outbreak in Kahramanmaraş and the commotion it sparked in many other parts of the country, Turkey was stunned by the cold-blooded murder of one of its most prestigious public figures, Abdi Ipekçi, editor of *Milliyet*. The murder was intended to undermine Turks' confidence in themselves. The murderer was Mehmet Ali Agca, but his identity was not known until the end of June. The circumstances of the Ipekçi murder and the controversy still surrounding it will be discussed in detail in Chapter 8 below.

It would be tedious to attempt to recount even the major terrorist incidents during the final period before military takeover. Though there were still periods when life in some parts of Turkey seemed to go on at a normal pace for weeks at a time, labor extremists were becoming more deeply committed to terrorist intimidation of workers who tried to maintain production. More urban 'liberated areas' were set up and the concept was extended to the east. In the remote Black Sea coastal town of Fatsa an ultra-leftist mayor declared the area a liberated commune. Leftists publicized the mayor as a kind of Robin Hood figure and alleged that the Demirel government had been quick to eliminate the Fatsa commune—when the military were ordered to march in—but soft on rightists in other parts of the country.

Extremists were encouraged or incited by propaganda from the two Soviet-backed clandestine radio stations broadcasting from East Germany. There was a vast outpouring of printed propaganda from both leftist and rightist publishing houses with little visible financing. One Turkish researcher has identified 270 periodicals used for leftist propaganda during the final period of terrorism and 61 leftist publishing houses.[12] Rightist propagandists were less numerous but active; some specialized in anti-Jewish materials.

Ecevit's last government fell in October 1979, demoralized by terrorism and economic decline, and Demirel took over again after partial elections in what seemed like an endless game of musical chairs. The security situation was becoming desperate and without a more coherent economic policy, continued Western economic aid was in jeopardy. Was Turkey capable of governing itself? Was it going the way of Iran?

Economically the tide began to turn on 24 January 1980 when Demirel announced a sweeping economic reform program—meeting all IMF conditions—and gave its principal architect, Turgut Özal, an outspoken advocate of free market principles, unprecedented authority to implement it. The business community and the public responded with enthusiasm and discipline. For a brief period political bickering almost ceased. Terrorism, however, did not. It became worse.

It was as if the terrorists had been ordered to prevent economic stabilization at any cost. Weapons continued to flow into the country in unprecedented quantities and terrorists appeared to have more money than ever at their disposal. Where did the funds and arms come from? Bank robberies? Thefts from police and military stores? Blackmail of businessmen? There was little evidence that any of these sources was significant.

Military and security authorities were intercepting sea shipments of arms with increasing frequency—whole shiploads with bills of lading that read 'spare parts', to be off-loaded to smaller boats in the Sea of Marmara. Coastal boats bringing arms slipped into remote harbors on the Black Sea. International freight trucks carrying legitimate goods from Europe to the Middle East also brought arms and sometimes even smuggled men. Usually these trucks were Bulgarian-operated. An enormous 'mafia' of Turkish smugglers based in Sofia fed other illicit channels, bringing in TV sets, electrical goods, watches and American-type cigarettes. These illicit channels had developed during the period when the Turkish economy, with a weak currency and declining domestic production, had been largely driven underground. Weapons and money that flowed in for terrorists were mixed into 'normal' smuggling channels.[13] But money also came as ostensible remittances from Turkish workers in Germany, as contributions to worthy causes and as false business transactions. Undoubtedly a good deal was disbursed directly from the embassies and consulates of communist governments in Ankara and Istanbul.

Martial law notwithstanding, irrational political and sectarian clashes continued to break out in all parts of the country with both the causes and the instigators often difficult to identify. Terrorism had developed a momentum of its own. Parents feared sending their children to schools where they might be shot in outbreaks that seemed to occur without provocation or warning. People stayed off the streets at night. Terrorist and subversive incidents registered on police records during the final year before military assumption of power totaled 23,841 and 2,812 people were killed during this period. By the later summer of 1980 an average of 28 people countrywide were being killed daily.[14] Highly respected former Prime Minister Nihat Erim was gunned down by three men and a woman on 19 July 1980 as retribution for serving as head of the above-party government that brought terrorism under control in 1971. While Erim's funeral was taking place, Kemal Türkler, head of the radical labor federation, DISK, was assassinated.

The economic recovery program which had got off to such a good start early in the year was being jeopardized by strikes and confusion. Demirel's government could not enforce discipline. Ecevit joined with Erbakan in early September to bring a vote of censure in parliament against Foreign Minister Erkmen, who resigned. There seemed to be no end to the political gamesmanship. Erbakan staged a mass rally in Konya with thousands of his NSP followers clamoring for restoration of Muslim law and repeal of Atatürk reforms. That was the straw that broke the camel's back. On 12 September 1980 General Kenan Evren, Chief of Staff of the Armed Forces, announced that the military leadership had designated itself the National Security Council and taken control of the government. The country heaved a collective sigh of relief. There was no resistance. Instead there was jubilation. With quarreling politicians silenced and massive arrests of terrorists, the country quickly returned to order.[15]

Balance Sheet of Terrorism

The full scope and nature of terrorism in Turkey did not begin to be realized, even among Turks themselves, until after the military took power and the clean-up of terrorism got under way. Prodigious quantities of weapons, ammunition and explosives came to light. Most of them were discovered in hide-outs, in former 'liberated areas', in premises of organizations such as TÖBDER, DISK and groups associated with the National Action Party. During the first 18 months of military administration, more than 800,000 weapons—enough to supply each man in the Turkish armed forces a gun with enough left over to give each combat soldier a second weapon as well—were collected or surrendered to the police. Most of these were pistols, but the total included over 64,000 high-powered rifles, over 6,300 automatic rifles and more than 8,000 shotguns. Over 6,000 automatic pistols and machine guns were taken from terrorists as well as 24 rocket launchers. More than 5,300,000 rounds of unused ammunition for all this weaponry were also collected, along with nearly 23,000 bombs, grenades, mines and other explosive devices. The nationwide haul from terrorists in statistics released by the government as of February 1982 also included 26,242 stabbing and cutting instruments and 94 radio communications sets.[16]

The list of origin of all this lethal hardware reads like the catalogue of an international arms dealer: Soviet Kalashnikovs, Belgian G-1 and G-3 infantry rifles, US M-1 rifles, German and French Mausers; pistols of a dozen other makes; Belgian Brownings, Czech Vizors, Italian Berettas, Spanish Astras, Lamas and Stars, German Walthers,

US Smith & Westons, Turkish pistols from the military arsenal at Kirikkale; British Sten guns; US Thomson submachine guns, German MP-5s, Czech Akreps.[17] Only a few of these weapons were of Turkish manufacture. Few of foreign make had been stolen from Turkish military or police arsenals. There was no normal point of origin in Turkey itself for them. Turkish authorities calculate the value of all these arms and ammunition at $300 million. This figure relates, of course, only to what has been confiscated; it does not take into account what was expended, lost, destroyed or still remains hidden. Qaddafy may have supplied funds for some of these weapons; Palestinians a bit; Syrians some more. But where do they get their weapons and ammunition? For the great bulk of these lethal tools of terrorism there is no other logical source than the Soviet bloc, no matter what the trademark or original point of manufacture may be.

What about the terrorists themselves? The figures are almost as shocking. During the first year of military administration—from 12 September 1980 through 11 September 1981—there were *ten times* as many arrests as there had been in 1971–2 when the clean-up after the first great terrorist wave took place: 43,140 terrorists and terrorist collaborators had been taken into custody by 11 September 1981. During the following year, the government released a large number of statistics on these people. Eighty-five per cent were under 35 years of age; 57 per cent between the ages of 16 and 25. Of the entire group, 28 per cent had only elementary school education, 36 per cent secondary education and only 14 per cent had attended universities. At the other end of the spectrum, 22 per cent had not completed elementary school at all. University students played a minor role as terrorist rank-and-file during the second wave. Many terrorists in leadership positions had previous university experience, but most were no longer students. Only 23 per cent of all terrorists were classified as being students of any kind at the time of their terrorist activity. Slightly over half of the terrorists captured during the first year of military administration—21, 864—were classified as leftist activists, only 14 per cent as rightist activists, 5 per cent (mostly Kurds) as separatists and 30 per cent defied or refused classification or were not sure themselves to which category they belonged.[18]

There are many more statistics available and a great deal of additional data is continually appearing as interrogations and trials of terrorists in Turkey have gone forward. During much of 1982 the national television service, TRT/TV, broadcast almost nightly round-ups of confessions and proceedings at trials of terrorists in all parts of the country. Additional arrests have continued to be made, though on a much smaller scale than during the first year of military control. A sizable portion of those originally arrested were found not guilty. On the other hand, perhaps as many as 15,000 known terrorists have escaped abroad. Many have obtained political asylum in Western Europe. A few were captured by the Israelis when they overran PLO camps in Lebanon in the summer of 1982. Arms caches continue to be uncovered in Turkey. Terrorist cells whose members have been trying to secrete arms and other gear for future use also continue to be discovered.

General, now President, Kenan Evren summed up the situation on the first anniversary of the military assumption of power:

> Turkish society was dragged near the brink of disintegration with intense subversive efforts and propaganda which were undoubtedly masterminded and conducted from foreign countries . . . So-called leaders . . . dared to form terrorist organizations . . . to direct and bend our country . . . by infiltrating . . . associations, schools, trade unions, political parties and public institutions.

> Certain countries aided the development of Turkish terrorism under the guise of friendship, economic and cultural agreements . . . It is clear that terrorists have received both financial and arms support from abroad . . . either directly or by countries sending weapons and equipment through smuggling with connivance and encouragement of the countries concerned. The aim . . . of terror in Turkey has been to isolate the country from its alliances and to pressure and dominate Turkey through subversive organizations claiming to represent the 'democratic masses'.

Though there is a great deal yet to be learned about terrorism in Turkey, we already know enough to justify two basic conclusions. Terrorism in Turkey was:

* deliberately fomented on a massive scale by the Soviet Union utilizing surrogates such as Bulgaria and Syria as principal channels for arms and Palestinians as major 'subcontractors' for training.

* The Soviet *modus operandi* included multi-faceted infiltration and build-up of rightist groups to serve as a foil for the left and

accelerate the destabilization process.

Turkish authorities believe that support of terrorism during the 1975 to 1980 period may have required outside funds totaling at least $1 billion—the equivalent of American and other NATO military aid for Turkey during this period.

This is the context in which Mehmet Ali Agca grew to maturity and in which he was recruited to terrorism. But he was an atypical terrorist, selected for unusual tasks and in all likelihood given special training. I will examine his evolution against the background of the Turkey of his time in Chapter 8. However, it is clear from the evidence in this chapter that traditional Soviet ambitions toward Turkey had enjoyed a most fruitful period during the 1970s. Very large amounts of money had been spent but significant results had been achieved, not the least of which was the recruitment of Agca himself and others like him. As we shall see in the next three chapters, the Soviets prefer to subcontract their more exotic subversive adventures. Access to a pool of experienced foreign assassins is therefore a worthwhile investment, particularly if it is difficult for the West to link them directly to the KGB. The links in the Agca chain pass through Italy and Bulgaria and we shall consider these next.

4

TERROR IN ITALY

Whose Puppets?

Italy's 87-year-old president, Sandro Pertini, a lifelong democratic socialist by conviction, spent a total of 15 years in prison and exile during the Mussolini era. This experience did not leave him embittered. It deepened his understanding of the real meaning of freedom. It also gives him better credentials as an opponent of fascism than any of the Italian terrorists who have claimed they were fighting it. In reality fascism is no force in Italy. Communism is. The relationship of communism to terrorism in Italy is curious. This is one of many issues on which Italian communists are sharply divided. President Pertini knows this. He is a keen student of terrorists and their mentality. In the spring of 1982, speaking at Johns Hopkins University on a visit to the United States, he reviewed recent developments in the fight against terrorism in Italy:

> for me the indication that Italian terrorism is about to be defeated is this: terrorists are now talking . . . It means that they are not guided by any true political belief . . . It indicates that they are feeling the ground eroded out from under their feet. They are not fighting for some higher and noble cause . . . If they are talking, it is because they are all puppets! They are in the hands of some puppeteer who would want to blow up this democratic bridge which is Italy! He is not yet defeated, but we are on the right road. [1]

President Pertini has a habit of speaking out on terrorism. More than a year earlier he created a diplomatic storm when he told the Hamburg newspaper *Die Welt* in an interview:

> I don't know, I only suspect it, and therefore I can only express my suspicion. How is it that terrorism was unleashed in Turkey, in a land that has a 1000-km common border with the Soviet Union?

How is it that it is so strong in Italy, which is a democratic bridge between Europe, Africa and the Middle East?[2]

A few days later the Soviet Ministry of Foreign Affairs summoned Italian Ambassador Walter Maccotta and lodged a formal protest against the Italian president's remarks. Moscow's sensitivity provoked extensive debate in Italy. Evidence of Russian support for subversion in Italy could still be dismissed as unconvincing by intellectuals who took pleasure in explaining terrorism as a manifestation of the ills of their own society; and by squabbling politicians who lacked the courage to face the consequences of publicizing evidence of Soviet bloc complicity their security officials provided them.

Italy was like Turkey in this respect. It was like Turkey in other ways too, but there were also important differences. Terrorism in Italy never came as close to wrecking the functioning of government or the operation of the economy as it did in Turkey in the late 1970s, but it was more persistent and insidious.

Terrorism developed in Italy in the late 1960s, much as it had in Turkey.[3] It was a student and intellectual phenomenon at first, but there seemed to be a broader base for it in the Italian communist movement. Italian communist leadership broke with Moscow over the invasion of Czechoslovakia in 1968. As a result tensions *within* the Italian Communist Party were greater than the strain between the communists and the other parties. There is a parallel here to what happened to the much weaker Turkish Labor Party in 1968–9. Extremist organizations were brought into being by people who had been part of the party but now turned toward violence, operating either autonomously or completely separately from it. Do we see here a common operational principle applied by Moscow to both countries, and to others as well? It is a hypothesis worth pondering. Defectors should eventually provide more insight. So, perhaps, will revelations among Italian communist leaders themselves. Ferment within the party, as it tries to come to terms with its complicated past relationship to the Soviet Union, provides a continual source of new information.[4]

'Our Jesus Christ'

Terrorism in Italy had more elegant theoretical foundations than terrorism in Turkey. There are at least three reasons for this: (1)

There was a richer tradition of political philosophy with strong anarchist and totalitarian currents to draw on. (2) And there was time. During the very period when an elaborate and highly professional structure was being created to support the Red Brigades in Italy (*Potere Operaio* [Workers' Power] which came into being in September 1971) an above-party government in Turkey, backed by a determined military leadership, was arresting terrorists by the hundreds, confiscating their arms and disrupting their organizational structure. While Turkish terrorists had to start all over again in 1975–6, the development of terrorism in Italy was steady, with violence escalating year by year during the 1970s. By 1975, 702 terrorist incidents were counted during the year. There were 1,198 in 1976; 2,124 in 1977; 2,365 in 1978; and 2,750 in 1979.[5]

(3) Finally, terrorism in Italy benefitted from the leadership of eminent and widely respected personalities. The millionaire leftist publisher, Giangiacomo Feltrinelli, until his death in 1972 while trying to blow up an electric pylon, provided funding and protection and a direct link to the East. He visited Czechoslovakia at least 22 times before he died.[6] The intellectual foundations were laid by Antonio Negri, a University of Padua political science professor. He was involved in the break-up of *Potere Operaio* into several inter-linked ultra-left groups in 1973. One of them, *Autonomia*, was dominated by Negri. With a record of impressive scholarship, Negri affected a posture of intellectual detachment. An investigative journalist who was the first to expose many of Negri's direct terrorist connections (and was later murdered) wrote of him:

> Of all the leaders of the *Autonomia*, Negri was the one who put himself on display the least . . . His revolutionary vigor seemed merely an intellectual abstraction rather than an exact political project.[7]

Carlo Casirati, a convicted criminal recruited by *Autonomia* to organize bank robberies, called Negri's seeming detachment a ploy: 'Negri was the man through whose hands everything passed. He was our Jesus Christ.'[8] The whole *Potere Operaio* complex, in spite of its name, was noteworthy for its lack of workers. Known among the inner circle as 'The Organization', it attracted a vast agglomeration of new leftists, intellectuals, counterculture enthusiasts and apologists for terrorism and violence. Claire Sterling has estimated that as many as 200,000 people eventually became involved, most of them unwitting, of course, of the ultimate purposes of the ventures they were supporting.[9]

Until the late 1960s, violence in Italy, which was always endemic in the south with such groups as the Mafia in Sicily, the 'Ndrangheta in Calabria and the Camorra in Naples, was apolitical or gravitated more toward fascist remnants than toward the left. Feltrinelli is said to have been obsessed with fear of a rightist takeover in Italy. There was little evidence to support this obsession, but it served as a convenient rationalization for the extreme radicalism of the Red Brigades and justified violence. Former Catholic sociology students from the University of Trento (e.g. Renato Curcio) and communist youth activists from Emilia formed what came to be called the 'historic nucleus' of the Red Brigades, centered in the Milan area.[10]

Communists as Targets

The Red Brigades were targeted as much against the revisionist leadership of the Italian Communist Party as against the legitimate Italian government but the party was slow to acknowledge or even recognize this aspect of the situation. Many non-communists claimed the Red Brigades were a secret wing of the party, but until 1977 Italian communists claimed that they were merely an extension of neo-fascist conspiracy. This theory fits neatly into the line of the forged US Army Field Manual in Turkey, and was propagated by other forgeries and disinformation spread by Soviet outlets in Italy.

During 1978 Italian communist leaders began to acknowledge left-wing terrorism for what it really was and to admit the threat it posed to their own position; for example, the party journal *Rinascita* declared on 20 January 1978:

> For a long time the Red Brigades were thought to be merely a disguise for fascist terrorism, perhaps carried on using the more traditional technique of infiltration. Today it must be admitted that around 1970 left-wing terrorism appeared in Italy.

What was going on was a struggle both between the leadership of the Italian Communist Party and Moscow hard-liners and between that same leadership and die-hards in the Italian movement itself.

Unlike most communist parties, the Italian one has been the subject of a good deal of academic survey research.[11] A lengthy report published by two University of Bologna sociologists in a scholarly journal in 1978,[12] revealed that ten years after the invasion of Czechoslovakia only a quarter of the Italian Communist Party's membership shared the party's own official view of it. Thirty-five per cent of the respondents held that 'the USSR did well to suffocate in time the danger of a division within the socialist world' while another 33 per cent thought the USSR was wrong to intervene though the Prague Spring was an 'experiment dangerous to socialism'.

The Soviet invasion of Afghanistan in 1979 and the suppression of Solidarity in Poland in 1981 caused rethinking among rank-and-file die-hards. By March 1983, when the Italian Communist Party held its 16th Congress, no more than 6–8 per cent of the membership was believed to support Armando Cossutta, who campaigned to draw the party back to a pro-Soviet position. He was decisively defeated. The plot against the Pope, which the Italian communists have never debated publicly, may also have continued to be a factor in this continuing erosion of pro-Soviet attitudes. The 16th Congress was a remarkably open affair—without precedent for a communist party in modern times. A spokesman for the majority position declared:

> Our party has made a concrete assessment of these facts—first of all the intervention of Afghanistan, preceded by the other, very serious intervention in Czechoslovakia—and has judged them unjustifiable on principle and fraught with negative consequences for the cause of detente, the independence and sovereignty of all nations and the substance and image of socialism . . . We distinguish among these countries and don't lump them all together. But how can one pass over the seriousness of the fact that, in Poland, after 35 years of communist rule, the crisis was so serious that there was a general resurgence of the working class and the toiling masses?[13]

With this kind of ferment infecting it, the Italian Communist Party was not a reliable instrument for development of terrorism. The Red Brigades were kept separate from it.

Turning Point—The Moro Murder

The most spectacular of all Red Brigades actions in the 1970s—the kidnapping and murder of former Italian Prime Minister Aldo

Moro—was mounted to prevent the leadership of the Communist Party from backing, and perhaps eventually joining, the government. The party had committed itself to 'Eurocommunism', a notion more popular and acceptable in Western capitals than in Moscow in the late 1970s. Christian Democrat Moro had formed a government with communist backing and was on his way to a parliamentary debate preceding a vote of confidence when he was ambushed and captured on 16 March 1978.

During the 55 days they held him, the Red Brigades claimed to have conducted a trial of Moro, issuing nine communiqués to the media and even distributing photographs. When the authorities refused to negotiate for his release, he was executed and his body was deposited in the trunk of a car half way between the headquarters of the Communist and Christian Democratic parties. While Moro was being held, the Red Brigades had the resources to carry out two murders and six leg-shootings in major Italian cities. Italy, though accustomed to terrorist brutality after nearly a decade of it, was nevertheless shocked.[14]

The Moro affair was the high point of terrorism in Italy, but it also caused a reaction that led to effective counter-measures. Political infighting and confusion among Italy's democratic parties were gradually overcome as a hindrance to action by the government to bring terrorism under control. Police were allowed to bug telephones and hold suspects. A law rewarding repentant terrorists for full confessions with reduced sentences was enacted at the request of General Alberto Dalla Chiesa, who was put in charge of an anti-terrorist unit that was given special powers for co-ordinating Italy's competing police and security organizations. The Red Brigades retaliated by declaring Italy to be in a state of civil war. Their foreign supporters increased the flow of arms, bombs and money for them. But the population, sensing the possibility of receiving protection from the government, reacted strongly against Red Brigades attacks on journalists, judges and respected public figures.[15]

The Soviets reacted to the Moro murder in a very different way. Shortly after the body was discovered, Soviet propagandists began suggesting an American link to the atrocity. The fabricated US Army Field Manual was cited as proof that the action conformed to well-known American operational doctrine. Propaganda fabrications, planted in newspapers in various countries were then requoted as authoritative judgements. In December 1978, the international communist mouthpiece *Problems of Peace and Socialism* (published in

Prague), declared:

> Let us note what another Italian journal has suggested . . . the suspicion that the Red Brigades or those who manipulate them in Italy are pro-fascist organizations skilfully camouflaged as reds
> . . .

This article goes on to speculate that the abduction of Moro and his subsequent murder must have been masterminded by the CIA. These allegations have continued to be repeated ever since in Soviet articles and material put out by known and surrogate Soviet propaganda outlets. There is a remarkable parallel with rapid Soviet reaction to Agca's shooting of the Pope.

Curbing Italian Terrorism

General Dalla Chiesa did not have to wait long for his club-and-carrot methods to begin to work. More and more Red Brigades members began to repent and defect. Patrizio Peci, who decided to talk in early 1980, provided information that resulted in the arrest of more than 400 terrorists. He reported that Red Brigades members continued to go to Czechoslovakia for training through the 1970s and testified that they received quantities of weapons shipped through Hungary and Austria. The damage Peci did to his former colleagues did not go unavenged. His brother Roberto was murdered in retaliation in the summer of 1981.[16]

Red Brigades activity leveled off during 1980 but was still at a high level. The basic pattern remained the same: domestic violence against symbols of the Italian establishment. Targets included industrial executives, prominent newspapermen, a prison doctor and many policemen and civil servants. The most spectacular terrorist episode of 1980 was the bombing of the railway station in Bologna at the height of the summer holiday season on 2 August 1980 in which at least 80 people were killed and more than 200 injured. No specific motive for this attack, other than terror itself, has been advanced. A neo-fascist group, the Revolutionary Armed Nuclei, first claimed and then denied responsibility. Although it has been assumed that a right-wing group was responsible for this particular bloody attack, the actual sponsorship of the action still remains obscure. It may have been an example of the Moscow technique—which was reaching a crescendo in Turkey at this time—of encouraging both the left and right to as many irrational actions as possible with the aim of heightening destabilization.[17] At the end of the year 1980 the Red Brigades' kidnapping of a high magistrate brought more publicity than any event ever since the Moro operation, but this victim was luckier. He was ultimately released unharmed.

The Bulgarian Connection

Despite the success of the Italian authorities in persuading some of the Red Brigades to talk, terrorist operations still continued if diminished in scale. On 17 December 1981, four Red Brigades disguised as plumbers burst into the Verona apartment of General James Dozier and kidnapped him. General Dozier was the highest ranking US officer in NATO's Southern European Command and the first American targetted in Italy.

His abduction triggered the largest manhunt in Italian history. The Italian police and security services, alerted and hardened by the experience of pursuing the Moro kidnappers and the plot against the Pope, and benefitting from the confessions that several hundred defected or captured Red Brigades members and their supporters had provided, were better equipped to act quickly. They had help from American and other NATO services. Forty-two days after the bound general was led away, Italian commandos stormed an apartment in Padua and freed him, gaunt and bearded but unharmed. The episode had much wider implications than the previous terrorist attacks because in the wake of Dozier's rescue, Luigi Scricciolo, head of the foreign department of the Social Labor Federation (UIL), was arrested. This arrest turned out to have very significant consequences because it established the Bulgarian connection in Italian terrorism, including the plot against the Pope.

Scricciolo was betrayed both by his wife and his cousin, Loris Scricciolo, but he had been held in such high respect in both political and intellectual circles that he was at first widely regarded as the victim of a family grudge. According to the cousin, whose allegations were soon confirmed by Antonio Savasta, who had led the Red Brigade team that kidnapped Dozier, the Bulgarian secret service had shown a direct interest in the operation. The Bulgarians had been so eager to get into the management of the case, in fact, they had aroused Red Brigade resentment. In return for a share in 'directing the captivity', the Bulgarians had promised more arms if NATO secrets were pried out of Dozier. The Bulgarians relayed offers of help from terrorist groups in France, Spain and Germany and encouraged the Red Brigades to heighten their efforts to destabilize Italy during the time Dozier was being held.

Luigi Scricciolo's wife provided valuable information confirming his Bulgarian ties. By mid-summer 1982 he was talking freely to Judge Ferdinando Imposimato, in charge of the investigation of this case. He confessed to being a Bulgarian agent since 1976, passing subsidies to Italy's peace movement for mounting anti-NATO demonstrations and serving as a link to the Red Brigades on a wide range of interests. Scricciolo had other information of extraordinary interest which linked him and the Bulgarians to Agca, but before we turn to it, we must go back a year to another chain of events that had led to the unraveling of the first skein in the Bulgarian connection in Italy.[18]

One of the *pentiti*, as they came to be called in Italy—repentant terrorist defectors—in the spring of 1981 identified Maurizio Folini as a prime link between Italian terrorism, PLO elements, the Bulgarians and the KGB. Folini was in charge of weapons procurement for a terrorist group with close relations with Libya. His network provided weapons to both rightist and leftist terrorist groups. Investigation of these connections by the Italian security authorities uncovered a maze of interlocking relationships with Syria, Turkey, Armenians and anti-Sadat Egyptians. There were Iranian connections as well. Weapons and ammunition were only one part of the operations of this ring. Drugs were another. Heroin procured in Lebanon and Turkey from sources as distant as Pakistan and South-east Asia was shipped via Bulgaria to Europe. The ring appears to have been partially self-supporting, but subsidies deriving ultimately from the Soviet Union could be drawn on to finance high-priority terrorist operations. Folini and others arrested as a result of the investigations following the exposure of this ring provided the first incontrovertible evidence of direct Soviet, Bulgarian and Libyan support of Red Brigades operations. In Italy itself, contact with members of this group, who were located primarily in the north, seems to have been largely a Bulgarian responsibility. But there may well be Soviet connections that have not yet been publicized.[19]

The whole case was placed in the hands of an investigating judge, Carlo Palermo. As of early 1983, he had indicted more than 40 people in Italy as principals and accomplices in the operations of this ring and had had nearly 300 arrested. The systematic exposure of all the links in this enormous chain of subversive connections may take years. Already the investigations have resulted in identification of Bulgarian 'diplomats' in Italy with ties to both Scricciolo and the plot to kill the Pope.[20]

Scricciolo's duties as a Bulgarian agent were all the more important in 1981 because of his connection with Lech Walesa. As a spokesman not only for the Italian labor confederation, but also as a representative of associated Western labor groups, Scricciolo had traveled to Poland to offer Walesa advice and help in setting up Solidarity— typewriters, duplicating machines and money. When Walesa made his historic visit to Rome in January 1981, Scricciolo was his host. All the while he was reporting everythingWalesa did, everything he told him, to his Bulgarian case officers. Such information must have enjoyed the highest priority for transmission to KGB headquarters in Moscow. How it was reported we do not know. Perhaps it did not go via Sofia at all, but directly to the KGB in Rome. Scricciolo was the kind of gold-chip secret agent any intelligence service would envy. From the viewpoint of professional technique, his relationship to Walesa—disguised as a man committed to helping him—was ideal.[21]

The Watershed of Italian Terrorism

1981–2 was the turning point for Italian terrorism and also for Soviet efforts to use the terrorist network for its own subversive purpose. Incidents declined steadily: 849 in 1981, 603 in 1982. Over the same period increasing evidence came to light of Soviet sponsorship of these activities.

Two daring terrorist actions—the attack on the Pope and the kidnapping of General James Dozier—generated reactions which were beyond the capacity of the Russians to dampen or divert. In both there was an element of simple bad luck. If Agca had succeeded in killing the Pope, the subsequent unfolding of the case might have been very different. It might never have unfolded at all. A dead Polish Pope would have been deeply regretted but quickly forgotten and it is almost inconceivable that his successor would have been from Eastern Europe. A prime Soviet aim would have been achieved. The Dozier kidnapping was a dramatic attempt against a senior US military officer. It followed the abortive assassination attempt, by rocket, against General Kroesen, US European Commander in Heidelberg on 16 September 1981. Both these episodes may have been motivated by a desire to divert attention from the attack on the Pope. In abducting Dozier when they did, the Red Brigades overreached their capacity to intimidate and maintain their momentum. They—and their backers—underestimated the capacity of the Italian authorities to strike back and then capitalize on the gains they had made by intensifying the pursuit of terrorists on all fronts.

The story of terrorism in Italy is still unfolding. Terrorism there is in all likelihood still not at an end. But there can be little doubt that it has been severely crippled. Several books will need to be written to record and interrelate even what is known now. More information is continually coming to light.

However, from what is already known one can establish the broad outlines. The terrorist network had been created in the confusion of Italian politics in the 1970s. It had been subsidized and manipulated by a variety of East European intelligence services of which the Bulgarians appear to have been the most active. These East Europeans and their ultimate Soviet sponsors had become so accustomed to using Italy—the 'Playground of Terrorism'—that they took it for granted that the Polish Pope could be murdered there with impunity. They were so confident they became careless. To the question why Sergei Antonov, the Bulgarian airline chief in Rome and a crucial link to Agca, had not been recalled to Sofia after Agca's attack on the Pope, Velichko Peitchev, a former Bulgarian official who defected in 1973, answered:

> They've been operating in Italy so long without being bothered—why should they worry in this case.[22]

With the plot against the Pope and the Dozier kidnapping, the Bulgarians overreached themselves and were exposed. However, before we return to the detail of Agca's adventures let us look first at three more essential features of the background of his plot: the evolution of support for terrorism and subversion by the Soviet Union and Bulgaria and the features of the Polish situation which explain Russian behavior there.

5
THE RUSSIAN TRADITION OF TERROR

Marx on Russia and Terrorism

To a degree far beyond anything that can be found in Western European tradition or experience, political intrigue, brutality, terrorism—'the habit of violence'—have characterized Russia's history.[1] While Western Europe and the United States were evolving in the direction of more open, participatory societies in the late nineteenth and early twentieth centuries, Russian evolution was tragically directed toward greater entanglement in terror and intrigue on the part of both the state and its enemies.[2] Karl Marx wrote in 1853:

> There is no more striking feature in the politics of Russia than the traditional identity, not only of her objects, but of her manner of pursuing them.[3]

Marx was no friend of Russia. His mid-nineteenth century writing, especially when he was serving as correspondent for the *New York Tribune* in the 1850s, is among the most critical that can be found on the Tsarist Empire. His daughter Eleanor and her husband, Edward Aveling, collected this correspondence for publication in 1897 because, as she said, of

> the remarkable historical acumen shown, the great power of piercing through the semblance of things to the things themselves; the accuracy with which, in almost every case, events and consequences likely to follow have been foretold.[4]

She was especially struck by her father's views of Russia:

> One thing has remained constant and persistent: the Russian Government's policy of aggrandizement. The methods may vary—the policy remains the same. Today the Russian Government . . .

76

is, as it was in the [1850s], the greatest enemy of all advance, the greatest stronghold of reaction.[5]

Soviet writers occasionally cite Marx's denunciations of the Tsarist system, but writings like this on Russia are ignored or suppressed. They are too uncomfortable. They support the sharpest criticisms that are made of the Soviet system today, both from within the USSR and from the outside.

Marx had less to say on terror and violence than he had to say on Imperial Russia, but what he did say was equivocal. He does not appear to have been as opposed to terror as long as it supported revolutionary change. In the wake of the revolutionary events of 1848 he wrote:

> There is only one way to *shorten* the murderous death agonies of the old society, only one way to shorten the bloody birth pangs of the new society . . . only one *means*—Revolutionary terrorism.[6]

The degree to which Marx and Engels approved of terror in subsequent years will always be subject to debate. For our purposes in this brief survey the operative issue is how Marxism came to affect what actually happened in Russia.

The Leninist Legacy

Marxist ideas, as they became part of the ideological ferment which infected the Russian Empire during the second half of the nineteenth century, contributed to consolidation of the view that violent change was going to be needed to set Russia on a path toward sustained political and economic modernization. Bakunin, Kropotkin, Nechaev, the People's Will, the Social Revolutionaries, along with the extraordinary double agent Azev, are all part of a line of development which culminated in Lenin, 'The High Priest of Terror', as the historian Albert Parry termed him.[7]

This course of development was not inevitable. There were other men and organizations, other currents of thought that at the time seemed stronger. The historical balance was tipped at crucial junctures during the years before 1917 in ways that in retrospect seem almost accidental. But in the end Lenin and Bolshevism triumphed and this is the legacy most relevant for the history of the Soviet Union and the problems it represents for the world today.

Other distinguished traditions in Russian history and intellectual life are not dead. They are simply not operative to a high degree in Soviet policy and actions. Nothing said subsequently in this chapter—or for that matter written or seemingly implied anywhere else in this book—is meant to belittle or disparage the positive side of the Russian revolutionary tradition. It is alive today in the unconquerable minds of men such as Andrei Sakharov and Alexander Solzhenitsyn and thousands of others who produce a steady flow of *samizdat* (underground literature). For these Russians the modern course of Russian historical development and the specific actions described below are tragic and painful.

Albert Parry explained Lenin's thought processes very simply:

> The centrality of Lenin to modern terror is now beyond dispute . . . Lenin believed capitalism to be violence; the revolutionary use of violence was not more than a wholly proper countervio- lence.[8]

This is the argument used by the Baader–Meinhof gang and the Italian Red Brigades. Most of the philosophy of these and other modern terrorist groups can be found in Nechaev's *Catechism of a Revolutionary*, drawn up with Bakunin's participation, in the late 1860s. Lenin wrote in 1901:

> In principle we have never rejected terror nor can we reject it. Terror is one of those military means that can come in handy and be even necessary at a certain moment of a battle, when the troops are in a certain shape under certain circumstances . . . [9]

After seizing power in November 1917, Lenin soon found that 'certain circumstances'—staying in power and outwitting his opponents—argued for violence. Terror became the main method by which the Bolsheviks consolidated their hold on Russia and destroyed their rivals. Class war meant then, as it has meant ever since, resort to terror when it was waged at full intensity:

> The operative word in what Lenin called the class war was not class but war. This involved not merely an acceptance of terror and a loving concern with the idea of its application, but also a pedantic elaboration of terroristic methods that distinguished him from

other socialist leaders.[10]

The notion that it was Stalin who brutalized the Soviet system is comforting but it is an illusion. Solzhenitsyn's *Gulag Archipelago* makes clear that it was Lenin who started the system.[11] The history of Soviet Russia falls into periods of terror, relieved by periods of relative relaxation, with regional variations. In the country as a whole, terror dominated during collectivization and, with only a brief period of relief, intensified again during the period of the great purges. Substantial internal relaxation became necessary to enable the country to defeat the German invasion, but terror was reimposed even before the war's end when several nationalities considered collaborators were uprooted and deported to Central Asia and Siberia.[12] It continued with the dispatch to forced labor camps of millions of returned prisoners of war, laborers and alleged traitors (primarily Russians and other Slavs). The Baltic States and the Western Ukraine were systematically purged in the period 1945 to 1950.

Since Stalin's death in 1953, terror as a tool of domestic governance has been applied in more differentiated, subtle and sophisticated ways but it has never been absent from the Soviet internal scene. Only through periodic application of violence has the USSR been able to maintain control over the captive peoples of Eastern Europe.

None of this history proves, of course, that the Soviet Union has been supporting international terrorism, but it provides essential background. A system relying on deliberate and continual application of techniques of subversion and violence to maintain itself in power over its own population would naturally incline toward similar methods for extending its influence abroad.

Soviet Covert Operations Abroad

Covert activity abroad has been a feature of the Soviet system from its earliest days with varying patterns of collaboration and rivalry between international communist co-ordinating organizations and intelligence operations. There is a large memoir literature dealing with the period preceding World War II;[13] it expanded enormously after 1946. Several comprehensive studies of Soviet intelligence and subversive operations, which take most of the defector memoirs into account, have appeared in the past two decades.[14] This material leaves no doubt that the Soviet Union has devoted enormous

resources to clandestine operations, expanded its capabilities continually, extended its geographic range of operations and refined its
techniques. It is still doing so. There is no basis for an assumption that
the Soviets have ever downgraded the priority or restricted the
momentum of clandestine operations in spite of periodic exposures
and temporary setbacks in several countries, some of which are well
documented. Priorities in respect to countries and areas of operational emphasis are, of course, adjusted from time to time. The
dominant characteristic of all Soviet covert operations has always
been careful preparation, patience, perseverance and effort in depth.
Eastern European intelligence services which were rapidly built up as
the Russians consolidated control over these countries were already
given important auxiliary tasks in the 1950s.

Ladislav Bittman, a Czech intelligence officer who fled his
country's service after the Soviet invasion of 1968, has provided one
of the best first-hand descriptions of the value of the East European
services to the Russians:

> The activities of the satellite intelligence services are usually under-
> estimated by the West, but these offshoots from the Soviet appara-
> tus play an important role in the Soviet overall scheme . . . The
> satellite services permit the Soviet Union to increase its intelligence
> activities by roughly 50 per cent . . . Despite the fact that most of
> the information obtained and the operations conducted by satellite
> countries are useless to themselves, their intelligence organizations
> finance this activity and in the event of failure—such as the ex-
> posure of agents—assume responsibility and the risk of enemy
> retaliation. The existence of subsidiary intelligence services also
> facilitates   approaching   and   recruiting . . . non-Communist
> citizens—men who would refuse a direct Soviet proposal for
> reasons of nationalism or anti-Russian feeling.[15]

Note how these factors are all relevant in the case of Mehmet Ali
Agca.

During the 1950s it was already apparent that Soviet operations
conducted within the formal government structure enjoyed higher
priority than those undertaken through communist party channels.
This trend has continued. It has made possible the support of non-
communist, nationalist and even rightist groups. Power politics long
ago outdistanced ideology as a criterion for judging the worthiness of
groups and individuals for covert support and exploitation. The

Soviets have often displayed remarkable imagination—and opportunism—in manipulating and camouflaging raw power considerations under various kinds of ideological cloaks which make them more respectable, especially in the Third World.

American reaction to the Korean invasion in 1950, coming in the wake of the dramatic Western response to the Berlin Blockade, left Stalin acutely frustrated in his final years in power. He eventually found it impossible to control all the intrigue that swirled around him. The circumstances of his own death in 1953 are still obscure. Khrushchev, once he had gained a firm hold on power, was daring about competing with the West for influence on a much more flexible basis but he suffered a severe setback when Kennedy forced him to back down during the Cuban missile crisis. East–West competition during the past 20 years has been profoundly affected by decisions the Soviet leadership group took in the period immediately following this 1962 humiliation. These may well have been Khrushchev's decisions, even though he was unable for long to maintain his hold on power. The missile crisis weakened him.

The former Czech general, Jan Šejna, who like Bittman fled in 1968, maintains that the Soviet Union had committed itself by 1964 to a broad, long-range expansion of covert operations in all major Western countries and that this plan included expansion of East European surrogate capabilities, as Bittman described them.[16] The plan included encouragement of Castro's ambitions to revolutionize Latin America and the entire Third World. The Tricontinental structure (African, Asian, Latin American Peoples' Solidarity Organization) began to operate out of Havana in 1966 and rapidly expanded as a propaganda and operational instrument for encouraging anti-Western revolutionary ferment wherever the ground looked even mildly fertile. Castro had no financial means of his own. Cuba has remained dependent on Soviet funding and material support for every major foreign operation it has undertaken.

Lessons were learned from all these experiences. And more were learned from the student and intellectual ferment which welled up throughout the West in the late 1960s. There is evidence of direct Soviet involvement in some of it. The Russians encouraged and publicized most of this ferment through overt and covert propaganda channels. A wide variety of surrogate arrangements were used. Many countries proved amenable to Soviet purposes: for instance, Syria, South Yemen, Iraq and Libya, all served as channels, along with Cuba, for support of Eritreans and other anti-Ethiopian activities in the late 1960s and early 1970s. North Korea was especially useful in other areas where the Russians were competing with the still active Chinese communists for influence on liberation movements and guerrilla organizations. The Palestinians began to be developed as a major operational force in the late 1960s when they were susceptible as a result of the Israeli victory in 1967. By this time, the controled intelligence services of Eastern Europe had reached a relatively high degree of effectiveness. The best were the East Germans, Czechs, Bulgarians and Hungarians. Soviet exploitation of the Czechoslovak service seems to have increased, rather than declined, in the wake of the invasion at the end of the summer of 1968.

It was at the turn of the decade that a shift from relatively diffuse agitational and propaganda activity toward more tightly controled conspiratorial and violent operations occurred: terrorism in its more dramatic and alarming forms. The shift coincides with the assumption of KGB leadership by Yuri Andropov. Cuba had encouraged hijackings of aircraft from the US and Latin America in the late 1960s. Hijackings spread in the 1970s. Palestinians had a natural affinity for terrorist actions and Qaddafy, very soon after he established his hold on Libya, displayed a strong desire to make a mark in a much larger arena. If Andropov had come in to phase out ineffective operations and take new initiatives, the situation was made to order for him.

During the 1970s most of the long-standing clandestine broadcasting operations which the Soviet Union had sponsored since the 1950s were terminated. By the end of the decade, only those broadcasting to Turkey (two stations) and Iran (one station in two languages) remained. These stations exacerbated the political deterioration which afflicted both countries in the late 1970s. Meanwhile, evidence of intensified Soviet effort in the field of disinformation, subversive propaganda and forgery began to accumulate. Some of this material was designed to serve tactical purposes. Most of it was aimed at undermining confidence in Western governments and at disrupting US relationships with allied and friendly states.[17] In the broadest sense, its purpose was to foster alienation, suspicion and resentment in Western societies, fan tensions and help build a climate where terrorism and violent destabilization would seem credible and natural as manifestations of social strain and resultant political dissatisfaction.

Spreading Violence

Violence spread as the US became bogged down in Vietnam, NATO was beset by increasing strain and OPEC price increases caused economic crisis. This was a time when most democratic countries were coping with social and political tensions by accelerating efforts to achieve more complete democracy, broader social justice and rectification of economic, ethnic and regional imbalances. Violence reflected local causes in many instances and fed on indigenous grievances and frustrations. There nevertheless often seemed to be insidious processes of exacerbation at work. Casual violence escalated into organized, irrational terrorism. Generally leftist in ideological underpinnings and rationalizations, terrorists sometimes directly attacked rightist groups and ideas. But many terrorists' ideological motivations became more vague as their commitment to violence intensified. The most dedicated terrorists sometimes came from the most affluent levels of society. Intellectuals became fascinated by terrorism. Extreme nationalism was a factor in some cases, but was often entirely absent. A curious form of abstract internationalism, devoid of real humanitarianism and nihilistic at its core, was the most characteristic motivation—or rationalization for action. More often it seemed to be mere lust for power or self-dramatizing adventurism. We see these last three characteristics in Mehmet Ali Agca.

What was most surprising about practitioners and theorists of violence was that attitudes toward the Soviet Union were seldom hostile, often equivocal, sometimes surprisingly indulgent in the light of other goals they claimed to be pursuing. Such equivocation and generosity was almost always reciprocated by the Soviets themselves. They showed remarkable understanding, sympathy and at times open enthusiasm for disaffected 'revolutionary' groups working to destroy Western societies in spite of the fact that both sides knew that the most minor actions of the same type in Moscow or Minsk would provoke immediate KGB repression.[18] As Claire Sterling observed, the terrorists

have never tried to dismantle a society under Soviet sponsorship. They haven't lifted a finger against some of the most appalling tyrannies on record, either. Uganda under the maniac rule of Idi Amin did not make their list. (In fact, Palestinians volunteered to act as his personal bodyguard.) Nor did the Central African Empire under the cannibal reign of Emperor Bokassa . . . Yet the nearly empty desert sultanate of Oman has been high on their list and so has a stretch of Saharan sand staked out by the Polisario guerrillas, demanding statehood for a population of 80,000.[19]

To a remarkable extent, there *is* a common denominator in a very large percentage of terrorist activity: it supports direct or indirect Soviet political or ideological objectives. When Ethiopia was a Western-oriented country, dependent on the United States for its principal military support and offering modest military facilities for US use, insurgency in Eritrea was sustained by communist and radical Arab countries, Libya prominent among them. Cuba was an early patron of Eritrean rebels, some of whom received their first serious guerrilla training on that island. Since the Soviets fully embraced the Ethiopian Revolution in 1976, all of these countries have discovered that the Eritrean insurgency is not a genuine 'liberation' movement.

Reluctance to Believe

Despite much important evidence linking the Soviets to terrorism in the West, there has been great reluctance among Western commentators to believe it. The Russians have known how to exploit this Western uncertainty and that accounts for much of the success of their disinformation efforts.[20] Western commentators showed a similar reluctance to recognize the scope and depth of the Soviet purges of the 1930s, even in the face of publicity and partial evidence at the time. The first comprehensive documentary study was too impressive to be dismissed lightly, but it still met with skepticism.[21]

The chain of revelations which Khrushchev set in motion three years after the death of Stalin finally provided *evidence* which destroyed the cumulative body of apologetics and rationalization that had been produced during the previous two decades about the great purges and the forced labor system. The monumental works on Robert Conquest[22] and Alexander Solzhenitsyn[23] have exposed these appalling features of the Soviet system in such detail that it is no longer possible to ignore them. There are other, similar cases of Soviet state crime, equally relevant, which have never been widely acknowledged—for example, the Katyn massacre, which will be discussed below. These past experiences must be taken into account when we examine the possibility of Soviet sponsorship and support for various kinds of subversive activity, including assassination, during the past two decades.

Do the Soviets Sponsor Assassination?

The history of Soviet involvement in assassinations and mysterious deaths is directly relevant to the plot against the Pope. John Barron, in his classic book on the KGB, traces Soviet murder and kidnapping of *foreigners* back at least as far as 1926.[24] The KGB's predecessor, the OGPU, became so notorious in the 1930s as an organization committed to liquidation of enemies of the Soviet state that it may have been credited with more victims than it actually disposed of.

In 1936 the NKVD, the successor to the OGPU, set up a Special Tasks Section which soon became known by its gruesome nickname, 'Wet Affairs' (*Mokrye Dela*). Whatever the official designation of this unit has been since, it has always been known informally, both within the Soviet Union and outside, by the same term.

Walter Krivitsky, one of the OGPU/NKVD's chief operators in Western Europe, provided one of the first authoritative inside accounts of the conduct of wet affairs (and other kinds of subversion as well) in 1939.[25] Krivitsky, commenting on Soviet assassinations, wrote: 'Any fool can commit a murder; it takes a genius to commit a natural death.' Suicide is nevertheless a messy form of 'natural death' and one that in contrived circumstances usually generates suspicion of foul play, such as the purported window-leap suicide of the Czech patriot, Foreign Minister Jan Masaryk, on 10 March 1948. In recent years the Soviets have preferred traffic accidents as a method of committing 'natural deaths'.

The most famous killing linked to the Soviet Union in the period up to the beginning of World War II was the murder of Leon Trotsky in Mexico on 20 August 1940. No 'natural death' could be contrived for Trotsky, Stalin's arch-enemy. His killing came as the final, brutal episode in a chain of assaults. His villa had been attacked three months before by a gang in NKVD hire but he escaped alive even though more than 200 bullets entered his bedroom. The true identity of the assassin who succeeded was only established in the 1970s. He was a Spaniard. He revealed nothing of his personal history or backers during 20 years in prison and went to Czechoslovakia on release in 1960.

In the violence and oppression which accompanied Soviet occupation of Eastern Europe at the end of World War II and which continued during the forced imposition of communist governments on these states, kidnapping and murder became commonplace. These actions were simply an extension of practices inside the USSR where such methods had become part of standard Soviet security operating procedure. There were, of course, swings of the pendulum from extreme harshness to some degree of leniency, from freeze to thaw and back again.

Stalin's death in 1953 brought expectations of relaxation and some easing of conditions. Lavrenti Beria, head of the MVD (successor to the NKVD) since 1938, lost out in the power struggle among Stalin's successors. He was removed in June and executed in December 1953. Wet Affairs was dissolved in June too, but reconstituted in September. By the time the MVD was reorganized and formally established as the KGB the next year, the post-Stalin leadership had discovered that Wet Affairs was an indispensable arm of the Soviet state. During the Stalin era when Beria was in charge, this section appears to have had operational autonomy. Under Khrushchev the leadership examined and approved in advance all significant operations. This procedure is believed to have continued ever since. This is a crucial fact in judging responsibility in planning and execution of the plot against the Pope. The evidence rests on the testimony of many high-level defectors over a period of nearly 30 years.

Evidence from Soviet Defectors

Nikolai Khokhlov

One of the most dramatic of these defectors appeared in Germany in February 1954. His name was Nikolai Khokhlov, a native Russian and veteran MVD operator. He had been sent to assassinate Georgi Sergeevich Okolovich, head of the Russian émigré organization, NTS. Instead he came to the man's apartment, and exposed the plot to him as well as his plan to defect. The information he provided led to the apprehension of other Soviet agents who had been assigned to support him. He delivered the devices he had been given to carry out the killing to American authorities in West Germany and provided an enormous amount of information on Soviet wet affairs techniques and operational planning.

As a Radio Free Europe official, I spent a day with this man in the spring of 1954 in a house in the Taunus hills where he was being interrogated. We made plans for him to broadcast his story. I listened to him recount how he had spent several years as an 'illegal' in Soviet-occupied Romania immediately after the end of World War II. He had been selected as the war was coming to an end, rigorously trained to speak flawless Romanian and sent into the country in the wake of the Soviet armies to establish himself as an underground agent reporting back to Moscow on the attitudes of the population. He married a Romanian woman and lived as a Romanian for several years, gaining high marks in Moscow for his reporting. Then one day he simply disappeared. He was recalled to Moscow to be trained for new and more demanding assignments: Wet Affairs.

Khokhlov's revelations were widely publicized in the Western press and broadcast back to Eastern Europe and the Soviet Union. He wrote a book, *In the Name of Conscience*, which appeared first in German and then in English in 1959.[26] He had not been forgotten in Moscow. In September 1957 he was stricken with a sudden illness that quickly worsened. It was eventually diagnosed as poisoning by irradiated thallium. A small amount of the substance had apparently been placed in his food by an unseen hand. Of course, there was no proof that the attempt to kill him by radiation poisoning had its origin in Moscow. But from where else would such an initiative have come? Irradiated thallium is not accidentally ingested in the course of daily life.

The activities of exiled political activists have always aroused fear in the Kremlin to a degree that is difficult to comprehend in the West. But Soviet leaders have not forgotten that Lenin was just such a man, regarded as an eccentric dreamer in exile in Switzerland. Yet once assisted by the Germans to return to Russia after the revolution in March 1917, he had seized the political initiative by October and laid the groundwork for Bolshevik seizure of power. From Lenin and Stalin onward, every Soviet leader has been concerned to remove the threat of foreign challenge. Khrushchev, or others around him, were intensely preoccupied with this problem in the 1950s. Khokhlov's defection and the adverse publicity following it did not discourage further operations along the same line. Some succeeded, some failed and some have undoubtedly never come to light.

Bohdan Stashinsky

Of the operations we know about, the greatest successes, capped by ultimate failure and exposure, revolve around the activities of a young Ukrainian, Bohdan Stashinsky, who was compromised into serving the KGB and sent to establish himself as an 'illegal' in West Germany. After careful training and meticulous preparation, he succeeded in blowing prussic acid vapor into the face of a Ukrainian exile in the hall of the building in Munich where he had his office. The man collapsed and died immediately as if from a heart attack. Two years later, after both adventures and misadventures, Stashinsky was back in Munich again where he assassinated the famous Ukrainian resistance leader, Stefan Bandera, by the same method. This time the police were more alert—or perhaps more suspicious—and they found flakes of glass from the crushed acid container on the victim's face and traces of prussic acid in his body. It was clear that Bandera had been murdered. The Soviet press claimed that a prominent anti-communist political leader, West German Minister for Refugee Affairs, Dr Theodor Oberländer, had had Bandera killed to cover up his own alleged Nazi past. There was nothing to substantiate such allegations, but they were repeated steadily and treated with more respect than they deserved.

On return to Moscow, Stashinsky was personally congratulated by KGB chief Shelepin and awarded a decoration accompanied by a document signed by Marshall Voroshilow, Chairman of the Supreme Soviet of the USSR. In spite of the brilliant future which lay ahead of him in the KGB, Stashinsky fell into a situation which led to his defection in August 1961. It involved marriage with an East German girl who detested communism, birth of a child who died and a series of increasingly crude efforts by the KGB to manage his personal life.

Stashinsky arrived in the West ready to confess his murders and face trial but even hardened American and West German intelligence experts were initially skeptical of the lurid tales he had to tell. He had, in effect, to help convict himself. Documents were found to verify his movements in West Germany and witnesses who corroborated his recollections of circumstances surrounding his tracking of the two assassinated Ukrainian exile leaders. Police even opened the lock housing of Bandera's apartment door and found a piece of key Stashinsky said he had broken. His trial in Karlsruhe in October 1962 coincided with the Cuban missile crisis. It was a time when much of the world still found evidence of high-level Soviet scheming and duplicity hard to overlook. Stashinsky was obviously guilty and welcomed the verdict. He won the sympathy of the court. The presiding judge called him

an intelligent and gifted person, gentle and peace-loving by nature.

Had it not been for the Soviet system, which, just as did the Nazi system, regards political murder on behalf of the state as a necessity, he would probably be a schoolteacher somewhere in the Ukraine.[27]

Stashinsky made an eloquent statement at the end of the trial:

I wanted to unburden my conscience, and I wanted to give worldwide publicity to the way in which 'peaceful co-existence' really works in practice. I did not want to go on being used on murder assignments. I wanted to warn all those who live in danger of being liquidated . . . to take precautions.[28]

Stashinsky was sentenced to eight years imprisonment and is now, as far as is known, living somewhere in the world under a new identity.

Applying the Lessons

One cannot read the story of Stashinsky without being reminded of Agca. There are many differences, but both were promising and intelligent young men corrupted by a system that exploited them mercilessly. In both cases the Soviets leaped to blame the murders they had instigated on the West. Agca was only four years old when Stashinsky confessed and was tried. For all his voracious reading, he is unlikely ever to have heard of Stashinsky. Agca's career may nevertheless be partly the result of Stashinsky's fate. If it had not been for Stashinsky's defection and widely publicized confession, Agca might never have been selected to assassinate the Polish Pope.

According to several KGB defectors of the mid and late 1960s, the Stashinsky case had serious reverberations in the KGB and in the Soviet hierarchy. Supervisory officers were reported to have been demoted or transferred and a new policy on wet affairs abroad was adopted. They would not be abandoned as an operational technique, but they would be restricted and undertaken with greater precautions. One defector, Yuri Nosenko, claimed to have evidence that

the KGB concluded that future assassinations should be entrusted not to Soviet personnel such as Khokhlov and Stashinsky but to hired foreign criminals and illegal agents of other nationalities who could not be easily linked to the Soviet Union.[29]

Agca fits the pattern.

Andropov apparently reconfirmed and refined these principles when he took charge of the KGB in 1967. Not only would the East European and Cuban intelligence services be exploited more systematically to serve Soviet priorities; the supply of agents of non-Soviet bloc nationality would not be left to chance. Potential activists would be selected for training and deployment through co-operative organizations and countries. The potential of extremist organizations sheltering under the roof of the Palestine Liberation Organization was especially attractive.[30] In time Libya, South Yemen and Syria came to play an equally valuable part in the process. North Korea had long been helpful, but its usefulness for specific wet affairs operations was limited. For the Western hemisphere and much of the Third World, Cuba during the 1970s was converted into a mercenary country which devoted almost all its activities overseas to serving Soviet political and conspiratorial purposes. Somewhat more gradually, and no doubt at lower cost, Bulgaria came to play the same role for Europe and the Middle East.[31]

As we discussed in the previous chapter, Bulgaria had long been established as a Soviet surrogate in Italian affairs. However, to understand the nature and scope of Bulgarian activity, it needs to be seen in historical perspective.

6
BULGARIANS AS MERCENARIES

On Moscow Time

Bulgaria's leader, Todor Zhivkov, who came to power in 1954, declared on the occasion of a visit by Soviet Premier Nikita Khrushchev in 1962:

> We must say that our political watch-dial is exact to the second with the watch of the Soviet Union, that our watch is working to Moscow time. This is a matter of great pride for all Bulgarian people.[1]

The plot against the Pope has exposed the extent to which Bulgaria has adhered to Moscow time ever since.

The country went onto Moscow time in September 1944, but the shift was far from voluntary. Communist takeover in Bulgaria provides a stark example of how the Russians treat people who are supposed to be their friends. Sovietization in Bulgaria was faster and more brutal than anywhere else in Eastern Europe. In the first six months of Soviet occupation, according to official statistics which are probably too low, 10,897 persons were tried. Of these 2,138 were executed and 1,940 sentenced to prison terms of 20 years or more.

While Bulgaria was firmly locked into a Moscow stranglehold politically, economically it was treated with less brutality than other East European countries. In the first decade and a half of communist rule, Bulgaria received at least $1 billion in credits from the USSR. The money did not go into improving living standards. Bulgaria's communist leaders used it to industrialize Soviet-style. In the 1970s living standards improved modestly, but they leveled off and may even have fallen in the early 1980s. While Bulgaria is not, on balance, profitable to the Soviets in the way Qaddafy's Libya is, it has never fallen into the kind of economic disarray most of the other communist-dominated countries of Eastern Europe have experienced. It has made better use of Soviet aid than the Cubans have,

91

while at the same time serving Soviet purposes as a mercenary country in Europe and the Middle East.[2]

Despite current Bulgarian enthusiasm for serving Soviet purposes, the country's history is far from being a monotonous chronicle of Russophilia. Before we look more closely at how communist Bulgaria became one of the Kremlin's principal subcontractors for subversion and assassination, let us look back over recent Bulgarian history.

Bulgaria achieved its independence from the Turks at the Congress of Berlin in 1878, following the Russian–Turkish war of 1877. However, it was not foreordained to be a Russian puppet by the manner of its rebirth as an independent country. The predominant political influences came not from Russia but from two other directions: Central Europe, which supplied the first two Bulgarian monarchs, and America, which through schools in Bulgaria and in Istanbul at Robert College (an American missionary school), educated a large proportion of the officials who staffed the new Bulgarian government.

Of the 25 men who had completed Robert College by 1874, all but two were Bulgarians. The Class of 1871 had five graduates, all Bulgarian. These five men together went on, in the course of their careers, to provide two mayors, four national assembly members, three ambassadors, three cabinet ministers and two prime ministers. Bulgarians came as students to Amherst, Hamilton, Harvard, Princeton and Yale, but for the next two decades the majority continued to be educated at Robert College.[3]

Russians were popular too in Bulgaria in the wake of the 1878 liberation. The Bulgarians, who had no native nobility, would have accepted a Russian prince as their monarch. But the other powers were opposed. A German, Alexander of Battenberg, 22, related to both the British and Russian royal families, was installed as prince in 1879. Russian occupation armies withdrew but left behind 200 officers and numerous civilians who, like the carpetbaggers in the American South after the Civil War, took governmental positions and went into business. They soon alienated Bulgarians on all sides. As the popularity of the young Prince Alexander grew in his adopted country, his relations with the Russians deteriorated.

Soon Russian ambassadors in Europe were spreading tales of his alleged moral depravity and Russians in Sofia were supplying money to Bulgarian agents to organize clandestine activity against him. He escaped two assassination attempts in the spring of 1886 only to be kidnapped in August of that year. Bogdanov, the Russian diplomatic agent who organized the kidnapping, warned his conspirators not to kill Alexander for 'one day the truth will come out and Russia will have the heavy responsibility of having encouraged the assassination of a ruling prince'.[4] A counter-coup in Bulgaria enabled Alexander to return a hero, but during the ensuing confusion he finally abdicated in September 1886 in the face of unrelenting Russian pressure. In this crisis, diplomatic relations with Russia were broken and not restored until 1896.

The final Russian effort to subvert Bulgaria came in 1944. World War II was a political disaster for Bulgaria. It joined Germany but avoided a declaration of war against the USSR after the Germans invaded. Bulgaria refused to deliver its Jews to Hitler's gas chambers. The German link again brought the temporary dividend of 'restoration' of the coveted Yugoslav, Greek and Romanian territories lost in World War I, but the gains were short-lived. King Boris, who had succeeded his father King Ferdinand in 1919, died mysteriously on a flight returning from a visit to Hitler in 1943. He was succeeded by his six-year-old son, Simeon. Politicians began efforts to extricate the country from the war. A government of pro-Western political parties broke relations with Germany on 5 September 1944 but was shocked to find, a few hours later, that the Soviet Union had declared war on it! In the words of one historian:

> The Soviet government, which did not declare war on any of the former pro-German Bulgarian governments, suddenly declared war on an anti-German government which was about to sign an armistice with the Western Allies.[5]

Along with Russian invasion came a Soviet-backed communist coup.

Forging of a Satellite

With the advantages the Soviets gave them, Bulgarian communists had a head start over all the other East European communists in attacking, splitting and neutralizing rival political parties. Bulgaria in 1944 was still overwhelmingly a peasant country, with no sharp class distinctions, no significant large-scale industrialists or entrepreneurs. There were no large estates. Most of the population farmed their own land. The Agrarian Party had a natural majority. The Western Allies insisted on free elections, as provided at Yalta. The Soviet Union was determined to avoid the embarrassment of letting the Bulgarian population demonstrate that communism had only minority support. Old Bulgarian communist and veteran Cominform leader G.M. Dimitrov, who had taken Soviet citizenship, finally returned to Sofia in November 1945. The 'Fatherland Front', which the Soviets had set up as a government after they took over in September 1944, became a device for bamboozling Socialists and Agrarians into accepting communist domination. When elections took place in October 1946, they were held in an atmosphere of terror. The Fatherland Front got 70 per cent of the vote. The new national assembly convened to 'write' a new constitution, which was for all practical purposes a copy of the Soviet Stalin Constitution of 1936.

G.M. Dimitrov died in 1948 and was interred in a Lenin-style mausoleum. The process of forcing Bulgaria into a classic Stalinist mold continued without let-up. Agrarian Party leaders were driven into exile or arrested, put through show trials and executed. After Tito broke with Stalin, Bulgaria was one of the first to purge alleged Titoites. No chances with deviation were to be taken. Traicho Kostov, the most popular native communist, was tried and executed in 1949. The Western Allies had compromised a good many of their principles when they signed a peace treaty with Bulgaria in Paris on 10 February 1947 in the hope that they might retain enough influence to bring about improvements. The hope proved vain. The US broke relations in 1950. They were not restored until 1959. Moscow encouraged its Bulgarian satraps to every kind of excess. One provincial library even burned all books published before September 1944.

Junior Partners in Subversion

The new Bulgarian intelligence services were copies of their 'big brothers' in Moscow: the *Komitet za Durzhavna Signurnost* (KDS), like the KGB, and the *Razvedochni Otdel* (RO), like the GRU, the Soviet military security agency. Initially these services, especially the KDS, were oriented internally, putting large numbers of people considered politically unreliable into concentration camps or exploiting them as forced laborers. Bulgaria helped support the communist-instigated civil war in Greece and, later, terrorists who operated in Yugoslavia. By the end of the 1950s, with the country purged, tightly controled and mobilized on Moscow time, Soviet leaders began exploiting Bulgarians to supplement Soviet operations in more distant areas. Stefan Svirdlev, a KDS defector who came out through Greece in 1971, recalls:

> The Bulgarian secret service had been involved since 1947 in operations into neighboring countries. Permanent training camps were first set up in 1963. I personally visited the Semeonovo camp near Sofia and also Vraza and Berkovitsa in the north. Terrorists were taught how to carry out attacks, the use of explosives and secret codes. All kinds of weapons were demonstrated, techniques of sabotage and taking of hostages as well; and there were courses in advanced intelligence methods.[6]

Bulgaria developed technical assistance programs in the Third World and expanded its educational and cultural activities abroad. It also began training students from other countries. All these activities were used as cover for intelligence operations.

By the 1960s all East European satellite intelligence services were being intensively developed by the Russians to serve their purposes. There was even some degree of co-ordination among them. Bulgaria, however, was an exception. It already had a special place, as Ladislav Bittman, the Czech intelligence defector, noted:

> It is very difficult to assess the strength of the Bulgarian Intelligence Service. Although the Bulgarians are partners in the East European intelligence community, their achievements remain hidden from all but the Soviet Union, not because of their exceptional significance—rather the contrary. It is known that the level of loyalty and obedience to Moscow is highest in the Bulgarian Service. In view of Bulgaria's territorial position on the southeastern flank of Europe, it is probable that her intelligence service devotes special attention to neighboring Greece and Turkey as well as to Italy and Arab nations.[7]

A comprehensive study of Bulgarian intelligence operations has never been done and it is difficult to sort out hard-core covert operations from other types of activity. They were part of a continuum. At the beginning of the 1960s, Bulgarian ships were intercepted by the French delivering arms to Algeria.[8] Zhivkov boasted of these operations in a 1964 speech:

> We had assisted the struggle—the armed struggle—of the Algerian

people; we even sent them arms. (Radio Sofia, 7 December 1964)

In 1967 Zhivkov bragged of arms assistance to Vietnam (*Rabotnichesko Delo*, 26 April, 13 May 1967). Arms deliveries to several other countries have been acknowledged in regime media: Angola, Guinea-Bissau, Mozambique and South African communists. Asked whether the Bulgarians could undertake operations on their own, Svirdlev replied:

> In the Balkans the Bulgarians traditionally had a certain degree of independence, but all concrete decisions on NATO bases, relations with Greece and weapons go through Soviet hands.[9]

Another Bulgarian defector, a 74-year-old RO colonel who has been living under another identity in Switzerland for many years, claims that Bulgaria's agent-training facilities were under close Soviet control from the start:

> Although some instructors are Bulgarian, they are not really subordinate to the Bulgarian services but directly and exclusively to the Soviet KGB. The majority of instructors are Soviets and the orders come directly from Moscow.

This veteran has no difficulty understanding the Russians' preference for Bulgaria:

> Politically Bulgaria is the most completely subdued and loyal of all the satellites and the one where there is the least risk of any political upheaval . . . Furthermore, Bulgaria is situated at a crossroads. In the Middle Ages the Crusaders had to cross it. Today millions of tourists still cross it—so agents can pass through unnoticed. I mean to the eyes of Western intelligence services. For on Bulgarian territory itself, nothing, absolutely nothing, can escape the notice of the state security organization. There is an enormous surveillance apparatus in place which checks on people who transit in only a few hours. Two foreigners cannot have a meeting in a hotel in the capital or even in the street without the special services being informed.[10]

Bulgaria not only sent arms and trained foreign agents. It sent its own people: civilian and military 'experts' to help 'national liberation struggles'. Through the years such Bulgarian operations have been exposed—or admitted—in Indonesia, Syria, Egypt, Libya, Angola, the countries of the Horn of Africa and Afghanistan—all high priorities for the Soviets. A Bulgarian vessel delivered arms to Nicaragua in May 1983. A former Nicaraguan intelligence operative reported in June 1983 that 20–25 Bulgarians were advising Nicaraguan security services.[11]

Debacle in Egypt

Occasionally, expansion of Bulgarian operations abroad led to awkward incidents. Before the recent exposure in Italy which established the Bulgarian connection in the plot against the Pope, the most serious episode occurred in Cairo. In December 1978 members of the Bulgarian embassy staff resorted to weapons in an altercation with Egyptian citizens. As a result, Anwar Sadat broke diplomatic relations and sent Ambassador Georgi Vladikov and his entire diplomatic establishment back to Sofia. Sadat did not act in response to a single provocative episode but with knowledge of more extensive Bulgarian and Soviet efforts to undermine the Egyptian–Israeli peace process which had at that time reached a critical stage. The Cairo newspaper *Al Akhbar* declared on 6 December:

> The Bulgarian embassy's crime exceeded all limits and reached the point of opening fire on the Eygptian people in their own homeland . . . This is not all there is about the Bulgarian embassy. As we know, Bulgaria . . . is a very extreme communist state; it only says and does what Moscow wants. It has been carried away with its communist anti-Egyptian extremism, particularly since the peace initiative and the beginning of peace talks. The Bulgarian embassy has been a center of hostility and agitation against Egypt . . . It had strong connections with one of the rejectionist states . . . preoccupied with watching subversive and terrorist plots in Egypt. It was not an embassy, it was an arms cache . . . [12]

Bulgaria initially feigned shocked, hurt innocence. On the same date the official Bulgarian news agency complained:

> Certain circles in Cairo are probably angered that Bulgaria, like the other countries of the socialist community, condemns the policy of

separatist deals with Israel . . . the desire of these circles to divert the attention of the Egyptian public from the isolation to which they themselves have brought it by staging some dramatic spectacle is easy to explain . . . Why did they choose precisely Bulgaria? We are a small country and we do not threaten and we cannot threaten anybody either by paratroop landings or by economic and political repressions. It was perhaps precisely for this reason that they singled out the Bulgarian embassy in Cairo, the embassy of a country governed by communists . . .

But the commentator concluded on a threatening note.

No one has so far succeeded in intimidating the socialist states and in compelling them to change their principled policy on any issue . . . Behind the anti-Bulgarian action are concealed far deeper intentions of launching a massive campaign against all the socialist countries and against the progressive forces in the Arab World . . . They are not only plotting in a shortsighted way, but they are reckless as well. Let us recall an old Arab proverb: 'When Allah wishes to punish someone he first makes him mad.'[13]

Cairo radio had meanwhile called Bulgaria 'a cat's paw in the hand of the Soviet Union' and accused the Soviets of trying to undermine Egypt:

The Soviet Union, and behind it the Bulgarian government, fails to understand the true meaning of the sovereignty of the state or the meaning of diplomatic immunity.[14]

New Techniques in Assassination

Have there been no voices raised against the communist iron grip and Soviet exploitation of Bulgaria? There have been periods of cultural thaw and frost but there has never been a full-blown spring. Internally things have never gone much farther than complaints like the following outburst of writer Mladen Isaev in the official literary journal in 1967:

All over our blessed Bulgarian land, egoism, careerism, bureaucracy, narrow-mindedness, and callousness toward the people's destiny still exists. There are even more dangerous phenomena: perfidy, slander, cruelty. All these elements poison the atmosphere, stand in the way of our development. We have no right to watch this 'second reality' in silence, to play down its negative influence . . . To imagine it is possible to rid ourselves of all these phenomena by waving a magic wand would make us look silly and utterly unrealistic. They have widespread roots.[15]

Bulgaria has not lacked perceptive and talented people in its media. But inside the country they have had to speak in generalities like the passage just quoted. No matter how well such people have been treated by Zhivkov's regime, there has been a steady stream of defectors.

The most famous case is Georgi Markov, a writer who became a friend of Zhivkov and enjoyed the highest privileges of the new ruling class, including a BMW car. The Soviet invasion of Czechoslovakia disillusioned him. He took advantage of an opportunity to go to Italy on an official visit and stayed in the West. In Britain he had success as a playwright and went to work for the BBC. Radio Free Europe commissioned him to write a series of sketches of the luxurious life style of Bulgaria's communist elite. Markov described his personal experiences with Zhivkov at former royal palaces and hunting lodges. These RFE broadcasts coincided with the defection in June 1977 of one of the most familiar faces in Bulgarian TV, Vladimir Kostov. He condemned his government's policy of 'ever closer integration with the Soviet Union'.

In 1973 Bulgarian agents had kidnapped an earlier defector, Boris Arsov, from Denmark and secretly taken him back to Sofia for trial. He later 'died' in prison. It was a messy and embarrassing case. Defectors Kostov and Markov were scheduled for smoother 'natural deaths'. The KGB was the only credible source of the new technology the KDS employed: the poison pellet umbrella. It turned out not to be foolproof.

Kostov was attacked in Paris on 26 August 1978, developed a high fever for 48 hours and then recovered. He did not realize what had happened to him until he heard Markov had died on 11 September. Before he died in a London hospital after running a temperature of 104 degrees for four days though doctors could find no infection, Markov was able to recount how he had been attacked on Waterloo Bridge on 7 September by a man 'with a foreign accent' who thrust an umbrella at his thigh. Doctors found a skin puncture and eventually extracted a tiny platinum pellet, with four openings. Kostov in Paris, on hearing this, had X-rays which revealed a metal object in his thigh too. When removed and taken to London, it turned out to be identical with the one that had killed Markov.

Most of the toxin remained in the pellet taken from Kostov, for the sealer in the openings had not dissolved. British medical experts eventually identified the poison as ricin, a derivative of the seeds of the castor oil plant. It was known that research on it had been under way in Czechoslovakia and Hungary. Absolute proof of an East European connection? Of course not. But where else could such a device come from and who else would have a motive to use it? A London coroner ruled that Markov had been 'killed unlawfully' and the case has received intermittent publicity ever since. The Bulgarian press and radio reacted in exactly the same way it reacted in 1982-3 to revelations of direct complicity in the shooting of John Paul II.[16]

No other East European regime has been exposed using the poison pellet, nor have any cases of Soviet use of it come to light. It must have been developed as a more reliable successor to the prussic acid gun Stashinsky was given in the late 1950s.[17] Why was the poison pellet not used to murder Lech Walesa or the Pope? Was it considered? We have no way of knowing. The exposure of the Markov–Kostov cases might well have influenced Moscow to suspend its use, for it involves the risk of detection even after a seemingly 'natural' death and is irretrievably linked to the East. A pellet of the same poison that would dissolve without a trace would be another matter. How could it be detected? Perhaps it has already been used?

Subversion as Commercial Enterprise

Internationally the Bulgarian expulsion from Egypt, as well as the Markov–Kostov assassination cases, received little notice at the time. There were too many other crises. Iran was collapsing. Turkey was in the grips of spiralling terrorism. Here too the Bulgarians escaped lightly. Their hand was less publicized than it should have been and given a cloak of respectability by KINTEX, a rapidly growing Bulgarian state import-export agency founded in 1965.

Turkish officials knew well that Turkish smugglers had been welcomed in Bulgaria since the late 1960s and several Turkish mafia millionaires acquired villas in Sofia and on the seacoast. They were given warehouses for their contraband, naval escorts for their boats and used Bulgarian passports in true name or alias when they needed them to facilitate their ever-expanding operations in Germany and other parts of Western Europe. Much of this has been exposed in a detailed book published in 1981 by Turkish journalist, Ugur Mumcu.[18] Curiously enough he is a leftist and has often been an apologist for the Soviet Union. His unequivocal indictment of Bulgaria as a 'gangster country',[19] supplying both left and right in Turkey with arms, gains force in view of his own past orientation. He is equally harsh on some of his own country's officials for tolerating, and in some cases abetting, these massive smuggling operations.

Time and again in the late 1970s the Turks caught the Bulgarians red-handed. In 1979, for example, a shipment of new weapons arrived in Istanbul from a factory in Argentina and came to the attention of the government. The shipment was accompanied by a bill of lading issued only three weeks before, consigning them to KINTEX, the Bulgarian firm.

A whole shipload of 'spare parts' being shipped by KINTEX had been taken on by the Cypriot-flag vessel *Vassoula* in the Bulgarian port of Burgaz in June 1977, supposedly bound for Cyprus and the Middle East. But Turkish officials got a tip that the *Vassoula* was going to offload her cargo in Turkey. The 'spare parts', when the ship's hold was opened, turned out to consist of: 55 crates containing 495 rocket-launchers, 21 crates with 755 rockets, 55 crates of portable rocket-launchers, 1,667 crates of ammunition for the portable launchers, and 60 gas bombs. Investigation of the case continued into 1978, in the course of which the Ethiopian government claimed ownership of the cargo. Its true owners were never legally established. Meanwhile, Turkey had exchanged one weak coalition government for another and no effective action was taken against Bulgaria. Other vessels' cargos in all likelihood reached their intended destination. KINTEX could amortize a certain percentage of losses. It gained enormous sums smuggling American-type cigarettes and other contraband into Turkey and other countries in the Middle East.[20]

Turkey has been in a difficult position to retaliate against Bulgaria for this and numerous other proven cases of large-scale support of terrorism, many involving illegal use of another successful Bulgarian business adventure: the international transport truck operation. There are two reasons: Bulgaria controls Turkey's most direct rail and highway access to Europe and at least a million Turks use this route every year. Alternate routes through Greece have never been closed, but they are longer and subject to harrassment by Greek governments whose sense of NATO solidarity is weak. Worse still, Turkey has been importing at least 5 per cent of its electricity from Bulgaria, which has had a surplus thanks to the intense campaign to expand electricity generating capacity during the first years of communism. The importance of Bulgarian electricity for the Turkish economy is magnified by the fact that imported power is used primarily in the heavily industrialized, populous Istanbul area. Turkey is currently expanding its power-generating capacity and expects to be able to forgo Bulgarian electricity imports by the mid-1980s.[21]

Turkey's military leadership has also taken stronger measures against Bulgarian smuggling and subversion since September 1980, repeatedly requesting extradition of terrorists and smugglers and placing on trial those whom it has managed to capture or lure into its custody. Turkey has the possibility of retaliating against Bulgarian shipping through the Turkish Straits. General Evren is understood to have talked sternly to Zhivkov during his visit to Sofia in early 1982 and again in June 1983 when Zhivkov visited Ankara.

Controling the Bulgarians

The importance of the Bulgarian connection in disseminating East European subversion in neighboring states is reinforced by the stature of the Soviet ambassador to Sofia, Nikita Pavlovich Tolubeev. A former party official in the Ukraine, Tolubeev was assigned as ambassador to Cuba in 1970 after a brief spell in Cyprus. The 1970s were an extraordinarily productive period in the Soviet–Cuban relationship during which the Cubans supplied mercenaries in Angola in 1975 and rendered more extensive services for communism in Ethiopia after 1977. With these accomplishments to his credit, Tolubeev was shifted to Bulgaria in 1979. His career progression reveals direct association with the Central Committee *apparat*. Tolubeev, his former colleague in the Ukraine, KGB chief Chebrikov and Geidar Aliev (the Azerbaijani whom Andropov brought to Moscow as one of his principal deputies in 1982) all joined the Soviet Communist Party's Central Committee in 1971.

The KGB works directly under the Central Committee. The Central Committee secretariat supervises assistance for 'liberation movements', 'active measures' (covert action operations), relations with other communist parties and leftist movements and propaganda.

Since the Soviet relationship with Bulgaria resembles that between Moscow and a constituent republic of the USSR, it can be assumed that Tolubeev devotes little time to traditional diplomatic duties. He is likely to participate directly in the KGB relationship with the Bulgarian security services.

It has only been possible to outline the Soviet–Bulgarian intelligence relationship in this chapter. More detail may emerge as the Bulgarian connection in Italy is fully exposed. However, enough evidence exists from the testimony of former East European intelligence officers like Ladislav Bittman and Stefan Svirdlev to establish the intimacy of the union. This compares dramatically with the hostility and suspicion that permeate relations elsewhere in the Eastern bloc, such as between Poland and the Soviet Union. In trying to explain why the Kremlin might want to kill the Polish pope, we must now examine the history of Russian–Polish relations.

7
THE POLISH THREAT TO THE SOVIET STATE

A Thousand Years with Rome

For Russians a visit to Warsaw has often been the next best thing to a trip to Western Europe. Ever since the 1950s Poland has been known to Soviet citizens as a place where the air feels freer, cultural life is livelier, the atmosphere more Western in a dozen subtle ways. Polish newspapers are sought after in the USSR. No matter how Poles have seen their own situation, Russians see Poles as enjoying more freedom than they themselves are permitted. Sometimes they are resentful; more often they are envious. The persistence of curiosity about Poland is one of several reasons—there are much larger ones of diplomacy and strategy—why the country is seen as a menace by the Kremlin as long as they can find no way of making it a pliant part of the Soviet imperial system.

Russia's problems with Poland are deeply embedded in history. Poles know their history better than most peoples. If they did not, their country would never have survived. Poland has no natural boundaries. Its location has shifted by several hundred miles from west to east and back again in the course of a thousand years.

Poland came into the European mainstream with the conversion of its King Mieszko I to the religion of Rome in 966. Twenty-three years later (989) its Slavic rival to the east, the Kievan state, converted to the religion of Byzantium. The dichotomy is still of major import, as we shall see at the end of this chapter when we review the contemporary religious scene in the western parts of the USSR. John Paul II's influence, however, may be having a profound impact on this historic cleavage.

For several hundred years after its conversion, Poland's politics were played out in Central Europe, in alliance and rivalry with the various German states, the Swedes, Danes, Bohemia and Hungary. The Mongol invasion in the thirteenth century disrupted things for a while, but internal dissensions forced the Mongols to withdraw to the east, where they kept the Russians under their yoke for more than two centuries. The still pagan Lithuanian King Jagiello married Queen Jadwiga of Poland in 1386 and converted to Roman Catholicism. The two states were united, forming a mighty bulwark against Russian expansion westward. At its maximum extent the Polish–Lithuanian kingdom reached from the Baltic to the Adriatic and the Black Sea and embraced most of what are today known as Belorussia and the Ukraine.

One Polish king was killed fighting the Turks at the Battle of Varna (in Bulgaria) in 1444. Nearly two and a half centuries later another, Jan Sobieski, defeated the Turks before Vienna (1683). In the intervening years Poles and Turks both fought each other and fought as allies against the Russians. Polish armies occupied Moscow in 1610, but Russian power was growing and half a century later the Polish–Lithuanian kingdom yielded half of the Ukraine to Russia. By the eighteenth century, continual wars had undermined Poland and it fell into chronic social and political anarchy. At the end of the eighteenth century, within a period of 25 years, the Polish–Lithuanian state, which had lasted more than four centuries, was wiped off the map of Europe in three successive partitions between Russia, Austria and Prussia. This was not the end, however, but the beginning of modern Poland.

The Roots of Polish Resistance

Poles have a remarkable capacity to be at their best in adversity:

> The shock of dismemberment stimulated a process of national regeneration throughout the commonwealth. The two decades separating the First Partition from the Second (1793) were years of remarkable progress . . . The state income was doubled; new industries were created and expanded; the educational system was modernized . . . the arts revived; the armed forces were re-organized and re-equipped . . . The Poles proceeded to further dismantle their obsolete government and to modernize their social structure. The result was the Constitution of 3 May 1791 [still celebrated by Poles as their true national holiday].[1]

It was of no avail. The final partition came in 1795 and the frontiers of Russia advanced to within 200 miles of both Berlin and Vienna. Poles were a much greater problem for their Russian masters than for the

Germans or Austrians.

The Polish uprisings of 1830-1 and 1863-4 shook Europe. The Russians drafted as many young Poles as possible into tsarist armies and sent them off to fight in the Balkans and the Caucasus. Many fled to the Turks and some became famous officers in the Sultan's armies, fighting against the Russians in the Crimean War. Poles settled in a village near Istanbul, which still exists. The experience of opposing a common Russian enemy resulted in a residue of mutual good feeling in both Poland and Turkey when both countries underwent national renewal in the twentieth century.

During the 1863 rebellion, the Polish revolutionary government abolished serfdom and proclaimed renewal of the old links between the Poles, Lithuanians and Ukrainians. This hardened Russian opposition and the tsar sent in troops to subdue the rebellious Poles. With the failure of this uprising, the romantic period of Polish nineteenth-century history was past, though Poles continued to take part in revolutionary movements in Europe and serve in far parts of the world, following the example of Pulaski and Kosciuszko in the American Revolution. Over a thousand Poles took part in the Paris commune in 1871. Modern Poland's 200-zloty banknote bears the portrait of General Jaroslaw Dombrowski who fell in this struggle.

After 1864, Russian oppression in the Polish heartlands was ruthless. But while conditions were harsh in parts of the country where the tsars ruled, there were opportunities to be exploited in Prussian and Austrian Poland, even though Bismarck tried to force assimilation. During the last 50 years before independence was regained, Poles made the best of things in what became known as the policy of 'organic work'. Agricultural production grew and industry expanded. By 1890, though Russian Poland accounted for only 7.3 per cent of the Russian Empire's population, it had 25 per cent of the empire's industrial output. In all three segments of the partitioned country the population grew steadily, in spite of heavy emigration. There were ten million Poles by the end of the century. Polish culture and intellectual life flourished both in the divided homeland and in exile.

The writer Stanislaw Staszyc had consoled his countrymen after the final partition with the reminder that: 'Even a great nation can fall but only a worthless one can perish.' Poles were determined to prove they were not worthless. World War I provided them with the opportunity to restore their state; the nation itself had never died.[2] US President Woodrow Wilson set the framework for the re-emergence of Poland in the 13th of his famous 14 Points: a state guaranteed by international covenant with secure access to the sea. Independent Poland took form again after 10 November 1918.

From Rebirth to Re-partition

Independent Poland had existed less than two years when it was attacked from the north-east and the east by Bolshevik armies. In May 1920 Polish and Ukrainian forces captured Kiev, but the Russians soon gained the upper hand and by August were threatening Warsaw. Lenin's (and Stalin's) hope was to turn Poland into a communist state, a spearhead into the heart of Europe which was in political turmoil.

> If successful the Bolshevik plan would have created, already in 1920, what ultimately materialized in 1944 and 1945: a belt of vassal states encompassing practically all of Central and Eastern Europe.[3]

The Bolsheviks were not successful. They were decisively defeated by the Poles. The defeat was formally accepted by a realistic Lenin in the Treaty of Riga signed in March 1921. It left nearly five million Ukrainians and Belorussians inside Poland's eastern borders where they escaped collectivization and the purges that took a heavy toll among their compatriots under Soviet rule in the 1930s.

Stalin was patient for 18 years, but he had not forgotten. The pact he signed with Hitler on 23 August 1939 sealed Poland's fate and sparked World War II. British and French indulgence of Hitler from 1935 onward had merely encouraged his appetite and willingness to take risks. Wishful thinking about the Soviet Union's commitment to collective security proved naïve.

Stalin waited until Hitler's armies had decimated the ill-equipped Polish forces before he sent in his own army. With the Soviet invasion, all hope of establishing a center of resistance in the east where Allied help might be received was gone. Poland was formally partitioned between the two totalitarian states with each taking approximately half of the territory of the independent republic as it had existed between 1918 and 1939. The Germans got the bulk of the people and proceeded to turn them into slaves, with the Jewish portion slated for annihilation. A second treaty between the Nazis and the Soviets, 'a document so shameful that [the Soviets] have never admitted its existence',[4] committed the partners to suppress any 'Polish agitation' that might develop.

In their half of Poland, the Russians reduced the sparse population further by mass deportations. Captured troops were included among the deportees. Officers were segregated into camps in Western Russia under jurisdiction of the NKVD. Few were released. Over 15,000 disappeared. After Hitler invaded the Soviet Union in June 1941 and Free Poles were permitted to recruit for the Polish forces that fought with the Allied armies in the Middle East, North Africa and Italy, a determined search for the missing officers began. They could not be found.

The Katyn Massacre

In April 1943 the Germans announced that they had uncovered mass graves of thousands of murdered Polish officers in the Katyn Forest near Smolensk. The announcement confirmed the worst fears of Poles who had for two years been receiving scraps of information that the missing officers—some of them at least—had been killed. In Britain, Poland's wartime exile government was reluctant to credit German claims. Allied governments and Western public opinion did not want to believe that its now popular Soviet ally could be guilty of such an atrocity.

The Germans set up an international commission with members from 12 countries to examine the site. The Polish Red Cross was permitted by the Germans to conduct an independent investigation with a nine-member team. A separate German medical–judicial commission made another independent investigation. The reports of all three groups coincided in all important details. Eight mass graves were found, each filled with ten to twelve layers of corpses. Two Polish generals were found in individual graves. Without exception all these officers had been shot in the back of the head. Many had their hands tied with a type of rope that was proven to be Soviet-made. Many were gagged. Some had obviously struggled fiercely, for their clothes and bodies were riddled with bayonet cuts. The clothes these men were wearing revealed that the weather had still been cool when they were shot. Letters, diaries, Soviet newspapers in pockets yielded no dates later than the spring of 1940 . . . The Soviet government had controled this area until the late summer of 1941, when it fell to the invading Germans.

What we know now, pieced together from thousands of scraps of evidence gathered over many years, indicates that the killings began in the first week of April 1940. The operation was meticulously planned and executed by the NKVD—the predecessor of the KGB— under direct supervision from Moscow. There was nothing accidental about the murder of these men. It was prescribed to the last detail and carried out in great secrecy. In all, 4,443 bodies were found at Katyn before the German armies had to retreat and the area reverted to Soviet control.[5] What happened to the other 11,000 missing Poles? They have never been accounted for. There is good reason to believe that they, too, were shot and buried at other locations in Soviet territory now known only to aging NKVD/KGB veterans.

Who were the murdered officers? They were young, most of them in their 20s and 30s, some in their 40s. Most of them were not career military men, but reserve officers who had been doctors, lawyers, business and professional men. They were educated, successful, middle-class citizens who, had they lived and had the opportunity to continue in Polish life in any normal way, would have been natural leaders. They were not predominantly from the eastern half of Poland which the Soviet Union had by this time incorporated. They were captured there because their units had been driven back by the Germans. Most of them were from the cities of the center and the west. They were killed at a time when Stalin could not have looked forward to early communization of all of Poland. Throughout 1940 he was doing his best to accommodate Hitler by stepping up shipments of strategic materials. He handed over to the Gestapo several hundred German communist refugees.[6] He knew his recently purged army which had just suffered an embarrassing setback in Finland was too weak to challenge Hitler at any point in the foreseeable future and there is not the slightest indication that Stalin thought of doing so.

So why cold-bloodedly kill off potential Polish leadership? The answer lies in the style of Soviet political terror which was already well established by the time of the Katyn massacre. By 1940 mass killings of classes considered politically inimical had been taking place among Russians and other peoples in the Soviet Union as a matter of state policy for more than ten years. Soviets had been blasé about such things. Just how blasé is demonstrated by remarks made by Stalin's son, Yakob Dzhugashvili, captured by the Germans in 1942, when he heard about the discovery of the Katyn graves:

What is all that noise about 10,000 or 15,000 Poles being killed? During the collectivization of the Ukraine about three million

people perished! Why be concerned about the Polish officers . . .
Those were intelligentsia, the most dangerous element to us, and
they had to be eliminated.[7]

The Katyn massacre is relevant to the plot against Pope John Paul
II because it is an atrocity which Poles have never been able to forgive
the Soviet system. The Soviets have never denied that there was a
massacre at Katyn. They have erected a monument at the site which
Poles even occasionally visit officially. It carries an inscription condemning the Germans.

But for several years an obelisk to the victims of Katyn also stood in
Powazki Cemetery in Warsaw, erected sometime in the 1970s. It
disappeared in August 1981. Zdzislaw Rurarz, Poland's ambassador
to Japan who left his post after the Jaruzelski 'coup' in December
1981, says of Katyn:

I remember very well the people's reaction to the news about
Katyn in April 1943. We all knew about the German crimes; I
myself saw them. But this time we knew they were not lying. I
never met anybody in Poland, within the establishment included,
who would say that Katyn was a German crime.[8]

Western Disbelief

What was clear to Poles in Poland was less clear among the Western
Allies. The urge to disbelieve—or at least to ignore—was very strong.
There is evidence that the US State Department had received a report
from the US Embassy in Moscow on the disappearance of these Poles
as early as February 1942. By the time the Germans announced
discovery of the mass graves, classified US government files contained a good deal of reporting. A research team told President
Roosevelt that the Germans appeared to be telling the truth. A
diplomat who also held a US Navy commission, George H. Earle, was
named Presidential Emissary for Balkan Affairs in 1943 and assigned
to Turkey. He developed an intense personal interest in Katyn and
gathered material from many sources for a report which he laid before
President Roosevelt in May 1944. Roosevelt told him, 'George, this is
entirely German propaganda and a German plot. I am absolutely
convinced the Russians did not do this.'[9]

Earle returned to Europe but came back to the United States again in early 1945 and decided to write an article about Katyn for publication. On 22 March 1945 he wrote to the President advising him what he was planning to do. On 24 March he received a reply signed by Roosevelt which read:

> I have noted with concern your plan to publish your unfavorable opinion of one of our allies . . . I not only do not wish it, but I specifically forbid you to publish any information or opinion about an ally that you may have acquired while in office or in the service of the US Navy.[10]

Shortly afterwards Earle was transferred to Samoa.

The Death of Sikorski

By the time the Katyn massacre came to light, the Polish government-in-exile under General Wladyslaw Sikorski was well established in London, where it was treated by the Western Allies as one of them. By 1943 it had sizable contingents of Polish troops fighting with Allied forces in the Middle East. The relationship the London Poles established with the USSR after Hitler's Soviet invasion was always problematic. It became evident during Sikorski's December 1941 visit to Moscow that Stalin's real preference was for a group of Polish puppets but with German artillery fire audible in Moscow suburbs, he had to treat the London Polish government with a modicum of warmth.

Discovery of the mass graves at Katyn in April 1943 gave Stalin the chance he had long sought to break with Sikorski. The London Polish government and the German government, acting completely independently, requested an International Red Cross investigation of the massacre within an hour of each other on the same day, 17 April 1943. Moscow, which made no effort to seek an independent investigation itself, accused the Poles of collusion with the Nazis and broke diplomatic relations. Whether Stalin already had a plan for the elimination of Sikorski or was prompted to set one in motion in the wake of the break has been the subject of speculation ever since, for Sikorski was killed in a plane crash on take-off from Gibraltar on 4 July 1943.

During the last months of his life Sikorski had been dogged by peculiar circumstances. During a flight to Washington in December 1942, the engines of his plane failed on take-off from Montreal and American officials voiced suspicion of sabotage. Mysterious phone calls to ministers in the Polish exile government had announced a crash at Gibraltar six weeks before the real crash occurred. The plane in which the general was killed was British, under British control, though the pilot was a Czech. He was fished out of the sea unconscious after the crash; all others were killed. The pilot explained the cause of the crash as a locked steering mechanism. The Soviets did not mention Sikorski's death until five days later when *Izvestia* called it 'tragic' but went on to accuse him of lack of will to consolidate friendship with the Soviet Union.

A British commission of enquiry was established but at that time, of course, could not take into account what has since become the most suspicious feature of the circumstances surrounding Sikorski's death: the fact that the chief of British Intelligence at Gibraltar in 1943 and thus the man ultimately responsible for the security of Sikorski's flight was the infamous spy, Kim Philby. The German playwright, Rolf Hochhuth, in his 1967 play *The Soldiers*, accused Sir Winston Churchill of arranging Sikorski's liquidation, claiming evidence locked in a Swiss bank vault.[11] John Le Carré speculates in his introduction to a book on Philby that allegations of Churchill's instigation could be based on a false flag recruitment:

> If Sikorski *was* assassinated, is it conceivable that Philby planned the operation on behalf of his Russian masters, and that the assassin whom he hired believed he was working for the British?[12]

Sikorski's loss was a heavy blow for the Polish cause at a time when Soviet behavior was giving the Poles and their Western allies increasing concern about their ability to affect the fate of the country after German defeat. The mystery of the plane crash at Gibraltar may never be clarified. However, there is no mystery about the next major negative episode in Russian–Polish relations: the Warsaw Uprising.

Defeat in Victory

On 29 July 1944 Moscow's Polish language radio station called 'Poles! The time of liberation is at hand! Poles to arms!' The call was repeated on the 30th. Advancing Russian armies had reached the outskirts of Warsaw on the eastern side of the Vistula. General Bor-Komorowski, commander of the Home Army, ordered his troops into battle against the Germans on 1 August. The entire population of the capital joined in supporting the underground uprising, confident that the city would soon be freed. Sixty-three days later, the exhausted remnants of the Home Army capitulated to the Germans. Warsaw was a smoldering ruin. 200,000 more Poles were dead. The Germans systematically fired and blew up all standing buildings. Stalin's armies had halted east of the city and waited for the Germans to destroy Polish resistance. The Soviets refused to let Western planes bringing arms and supplies land at their airfields.[13]

Warsaw, a heap of snow-covered ruins, was finally taken by the Red Army on 17 January 1945. It was the Russians who called the shots in the years that followed. The Allied summit conference at Yalta in early February fed the illusion that the Western Allies would have some say in the organization of Poland's future government. Stalin was simply playing for time. He did the same at Potsdam in August. Poland's fate had long since been sealed.[14]

Political commentators later wrote about Polish provocation of the Russians and desire to pre-empt Soviet capture of Warsaw. Revisionist historians took up these themes in the 1960s and 1970s. Serious scholarship has since demonstrated that Soviet failure to support the Warsaw Rising was carefully calculated to ensure that Poland would be demoralized and malleable when it finally fell to the Red Army. The country was overwhelmingly Catholic, agrarian, and had been anti-Russian for centuries. The Russian-organized Lublin government which had been proclaimed on 22 July would need all the help it could get from the Soviets to establish itself at all.

World War II had begun over Poland, but no country suffered more from it and none came out of it with less to show for the sacrifices it made. More than six million Polish citizens, more than half of them Jews, perished during the war. For every 1,000 citizens of pre-war Poland, 220 died during the period between 1 September 1939 and 8 May 1945. (Comparable figures for Yugoslavia were 108 per 1,000 and for the USSR 40 per 1,000.)[15]

The Formation of Karol Wojtyla

Poland's fate during World War II is essential background to the plot against Pope John Paul II, because it predetermined the climate of Soviet–Polish relations since 1945. The war years were also the formative years for the future pope. Born in Wadowice, a small southern mountain town, in 1920, Karol Wojtyla grew up with good religious sentiments, like most Poles, but commitment to a career in the church was far from his mind when he went to Krakow at 18 and registered at the university as a student of literature. A handsome, blond, athletically inclined extrovert, he was interested in a career in acting. Cardinal Sapieha took him and several other young men into the episcopal residence in 1940 where he remained until the end of the war, deeply affected by the ordeal his country was enduring. Wojtyla took up the study of theology and aided the cardinal in his refugee and resistance projects.

He was ordained a priest in September 1946 and sent to Rome for graduate work in philosophy. He lived at the Belgian college there, developed friends among American, Irish and French students and wrote a dissertation on the seventeenth century Spanish mystic, St John of the Cross. But he explored the real world too, traveling to several West European countries to help Catholic War Relief serve Polish refugees, perfecting his languages, developing his natural talents for communicating with people in small and large groups. He returned to Poland in 1948, acutely conscious of the contrast between freedom in Western Europe and conditions in his homeland.[16]

The Western powers had long since given up trying to gain leverage on internal Polish events. Nothing symbolized Soviet domination more than the presence of Soviet Marshall Konstantin Rokossovsky as Polish Minister of Defense. The weak Polish Communist Party was already being purged. Patriotic communist Wladyslaw Gomulka could not be trusted as secretary-general at a time when Stalin saw the specter of Titoism stalking all of Eastern Europe. He was removed and eventually imprisoned. The numerically much stronger Polish Socialist Party was forced to merge with the communists to form the Polish United Workers' Party (PZPR) in December 1948. This party was not united, its Polishness was questionable and few workers felt that it represented their interests, but for the next few years it served Soviet purposes well enough.

Nationalization and industrialization were given high priority. Poland was required to provide the Soviet Union with coal at the ridiculously low price of $1.25 per ton and sell Moscow sugar at half the world price. In effect, Poland was forced to pay reparations, though from the time Hitler attacked the Soviet Union it had been a Soviet ally.

The peasantry, however, could not be collectivized in spite of persuasion and coercion by the regime. The party lacked the strength to risk an upheaval in the countryside. In this respect and many others

Poland stands in sharp contrast to Bulgaria during this period. Socialist realism was imposed on cultural life, but Polish culture was too vigorous to stay blighted; the habit of resistance to authority too deeply ingrained in Polish minds. The church was subject to steadily mounting harassment. It is the church which is at the heart of the story of Poland from the end of World War II until today.

The Resistance of the Catholic Church

With barely 23 million people in 1945, Poland gained one advantage from its new boundaries: it was a more homogeneous country than any other in Eastern Europe. It was at least 98 per cent Polish and 95 per cent Roman Catholic. The Russians feared the church. Their initial tactic was to try to break its power by fragmentation and ruse. They set up an organization called PAX and permitted it to conduct publishing and charitable activity in competition with the church. The only man they could find to head it was Boleslaw Piasecki, a discredited pre-war fascist. Try as he did to serve Soviet purposes, Piasecki was unsuccessful.

Stefan Wyszynski, who became Bishop of Lublin in 1946, was named Polish primate on the death of Cardinal Hlond in 1948. Poland was fortunate in this man who possessed a remarkable combination of talents—patience, political skill and inexhaustible but carefully modulated energy. He had to exercise all his skills to cope with regime pressures. He was elevated to cardinal in 1952. This did not deter the regime from arresting him in 1953. Several bishops and several hundred priests were imprisoned during the same period, but it was eventually the regime which fell into disarray, not the church.[17] Recalling these experiences in a sermon at the shrine of the Black Madonna at Czestochowa in 1966, Wyszynski reflected:

> Strike the shepherd and the sheep will scatter. Often this has been tried and proven to be so. But whenever it has been done in Poland, it has served only to draw the sheep together.[18]

Though Stalin died in March 1953 and soon some of the more odious features of the old dictator's system were dismantled in the USSR and elsewhere in Eastern Europe, the weakness of the Polish regime led it to continue Stalinist policies until a crisis developed. The crisis was both economic and political. Something very close to a national revolution occurred in Poland in 1956, culminating in the 'Spring in October' solution which avoided Soviet military intervention. Gomulka, newly released from prison, was restored to party leadership and put in charge of the country. He was immediately confronted by mass clamor for release of Wyszynski. He had him brought from confinement in a monastery to a hero's welcome in Warsaw. For a while the two were *de facto* allies trying to make reform work in Poland, but the relationship was never easy. The Communist Party (and the Kremlin) could not reconcile itself to the growing esteem which the church commanded among the Polish people. More and more men kept joining the priesthood—Poland is unique among Catholic countries in having twice as many priests today as it had in 1945!

By the mid-1960s, Wyszynski had become the object of a vicious anti-church campaign organized by Gomulka's government. The secret police produced anonymous letters and pamphlets aimed at discrediting the cardinal and even forged texts of his sermons. These tactics enhanced his standing with the public, which now included a maturing post-war generation brought up in the church. Adversity brings out a sheer biological assertiveness in Poles. Until the 1970s Poland maintained one of the highest birthrates in Europe.

Gomulka could not sustain the momentum that had brought him back to power. His party's credibility declined and its internal cohesion eroded as Poland, in spite of economic aid from the West, fell into crisis again. The situation came to a head in 1970 when Gomulka was swept from power by a strike wave that began on the Baltic coast and eventually engulfed the whole country. There was, in effect, a national uprising again. Gomulka was replaced by the Silesian party boss, Edward Gierek, who announced a period of 'renewal' which for a time was remarkably successful, thanks to far-reaching concessions to workers and peasants and even more to Western credits and imports. Gierek's good years were briefer than Gomulka's. The generosity of Western bankers obscured the irrationality of the regime's economic policies for a while but labor unrest became serious again in 1976.[19] A Committee for the Defense of the Workers (Polish initials KOR) was organized by a group of writers and emerged as a force catalyzing anti-regime attitudes. Uncensored publications proliferated. On all manner of issues, these free publications spoke up more sharply than the church. But everyone knew that behind this whole nationwide movement for broader freedom stood the church. Its moral strength was never greater. It had consolidated its position in numerous ways.

In the late 1960s the regime launched an intense anti-Semitic campaign against Jewish intellectuals some of whom had originally been supporters of the government. There were scurrilous attempts to fan latent traditional anti-Semitism among workers and peasants. The church opposed these attempts. They backfired. The church became the ultimate beneficiary of the failure of this campaign. Jewish and non-Jewish intellectuals rallied to the church in the 1970s—not in a religious, but in a political sense. The case of Adam Michnik, one of the founders of KOR, demonstrates what happened:

> Michnik, an avowed atheist . . . concluded that the prevailing attitude of the intellectuals was mistaken. The church, wrote Michnik, had become the most formidable opponent of the totalitarian system. As such it was the mainstay of all people fighting for greater freedom, be they believers or non-believers.[20]

Sheer lack of a workable alternative kept Gierek in power until 1980. Gomulka had lasted for nearly 14 years, Gierek 10. His successor, Stanislaw Kania, lasted less than a year and a half. The party collapsed during his tenure and Solidarity, the nationwide workers' movement which embraced more than a quarter of the population, was legally recognized in August 1980. Poland had experienced a true workers' revolution. This is what prompted Moscow to implement plans for elimination of the Polish Pope. The probable evolution of these plots will be taken up in Chapter 9 below. I will conclude this chapter by tracing the developments which led to the election of John Paul II and then sketch some of the broader aspects of Polish–Soviet relations that bedevil the Kremlin.

The Making of a Polish Pope

When Archbishop Karol Wojtyla of Krakow helped Cardinal Wyszynski commemorate the 1,000th anniversary of Poland's conversion in 1966, he was already recognized as a pre-eminent figure in the Polish church. His elevation to cardinal the next year was a tribute to the special brand of ecumenism that he had helped Wyszynski implement—making the church the champion of human rights of all citizens. Human rights included workers' rights. Wojtyla was keenly interested in them. These concerns alone would be enough to earn

Moscow's deep suspicion.[21]

Their fear of Wojtyla led some in the Kremlin to conclude, after Wojtyla's election in October 1978, that Zbigniew Brzezinski must have engineered it from the White House.[22] In reality, according to the most authoritative Vatican sources, Wojtyla's election had nothing to do with East–West politics or concern about the internal situation in Poland. There is some reason to believe that his selection was initially welcomed by some communists in Warsaw because it removed him from the Polish scene where he had already long been regarded as the logical successor to Wyszynski.[23]

Wyszynski's orientation was almost exclusively Polish, though he had a keen appreciation for Poland's geo-political position. No less Polish in spirit, Wojtyla had not only benefitted from deep exposure to Europe in his late 20s, he had also served as a member of the preparatory commission for the Vatican Council and participated in four sessions between 1962 and 1965. This work brought many foreign contacts and invitations to visit and lecture. He rapidly acquired an international reputation as a philosopher, visiting the United States in 1969 and the Far East, Australia and New Zealand in the early 1970s. He was back in the United States in 1976 for the Eucharistic Congress in Philadelphia and then traveled extensively in Canada. As a permanent member of the Roman Synod of Bishops, he traveled frequently between Krakow and Rome in the 1970s. Back in Poland he still found time for hiking and skiing outings with university students. Nothing of political or intellectual significance that occurred in his historic diocese escaped his attention.

All these characteristics and experience were important in Wojtyla's election. Cardinal Benelli of Florence, a close rival in the voting that led to Wojtyla's selection, had commented in a sermon in France just after the death of his predecessor that the qualifications for the new pope should include comparative youth, robust health and keen administrative abilities.[24] Karol Wojtyla had all these and a great deal more.

Those Polish communist officials who were pleased to be rid of Wojtyla soon realized that their pleasure was premature. Polish President Henry Jablonski came to Rome for the installation ceremonies and exuded formal pride. He assured the new Pope he would be welcome as a visitor in his homeland at any time. Perhaps this was only routine courtesy. John Paul II took it as a serious invitation and planning for the visit started in the next weeks. The Pope wanted to participate in ceremonies on 9 May 1979 commemorating the 900th anniversary of the martyrdom of St Stanislaus, an eleventh-century Bishop of Krakow who excommunicated King Boleslaw the Bold for oppressive behavior toward his subjects. This symbolism was too strong for the beleaguered communist regime in Warsaw, which argued for a later date. The first week of June was agreed upon and publicly announced. Cardinal Wyszynski then declared the saint's anniversary a movable feast and shifted it to 9 June. It became a climax of the Pope's extraordinary eight-day visit to Poland which started on 2 June 1979. Nothing like it had ever been seen in any communist country before.

The whole visit was a triumph. The regime had no alternative but to co-operate. There were no incidents between police and people during the entire time the Pope was in Poland. Soon after arrival he told Gierek:

> It is the Church's mission to make man more confident, more courageous, more conscious of his rights and duties, socially responsive, creative and useful. The Church does not desire privileges but only and exclusively what is essential for the accomplishment of its mission.

Everywhere John Paul II mixed with crowds, confident of his safety. It was estimated that more than six million people, one sixth of the entire Polish population, laid eyes on him during his public appearances. Everywhere he talked of the responsibilities of Christians, the duties of Poles, human rights and human dignity. He visited Auschwitz and said mass at another Jewish death camp at Birkenau to 500,000 people to whom he reflected on

> . . . how far hatred can go, how far one's man destruction of his fellow man can go, how far cruelty can go . . .

The Polish Pope left Poland freer than it had been at any time since the German and Russian armies invaded in 1939. Political ferment intensified in the wake of his visit but, following his example, Poles—intellectuals, workers, peasants, students—all avoided the confrontation with the authorities which could provoke or justify retribution. The party and government had reached the point of political bankruptcy. The country was well on its way to economic bankruptcy as well, as Western banks became alarmed at their overexposure. Worker protests spread and industrial activity declined. By the fol-

lowing summer strikes and slow-downs resulted in the formation of
the nationwide labor movement, Solidarity, with Lech Walesa at its
head.

With recognition of Solidarity conceded reluctantly on 31 August
1980 by a regime which had no alternative but to summon Soviet
troops, the church was no longer the only institution which cut across
all social classes in Poland and faced the government as an unques-
tionable representative of the entire Polish people. The church now
had a formidable partner in Solidarity. The Kremlin was extremely
alarmed. What was happening in Poland undermined Soviet preten-
sion to the legitimacy of a workers' state. Worse still, continual
warnings against military intervention from the American president
and West European leaders prevented the Soviet leadership from
putting an end to the foolishness in Poland the way they had done in
Hungary in 1956 and Czechoslovakia in 1968. Without the curse of a
Polish Pope matters could be different . . .

John Paul II's Slavic Consciousness

John Paul II's Slavic pride is strong. Time and again during his 1979
visit to Poland, he referred to himself as a Slav. At Gniezno he posed
the question:

> Is it not the intention of the Holy Spirit that this Polish Pope, this
> Slav, should at this moment of history manifest the spiritual unity
> of Christian Europe?

He went on to survey centuries of church missionary activity in
Eastern Europe from Yugoslavia and Bulgaria to Czechoslovakia and
Lithuania. Back in Rome, he declared the two great apostles to the
Slavs, the Byzantine saints Cyril and Methodius, co-patron saints of
Europe, along with St Benedict. Mere playing with history? So it
might seem to those who lack appreciation of the psychological
undercurrents that are growing stronger in Eastern Europe. The
action attracted no notice in the West, but its significance was not
missed in Moscow.

This travel-loving pope received invitations for visits to all conti-
nents. In late September he flew to Ireland and from there directly to
Boston for an historic visit to the United States during the first week
of October 1979. His next choice seemed peculiar: Turkey, at the end

of November. His ostensible purpose was to celebrate the Feast of St Andrew together with the Greek Orthodox Patriarch of Constantinople and thus further the process of reunification of two great branches of ancient Christendom. The real meaning of the visit was that it underscored John Paul II's concern for all the Eastern churches. Incidentally, whether intentional or not, this visit, at a time when Turkey was suffering drastically worsening terrorism underwritten by Moscow and Sofia, also demonstrated papal support for Turkey's Western orientation and its commitment to democracy and freedom. The pontiff paid tribute to Atatürk at his tomb in Ankara. The Turkish government, embarrassed at Mehmet Ali Agca's escape and threatening letter on the eve of the visit, took stringent security precautions and was gratified that the visit went off successfully. Some Western observers wrote off the Turkish trip as indulgence of an idiosyncrasy on the part of the Pope. Moscow saw it as a threat.

If, as Lenin and Stalin had hoped, the Soviet government had by now succeeded in eradicating religion in the USSR, the Polish Pope's preoccupation with the unity of Christian Europe could be dismissed as harmless addiction to symbolism. The difficulty is that religion in the USSR—be it Catholic or Orthodox Christianity, or Islam or Judaism—is much more than a question of history or art. It has substantive meaning. Religion in the Soviet Union is alive and gaining strength. The problem has several dimensions.

The Religious Threat to Soviet Communism

First, there are the Poles. According to the 1979 Soviet census, there were still 1,151,000 of them in the USSR.[25] Though their numbers have declined from 1,380,000 in 1959 (apparently because of emigration back to Poland, but there may also have been undercounting), 80 per cent of them are concentrated next door to Poland, in Lithuania, Belorussia, and the Ukraine. These Polish populations seem relatively stable. The position of the church is weaker among them than it is in Poland. Polish priests nevertheless find opportunities to visit them, helping make up for a severe shortage of priests of their own and they find ways of receiving both church and other publications from Poland.

Then there are the Lithuanians, nearly three million of them, as determined in their Catholicism as the Poles. The Pope, who speaks Lithuanian, is always mindful of them. The Lithuanian church has defended its traditions tenaciously since Soviet rule was reimposed in 1945 and generates one of the steadiest outflows of *samizdat* in the Soviet Union. The KGB has harassed Lithuanian Catholics relentlessly, closing churches and imprisoning priests and bishops, but religious loyalties have intensified. The impact of the Polish Pope on Lithuania has been second only to that on Poland. During his visit to Poland in 1979, the country's eastern borders were closed to prevent Lithuanian, Latvian, Belorussian and Ukrainian Catholics from traveling to Poland to participate. The same was true in 1983.[26]

The Catholic population of Latvia is at least 400,000. John Paul II demonstrated his interest in them by appointing a Latvian the first cardinal in the Soviet Union in February 1983, Bishop Julijans Vaivods, an 88-year-old veteran of the struggle against communism. He is believed to have appointed imprisoned Lithuanian Archbishop Stepanovicius cardinal *in pectore* (secret) in 1979.[27]

There is a scattering of Catholics in many other parts of the Soviet Union, including Siberia and Kazakhstan, where deportations of earlier years created communities which, since they were looked upon as outcasts, were sometimes able to maintain their religious loyalties with less harassment from the authorities than some of the larger groups in the western USSR. A far-flung underground religious network, in which Polish priests play a prominent part, serves these groups. How many are there of these Catholics? There are no accurate statistics, but their numbers must at the very minimum be reckoned in the hundreds of thousands.

Numerically the largest group of believers in the USSR receptive to the direct influence of a Slavic Pope is the Ukrainian Uniate Church. The influence of this church extends into Belorussia also. It came into existence at the end of the sixteenth century when the Polish–Lithuanian state dominated this region. The Uniates recognized the authority of Rome and were permitted to retain most of their Eastern Orthodox ritual. The Western Ukraine never belonged to the Russian Empire. When Poland was partitioned, it went to Austria. Most of the Western Ukraine was Polish in the inter-war period, with areas belonging to Czechoslovakia and Romania and some Ukrainians living in Hungary too. The Ukrainian cultural renaissance in the nineteenth century was centred in this non-Russian region, while the Eastern Ukraine suffered from tsarist assimilation policies and an influx of ethnic Russians. When Stalin got all Ukrainian lands under Moscow control in 1945, he lost no time moving against the Uniate Church. In a synod held in Lvov in 1946 Uniate bishops 'voted' to sever their link with Rome and recognize the supremacy of the Moscow Patriarchate.[28]

Within the Ukraine republic the seven *oblasts*, which only came under Soviet rule in 1945, have a population of nearly ten million. They are much more compactly Ukrainian than the population of the rest of this republic.[29] It was evident in the 1960s that loyalty to the Uniate Church persisted in these regions. Much more evidence of survival of Uniate sympathies developed in the 1970s, extending to the Eastern Ukraine and distant regions of the USSR where Ukrainians have settled in large numbers such as Kazakhstan.[30] It also became increasingly difficult to distinguish between religious senti- ment and nationalism—the first sometimes serving as a camouflage, sometimes as a catalyst for the second. Ukrainian dissidents have produced a prodigious quantity of *samizdat* and some have become well known outside the USSR: Chornovil, Dzyuba, Moroz. Thus here, as elsewhere in the USSR and in Poland itself, the election of a Polish Pope accelerated a process that was already well under way. In attacking these trends, Soviet communist critics have confirmed their strength:

> For the present leadership in the Vatican, the Ukraine is an object of particular solicitude. It is trying to use the still considerable active nucleus of the Catholic Church as a basis for extending religious influence over the population of the republic.[31]

An official publication of the Ukrainian republic boasted in 1981 of the amount of attention local newspapers were giving to 'criticism of Catholicism and Uniatism'. 23.3, 25.5 and 47.7 per cent of 'all materials published about the reactionary essence of religion and the church' in three regional newspapers was directed against it. By publishing such statistics communist agitprop officials want to demonstrate that they are hard at work—but the increasingly rancorous tone of their denunciations of the influence of Rome betrays a sense of frustration.[32]

Fears of the Polish Pope

Harsh criticism of John Paul II has been rare in the Soviet central press, for it immediately attracts attention abroad. But soon after his election he began to be attacked in the provincial press in the Ukraine and Belorussia. A pamphlet entitled 'In the Service of the Neo-Fascists' issued in Lvov, cultural capital of the Western Ukraine and seat of a major university, had this to say of him:

> Revanchists and enemies of democracy and socialism look with hope upon the new pope . . . for he has made it his goal to unite Catholics all over the planet into a single anti-communist force. It is dictated not by anxiety for mankind and its future but by the desire for religious authority over the planet.[33]

Such outbursts became more and more frequent in 1980 and 1981, as the assassination attempt against the Pope was being prepared.

Sometimes the Soviet press creates false issues in order to distract attention from real ones, but this is not what is happening in the case of religion. Communist officialdom would prefer to ignore it entirely. They cannot, out of fear that unopposed it will grow in strength. The Soviet journal *Questions of Scientific Atheism* revealed in 1981, in an article surveying contemporary Catholicism, that more than 800 publications criticizing Catholic dogma, the history of the church, the papacy and other aspects of the church's activities were issued in the USSR during the decade of the 1970s.[34]

Official concern is not confined to Catholicism. There are signs of revival in Russian Orthodoxy as well as among other traditionally Orthodox nationalities such as the Moldavians. Interest among intellectuals in church art and architecture has been growing for a generation or more. Where is the line to be drawn between esthetics and the rest of religion? Communists are worried, and in articulating their concerns they confirm the magnitude of the problem they face. A writer in *Questions of Scientific Atheism* recently observed:

> Empirical observations testify to a certain revival of religious faith, or at least interest in religion, in specific regions and certain sections of the population. Of late, a new type of believer has been emerging and becoming more and more noticeable who, compared with the old traditionalist believer, has a higher level of intellectual development, a marked tendency towards rationalistic justification of his faith, and an interest in the philosophical and ethical aspects of dogma and in the history of religion.[35]

Here is the crux of the problem. The judgement cited above, remember, comes not from an exile or a hopeful Western observer but from a Soviet official charged with combatting religion. He must be given credit for seeing his problem realistically. It is the problem the entire communist leadership of the USSR faces in dealing with the impact of a Slavic Pope. He has catalyzed ideological currents that have been gaining strength in the Soviet Union for a long time. In a very incipient way, these currents resemble what has happened in Poland under communism. The church provides a context within which thinking about fundamental issues of politics, society, individual morality, human rights and obligations—all blocked by the sterility and bankruptcy of official Marxism—can take place. Thus it becomes attractive even to those who have no interest in theology and dogma and feel little need for conventional spiritual consolation.

The Kremlin has no answer to this challenge to its increasingly questioned claim to have a 'divine right' to rule as interpreters of 'scientific socialism'. Its dilemma is well summed up by the Polish philosopher Leszek Kolakowski:

> Communism would be such a splendid idea if only there were no people; and in Poland in particular communism would be a marvelous thing if only there were no Poles.[36]

But there are—36 million of them—an irreconcilable mass in the middle of Moscow's East European empire. To try to cope with them, the Kremlin was driven to plot to kill John Paul II.

SECTION THREE
The Twisted Road to Rome

In the last section, we established why the Soviet Union might want to have the Pope killed and what kind of experience, resources and skills they had available for the task. In this section, we take up the story where I left it at the end of Chapter 2 returning to Ankara from Malatya in October 1981.

Gradually a great deal of information relevant to the plot was gathered in many places, but the most important development in the investigation came on 25 November 1982 when the Italian investigating judge, Ilario Martella, capped off a year of persistent work by having Sergei Antonov, head of the Bulgarian airline office in Rome, put under arrest on evidence of direct involvement with Agca. Two other Bulgarians, Ayvazov and Kolev, were implicated as well, but they had fled and diplomatic status would have made their arrest impossible even if they had remained in Italy. Agca had begun to talk to Judge Martella the previous May. He had given up hope of rescue and feared he might be killed in prison. What he had to say, combined with the confessions of Italian socialist labor leader Luigi Scricciolo, provided solid evidence of a direct Bulgarian connection to the shooting of the Pope. It also provided evidence of a sub-plot to kill Solidarity leader Lech Walesa. This kind of direct involvement was something no one working on the plot originally envisioned. Skeptics of the Eastern connection and apologists for the Soviet Union, in fact, tried to turn these revelations around: for the Bulgarians to be in direct touch with Agca in Rome was so astonishing, so unprofessional, so unlike what one would expect of an always super-efficient KGB that there must be some other explanation. In other words, the Bulgarian connection was proof of its impossibility!

But this kind of circular argumentation would not hold. There was a flood of preoccupation in the press with what had been revealed in Rome and governments, legislators and laymen throughout the Western world concerned themselves with the plot more intensively than before. Thus while exposure of a direct Bulgarian link in Rome dramatizes the Eastern origin of the plot a few of us expected from the first days after it occurred, it has also tended to draw attention from other facets of the case which may be equally, if not more, important.

I completed two reports on the papal plot for the *Reader's Digest* by the end of 1981 and then turned to other tasks, but after the fall of 1982 I was almost continually involved in work on the papal plot again, making two further visits to Turkey and two to Italy in early 1983. It would serve little purpose to recount chronologically these investigations and each development which has continued to shed further light on the plot. Except for occasional references to particular experiences, I will concentrate in this section on examining the present state of our knowledge of Agca, his evolution as an assassin, and the likely course of development of the scheme to shoot John Paul II.

8
THE EVOLUTION OF THE ASSASSIN

Agca the Student

Mehmet Ali Agca had just turned 21 when he committed his first known murder in early 1979. This murder is still far from explained. What we know about it will be discussed in detail later in this chapter. Though Agca was not identified as the murderer until almost five months after the act, the killing of *Milliyet* editor Abdi Ipekçi did not look like either an accident or the deed of a lunatic. It appeared to have political meaning. What was the meaning? Who wanted a message delivered? These questions are still being debated in Turkey.

If it had a political objective, the killing would be likely to have had organizational backing. At the time it occurred, this killing was interpreted exclusively in Turkish domestic terms, but as time has passed suspicion has grown that it may have had more than domestic motivation. The question remains open. It has bearing on Agca. Who was he working for? Whom did he think he was working for? What brought him to undertake the killing? Ideology? Money? Megalomania? Was he pressed or compromised into doing it? Or was he, after all, suffering from some form of mental imbalance?

The last of these questions can be disposed of most easily. He was put through psychiatric examination after his arrest in 1979. He was judged mentally normal. The same judgment was made in Rome in 1981. A Turkish official with long experience in dealing with drug traffickers, smugglers and terrorists, who sat in on Agca's interrogation in Rome in May and June 1981, had no doubts about Agca's sanity when he described him to me:

He has a sharp mind and catches ideas immediately. He is more the political criminal type than the simple terrorist who likes violent action for its own sake.

This parallels the judgement of Hasan Fehmi Güneş, Turkish Minister of the Interior at the time of Agca's interrogation in 1979:

Terrorist organizations in Turkey normally recruit semi-retarded illiterates as their hit men. Agca did not belong to this category. He was a clever, brave and determined man. He was highly trained . . . He was a man psychologically ready for interrogation and gave away nothing about his terrorist roots. He was obstinate and defiant.

In high school Agca was recognized by his classmates as a voracious reader, bright and quick, but he was not popular. He was intense, stubborn, cocky. So they gave him the nickname *imparator*—emperor. We have already seen him going around alone, holding himself aloof. We see another facet of him in another passage from his 1979 confession:

In school one day for amusement I was reading the magazines *Girgir* and *Çarşaf*. A fellow took the magazines from my hand and tore them up, saying, 'Who brought this crap to school?' Then he threw them angrily to the ground. My pride was hurt.

Çarşaf and *Girgir*, weekly humor magazines, enjoyed wide circulation in the mid-1970s. They were non-partisan, but biting in their humor and frequently poked fun at all political factions and made light of pompous politicians who took their quarrels too seriously. Agca's recollection may be significant for the use of the word 'crap', *ot* in Turkish (which means literally 'hay' or 'weeds'). In the 1970s rightists used it for persons who were neither opponents or supporters, i.e. were indifferent to political agitation or considered themselves above it. Recalling this period, one Ankara University student said to me in the summer of 1981:

The worst thing was to try *not* to take sides; I didn't want to be either a rightist or a leftist, but I found myself being attacked by both extremes. I finally gave up and joined the rightists so they could protect me against the leftists.

His roommate added:

Leftists and rightists, who were both really minorities, terrorized all the rest of us. Now we are all in the center—all Atatürkists again. We don't argue about politics. We study. We have time for other things we didn't before: sports, music, hobbies and sex. It's a great relief.

Agca's desire to avoid partisan politics seems to spring from a different source than that of these students, however. Perhaps it became self-reinforcing. Once on a course, he tended to stick to it. His mother made a revealing comment to me in the course of our conversation that strengthens this impression:

> Oh you couldn't convince him his judgment was wrong—he was absolutely confident of himself!

Agca's confession indicates that he continued his aloofness at the University of Ankara:

> After finishing high school I registered at the History and Geography Faculty. The school which was my ideal, political science or law, was impossible. During the period I remained in Ankara, I stayed in a dormitory that belonged to the teacher training school. This dormitory was under those of rightist views. On the whole I attended school, came from school. I did not hang placards, I did not want to get involved in the fights of the leading people at the school. I did not accept them at all.

Agca's dormitory, Beşevler, was indeed in the hands of the right during this period. The Ankara History and Geography Faculty, however, had a strong leftist element. The Political Science Faculty at Ankara was notorious for leftist agitation. Is the fact that this was Agca's first choice meaningful? We do not know. Agca seems to have made very little impression in Ankara. Professors at the university to whom I talked in the fall of 1981 were surprised to learn that he had ever been a student there! There was no requirement for students to attend classes. But what did Agca do? Security and police records confirm that he avoided entanglement in agitation. The Director of Security in Ankara gave me the following written answer in October 1981 to a query about evidence of association with the Gray Wolves:

> At the time of Agca's arrest, nothing was found on him indicating Idealist [Gray Wolf] connections. In his declaration to the police, he maintained he did not belong to any political persuasion, was not the supporter of any ideology, did not belong to any party, association or group with a political aim and had not collaborated

with such organizations. He maintained he was a terrorist acting entirely on his own. His name has not been found on any list of Idealist members.

Rightist or Leftist?

Did student friendships from Malatya continue in Ankara and later in Istanbul? Evidence is sparse. Turkish leftists have tried to fit Agca into a tightly knit rightist group which formed in Malatya when he was in his teens and provided the context in which he evolved into a professional killer in Ankara and Istanbul. They want to bolster the case leftists in Turkey began making as soon as Abdi Ipekçi was killed that the deed had to be the work of rightists. By the time Agca was caught he had already been categorized as a rightist. This allegation has been made over and over again.[1] It cannot be accepted as proven or even, necessarily, as probable.

Shortly after he was captured in Rome, Agca claimed that in the spring of 1977 he and a school friend, Sedat Sirri Kadem, crossed the Syrian border at Kilis and made their way to Damascus. They then were met by Teslim Töre, head of the pro-communist Turkish People's Liberation Army (THKO). Töre was a native of Malatya but fled Turkey in 1970 or 1971 when the first wave of terrorism was brought to an end. He has been closely associated with the PLO ever since. Agca said Töre arranged for him and Kadem to spend 40 days training in a Palestinian camp 20 km south of Beirut. Then he arranged for them to return to Turkey by an illegal route similar to that by which they had come. Agca claimed that during the next two years he was in contact with Töre's group in Turkey as well as with five other clandestine terrorist organizations, three of them leftist, two rightist.[2]

In the summer of 1982, Sedat Sirri Kadem's father, Mehmet, was interviewed in Malatya by a Turkish journalist.[3] He admitted that his son had been a friend of Mehmet Ali Agca. He described his son as having had 'behavior problems' in high school but said he had eventually gained credit for graduation in 1977 from the same high school Agca completed in 1976. Then his son, according to Mehmet Kadem, spent a year in vocational school in Malatya before going to Istanbul to study political science. He claimed to have heard nothing from him since July 1980 when he sent him TL 100,000 (then about $2,000) in response to an urgent plea for money. The elder Kadem described himself and his son as 'of social democratic views'.

There is no confirmation of his father's statement that Sedat Sirri Kadem became a political science student in Istanbul, but his move to the big city in the fall of 1978, the same time Agca officially transferred from Ankara, could be more than coincidence. The young Kadem may have misled his father about his student status. His high school record would not seem to have qualified him for entry into the University at Istanbul. On the other hand, organizational supporters might have arranged for someone else to take the entrance examination in his place. Terrorist organizations were sometimes able to do this in the confused situation that prevailed in Turkey in the late 1970s. Whether a student actually spent time at a university or not, the status was valuable because it gave automatic deferral of military service. A prominent Turkish criminologist, Professor Sahir Erman of the University of Istanbul, has contended that Agca himself is unlikely to have taken the examinations by which he qualified first for Ankara and then Istanbul universities. Documents of which I have copies look as if they had been filled out and signed by Agca and the photographs resemble him. But there is room for speculation. The question is best left open until further investigation in Turkey and, we hope, information from Agca himself, can settle it.

Claire Sterling found evidence that Sedat Sirri Kadem had been arrested as a DEVSOL (Revolutionary Left) terrorist in 1981, but I have been unable to determine his present whereabouts.[4] We know Agca maintained links with several young men from Malatya in Istanbul who had an orientation toward the right. Is it possible that Sedat Sirri Kadem might be a missing link to the left?

We still know the least about the relationships which Agca's family says were most important during his student years in Malatya—those with teachers. No teacher has come forward to admit close ties with Agca or to try to explain him. Names have been difficult to trace. Teachers in Turkey in the 1970s were intensely politicized. Some did little teaching and looked upon their students as raw material to organize for partisan fighting. The leftist teachers' federation TÖBDER was a major terrorist support mechanism. National Action Party organizers were active among teachers who were opposed to the left. Teachers were more polarized than students. If Agca, by the time he left Malatya for Ankara, had been identified as a promising recruit for major terrorist tasks, one or more of his teachers is likely to have marked him for special handling and alerted contacts in Ankara to welcome him. It may not be accidental that the dormitory where Agca stayed in Ankara belonged to the teacher training school, though he was not part of it.

The evidence we have, therefore, confirms Agca's own claim to have been in contact with both rightists and leftists. It also supports his contention that he was not motivated by ideology as it was conventionally understood in Turkey at that time. What did motivate him?

His brother Adnan's recollection of his scorn for the low pay of a teacher may provide an important clue. The most logical motivation is one which is easiest to explain. Agca had grown up in poverty. He knew what it meant to work and save. He took pride in helping his family. He was fired with ambition to lead a better life. Turkey in the late 1970s—Malatya in particular—was not a place where it was easy for a student to see a clear path into the future. The country was visibly faltering, both economically and politically. Short-cuts could be tempting, irresistible in fact. Agca was ripe for recruitment on the promise of *good monetary reward*.

The monetary appeal could be sweetened with an overlay of idealism tailored to fit the self-esteem of a quick-minded, stubborn, cocky loner who held himself aloof from the ideological turbulence in which his classmates were losing themselves. The recruiters did not want to be so crass as to depend on money alone.[5] We can probably see a reflection of the kind of rationalizations they used in a passage in Agca's confession written on 6 July 1979 as a justification for killing Abdi Ipekçi:

> Part of our people who were massacring each other would have seen the facts. Those who shed no tears for thousands of people, seeing on whose side the system is, would see the storm caused by the death of one person and would at least understand that no result could be obtained from killing each other. Perhaps anarchy would be directed against a few industrialists, bad administrators and exploiters. As in the case of Germany, it would for the most part subside, if not completely. The people would no longer be attacking themselves.

The language is convoluted, the Turkish even more tortured and dense than the English. What he appears to be saying is that by killing one prominent person he was hoping to shock Turks so much that they would stop killing each other, or turn anarchy—terror—into a movement directed primarily at industrialists, bad administrators and exploiters. The comparison with Germany may refer to the Baader–

Meinhof heyday and its aftermath, but the reference is unclear. The passage as a whole has a more leftist than rightist flavor. In this it is like many other Agca statements. But it is clearly a rationalization. It probably reveals more about the political orientation of Agca's sponsors than it does of Agca himself. He cannot convincingly be made out to be either a rightist or a leftist. In Agca both extremes touched and merged, to be employed for destructive purposes. It is the way terrorism developed in Turkey—both extremes against the vital center. This is the way it served Soviet purposes best, but there is no reason to assume that as the recruitment process started Agca had any idea he was to serve Soviet purposes at all . . .

Money Begins to Flow

Agca's 20th year, 1977, was crucial to his development as a terrorist. If he went for Palestinian training that spring, his sponsors had a good opportunity to assess his talents. If the seasoned terrorist Teslim Töre was as closely involved in the training trip as Agca claimed, he might have recommended him for special attention after he returned to Ankara. Every terrorist organization in Turkey had its men in the capital. The Soviet Union and all its Eastern European satrapies have large diplomatic missions in Ankara with trade, cultural and press representation. A sizable proportion of these people are known to be intelligence officers. They are watched, of course, by MIT, the Turkish National Intelligence Organization, and by security and police officers. But these organizations were severely strained in the 1970s by overwork and political interference. Their priorities were not always clear. Priorities changed frequently as coalition governments succeeded each other. A young Turkish student with no known organizational ties and no record of involvement in political agitation would not cause particular concern if he were observed in contact with an Eastern bloc intelligence representative. The contact would probably have been dismissed as too minor to merit follow-up when dozens of higher priority cases were demanding attention. And even if some officer intended to look into it, he might have been diverted by a dozen other preoccupations. The more Eastern bloc operators got away with in Turkey the bolder they became. It was the same as in Italy.

If Turkish intelligence people have evidence of direct contact between Agca and Eastern intelligence representatives in Ankara they have so far kept it to themselves. There may have been none. Agca may have been handled at arm's length, by Turks working as Eastern agents or by third-country operators—Syrians, Libyans, Iraqis—collaborating with the Russians or Bulgarians. All that we know is that somebody was in contact with him, somebody was seeing that he was kept obscure and clean and uncontaminated by ordinary terrorist connections that could have drawn him into premature trouble. But he was doing something for them—or at the very least absorbing well the training he was being given. The proof is that at the end of the year *he began to be paid.* An account was opened for him at the Beyazit (University) branch of the Türkiye Iş Bankasi in Istanbul on 13 December 1977 and the equivalent of about $1,600 deposited in it. He already had another account in the Akbank branch in the same area. It was a nice windfall for a poor student. It was only the beginning. The most curious thing about it is that Agca was not even living in Istanbul yet!

He did not take the university entrance examination again (with or without help) until the spring of 1978. He scored highest in science and lowest in English and qualified for one of the most sought-after faculties in the Turkish university system: economics at Istanbul. It is fairly common practice in Turkey for a student to take the examination a second time to change university or course of study. Agca's decision to do so could merely have reflected his own ambition. Why he shifted to economics from his earlier stated top choice of political science or law is not clear. Perhaps he had help in making the choice. The Economics Faculty of the University of Istanbul has many distinguished professors, but I could find no one there three years later who remembered having Mehmet Ali Agca as a student. It is possible that he never attended a class.

His university file includes certificates of draft deferral and clean police record in Malatya dated 9 October 1978, a medical certificate certifying absence of contagious disease and the list of twelve courses for which he registered for the 1978/9 academic year. It was a tough schedule with several economics courses, accounting, civil law and introduction to political science. The file's last entry is a computer printout of the same courses as of the end of the year with the notation that the student did not take any final examinations though fees for them had been paid.

There are other mysteries about Agca's move to Istanbul. It has never been established where he actually lived. A room he claimed was his when he was arrested looked unused for months. He claimed to have stayed with a cousin when he first arrived. The address given for the Türkiye Iş Bankasi account opened for him in December 1977 turned out to be non-existent. The Akbank account carried an address that belonged to a filling station. It would not be unusual for a student in Ankara to visit Istanbul once or twice a year—but two bank accounts nine months before he transferred from one university to the other for a student of limited means is extraordinary.

Thus one gets the impression that by this time Agca's student status may have been mostly a cover for other activity which was absorbing most of his time. He was in touch with a group of young men from Malatya most of whom were not students. There is some evidence that some of these young men were active on the fringes of the shady world of smugglers doing business in contraband and arms with regular links to Bulgaria and Europe, some also to Syria and to the Middle East. Many of the major smugglers originated from south-eastern Turkey. There was an active, close-knit group from Pötürge, a district of Malatya province south-east of the capital. Such regional ties are often important in Turkey in many aspects of life, but Agca's family roots were in Hekimhan, north of Malatya, and there do not seem to have been any major smuggling interests there.

Agca's sponsors are unlikely to have paid him in the manner they did for mere participation on the fringes of smuggling operations. There was no lack of unemployed manpower for such work. Nor would they have wanted him to become needlessly involved in the 'business' side of smuggling. What then *was* he doing in Istanbul during this period? Perhaps he was already proving himself in terrorist activities from which he escaped without a trace and preserved his anonymity. Killings were becoming at least a weekly occurrence in Istanbul during this time. Many have never been explained.

Whatever Agca was doing, he continued to be paid. His total earnings for the year 1978 were well above the average for a prosperous Turkish tradesman or middle-level official. Sahir Erman, the Turkish criminologist, laboriously pursued leads developed when the military prosecutor ordered a check of bank accounts in the name of Mehmet Ali Agca (rather a rare name in Turkey) throughout the country after Agca's arrest in June 1979. It was found that by the time Agca was ready to carry out the Ipekçi assassination, sums totalling at least $16,000 had gone into his bank accounts. The pattern was curious. Agca seems to have deposited little if any of the money himself. It was deposited for him with his name signed on the slips but the signatures, which vary, are not his. Withdrawal slips, however, always bear his true signature. Deposits were made in odd places, such as Üsküdar on the Asian side of the Bosporus and Gebze, a provincial town 50 km east of Istanbul along the Sea of Marmara. TL 200,000 was deposited in the Yapi-Kredi Bankasi in Gebze on 29 December 1978. This was equivalent to $8,000 at that time.

Confronted with evidence of this deposit in Gebze during his interrogation in 1979, Agca claimed that he had become apprehensive about being robbed when traveling by bus back to Malatya and carrying a sum of cash along. So he had got off the bus when it reached Gebze and gone to a bank to deposit the money. He admitted he withdrew it at the Malatya branch of the same bank on 4 January 1979. He redeposited half of it in an account in the Malatya branch of the Ziraat Bankasi on 15 January and claimed to have spent the rest of it buying his mother a sewing machine and TV set. It would have bought a great deal more than that. Professor Erman discovered that the signature on the Gebze deposit slip was clearly not Agca's.[6] The conclusion is inescapable that this movement of money had a direct relationship to the forthcoming assassination of Ipekçi.

More deposits may come to light than are now known, but what we know is enough to demonstrate that Agca was generously compensated and the method of payment was classically clandestine, of the type a sophisticated and experienced intelligence service would use. Would it not have been safer to pay Agca in cash? There would then have been no record for the courts to dig out later. But there would also have been no recourse for the depositors of the money if Agca simply took it and failed to deliver the services expected from him. His sponsors wanted a record. They may also have wanted a cumulative record that could be used to coerce him, if necessary, into more extensive co-operation later.

Who Killed Abdi Ipekçi

Who was Abdi Ipekçi? Descendant of an old and highly regarded *dönme* (Jewish convert) family, he was at the peak of his career and one of the most respected figures in Turkish public life when he was assassinated on the evening of 1 February 1979.

Nothing about the Ipekçi murder has been clarified. A complete reinvestigation of the case was ordered by the Turkish government in December 1982 and a committee with military and civilian membership was appointed to oversee the process. If the investigation is thorough enough to clarify all the uncertainties and questions in this case, its work may take years. At some point it will have to reinterrogate Agca.[7] Agca may have been telling his mother the truth when he insisted during his last meeting with her that he was not the assassin—that he had taken the blame for others. There can be little doubt that he was at least an accessory to the murder. He certainly knows more about it than he revealed during his five-month interrogation and trial in 1979—but there may be a good deal about the genesis and sponsorship of the operation that was hidden from him, just as in his shooting of the Pope.

There is perhaps more mystery about the killing of Abdi Ipekçi than there is about the attack on the Pope. When he shot the Pope, Agca was immediately apprehended and brought to interrogation without the opportunity to reflect or be coached by those who put him up to the deed. He was free for nearly five months after Abdi Ipekçi was shot. He returned to Malatya soon after and then went back to his 'normal' life in Istanbul, whatever that was. The fact that he had provided himself with a passport, issued in Malatya on 20 January 1979, is evidence that he—or someone—had considered the desirability of his fleeing abroad in the wake of the killing. But he did not. Why?

The mythology that grew up during the five months between the murder and Agca's capture has bedeviled those who have tried to get to the bottom of this case ever since. The left in Turkey rushed—or was pushed—to the judgment that Ipekçi had to have been murdered by the right. The blame was placed on Alparslan Türkeş, and his National Action Party. Türkeş, like all the other Turkish political leaders at the time, condemned the murder immediately and unequivocally. Not even any fringe group sympathetic to Türkeş intimated a desire to claim credit for it. When Agca was captured he was immediately labeled a Gray Wolf, though no evidence of membership or Türkeş sponsorship was produced or came to light. This characterization has been repeated ever since in Turkey and abroad as if it were an established fact. It has been diligently spread by Soviet commentators and communist media in many parts of the world.

Türkeş and over 900 members of his party were put on trial in Ankara by the Turkish military administration in April 1981 on charges of undermining the Atatürkist order in Turkey. The charges included abetting the Ipekçi killing. The trial did not go smoothly. Judges and prosecutors resigned. The trial was split into several separate cases and some of them were shifted to provincial centers, but the whole procedure is far from finished as of the summer of 1983. No convincing evidence of Türkeş' instigation of Ipekçi's assassination has been made public if it has indeed been presented to the court(s). Türkeş has argued that no motive for his party's abetting such an act can be demonstrated. Abdi Ipekçi did not single out Türkeş for unusually harsh journalistic treatment. He was more negative on Erbakan and his National Salvation Party.

Agca had no personal motivation for wanting to kill Ipekçi and no personal reason has been advanced for any of the other young men who seem to have been associated with him in this action. Money—as demonstrated by the sizable deposit into Agca's bank account at Gebze, sugared over with a supra-ideological rationalization of the kind reflected in the explanation he wrote after his capture—is sufficient to explain Agca's involvement.

But what about the people who paid the money and ordered the deed done? What was their purpose? What message were they sending? To whom?

Why Kill Ipekçi?

Abdi Ipekçi did not represent a party. He represented only his newspaper. It had long enjoyed the reputation of being the best in Turkey—less prone to sensationalism than most of the Turkish press, not as conservative as *Tercüman*, not left-leaning or ponderous like *Cumhuriyet*. *Milliyet* made a conscious effort to report both domestic and international news comprehensively and had some of the best reporters and columnists in the country. During a difficult period of domestic political strife and the strain of the US arms embargo, *Milliyet* had not lost faith in Turkey's pro-Western, pro-NATO, pro-EEC orientation nor advocated abandonment of the special relationship with the United States that had persisted since enunciation of the Truman Doctrine. Nor had the paper been pettily partisan in its domestic political reporting. Ipekçi was known to be personally sympathetic to Ecevit but he had more enthusiasm for Ecevit's ideals than for his performance in office. He was highly critical of some of the inexperienced and opinionated men Ecevit chose as ministers after his Republican People's Party returned to office in January 1978. He grew impatient with Ecevit's reluctance to face up to terrorism and came out editorially for extension of martial law long before Ecevit was forced to take action in the wake of the appalling violence in

Kahramanmaraş in December 1978.

I knew Abdi Ipekçi's views from having been a *Milliyet* reader, during my service at the US Embassy in Ankara in the mid-1970s. I met him twice. But the first time I met him was in Washington in July 1978 when he came to observe the final phase of the Carter Administration's campaign to persuade Congress to lift the arms embargo against Turkey. His main interest was in assessing how Turkish–American relations were going to develop once the embargo was lifted. He was unhappy with both extreme leftist and extreme rightist politicians in Turkey and was convinced that the best way to limit their influence was to rebuild a strong Turkish–American relationship. He told me of the initiative he had taken to get Greek and Turkish public opinion leaders together for periodic meetings to reduce the strain that threatened the Alliance in the eastern Mediterranean. He had no sympathy with the neutralism some Turkish leftists were pushing or for Erbakan's Muslim fundamentalism. He saw no serious threat in Türkeş if the two major parties remained strong and responsible and could bring themselves to co-operate for the good of the country. We talked of all these things. He asked me to have USIA (the US Information Agency) in Istanbul provide him with background on American policy developments so that he could be as constructive as possible in his editorials.

Our second meeting was in early January 1979 when I went to Turkey as the White House member of a mission headed by Deputy Secretary of State Warren Christopher for discussions with Ecevit and his ministers. The Guadeloupe Summit had just approved a Western economic rescue package for Turkey and it was time to hold comprehensive Turkish–American talks, the first in several years. The meetings went well. Ecevit was constructive and overruled his obstructionist foreign minister who had been blocking the US–Turkish prisoner exchange treaty in which several members of Congress were personally interested. We signed it the first day of our talks. Other aspects of the talks were also successful. I stopped over in Istanbul after these meetings to brief the US consul-general on them. Abdi Ipekçi had left word at the consulate that he was eager to see me, so I spent nearly two hours with him in his office in the *Milliyet* building on the afternoon of 13 January and left directly from it for the airport and return to Washington.

The total lack of security precautions at the *Milliyet* offices did not strike me at the time, for journalists had not yet become terrorist targets in Turkey. Less than three weeks later when I picked up the

Washington Post at breakfast at home on 2 February and read with shock that Abdi had been gunned down the night before, every detail of that afternoon came back to me vividly. He had wanted to hear directly from me how we thought our talks with Ecevit had gone. He showed me the weekend editorial he had drafted on the importance of the Turkish–American relationship and asked whether it reflected the mood of the meeting. It did. We talked about terrorism and martial law. We talked also about Iran, where the Shah's government had just collapsed and the country was degenerating into chaos. He hoped the United States would act to preserve something of its position there and spoke of the desirability of Turkey's helping to keep Iran oriented toward the West. As we were having our second round of tea, Turan Güneş walked in. He had been foreign minister in Ecevit's first government in 1974. Ipekçi and Güneş obviously enjoyed a close relationship. Both spoke with frankness of the weaknesses of Ecevit's current foreign and finance ministers and expressed skepticism that Ecevit's government would prove up to the task of getting the Turkish economy under control.

As the myth grew in the months that followed that Ipekçi had been murdered by Gray Wolves, I found it hard to see why Türkeş would have objected to most of the policy views Ipekçi had expressed to me. He and his principal lieutenants stoutly deny that they did. One argument went that Ipekçi was killed because he had favored martial law, which antagonized rightist militants. But it was just as likely to antagonize the much more numerous leftist militants. Türkeş and his party leadership were never really anti-Western. They were more eager for a close American relationship than the US was to have one. They never failed to come to the US Embassy if invited, but they were not frequently invited. Nor did they oppose Turkey's orientation toward Europe. They favoured an active Turkish European policy because they had so many followers among Turkish workers in Germany. There was very little in Ipekçi's basic policy positions that differed greatly from the positions Türkeş had endorsed as a member or supporter of the two previous Demirel-led governments.

The most serious questions about the Türkeş party do not relate to its policy positions, which were much less out of line with basic pro-Western Atatürkist principles than either Erbakan's National Salvation Party or the five little extreme leftist parties that operated in the 1970s. The doubts concern the extent to which Türkeş may have been dissimulating and above all whether he was really in control of his party or had a firm grip on its youth wing, the Gray Wolves.

Türkeş's party may have been infiltrated by foreign agents who sometimes acted to convey the impression they were following the party's
real, but hidden, agenda. Some members of the party may have had
hidden agendas of their own.

As evidence of many negative forces at work in the Türkeş party
has mounted, and as the basic case for Türkeş' instigation of the
Ipekçi assassination has failed to be proven, a new body of mythology
has developed among leftist publicists in Turkey. Abdi Ipekçi's killers
are alleged to have been hired by smugglers, by the Turkish mafia.
Why would they be so antagonistic toward him? Because it is claimed
he was going to publish a major series of exposés of smuggling
operations and their connections with terrorism. When I talked to the
Milliyet reporter assigned by Ipekçi to follow smuggling, he could give
me nothing to confirm this contention. He could not recall plans for
a major article series on smuggling. Nor could other senior reporters
who were close to Ipekçi and knew what his forward thinking was.

Another alleged reason for his killing suggested by leftists was
opposition to a change of ownership of the *Milliyet* publishing enter-
prise. The subject is extremely hazy. Why a change of ownership of a
newspaper would lead to murder of the most prestigious personality
connected with it is no more clear in Turkey than it would be in most
other countries. The journalist who has most artfully and suggestively
embroidered this kind of speculation is Ugur Mumcu, who also
dramatized minor episodes during Ipekçi's final weeks such as the
disappearance of a pocket address book and the loss of a set of keys.
While diverting attention to trivia, he has avoided analyzing what
Ipekçi was doing during the final months of his life in political terms.[8]

One chain of events stands out for its direct East–West relevance.
Zekeriya Sertel, an old Turkish communist who had been permitted
to return to Turkey after long exile, finished part of his memoirs in the
summer of 1978 and offered them for sale. Ipekçi was eager to buy
them for *Milliyet*. They were offered to *Cumhuriyet* which turned
them down. *Tercüman*, a moderately conservative, anti-communist
paper wanted them badly and was ready to pay a good price. Within
the *Milliyet* staff, there were two camps. One for, one against buying
them. Ipekçi succeeded in buying the memoirs and published them in
a series of 24 installments in September and October 1978. Entitled
'Nazim Hikmet's Last Days', the series chronicled the disillusionment
of the fugitive Turkish communist poet after he fled to the Soviet
Union in 1951. He died there in 1963. This memoir has never
appeared in book form, though it is an important document in the

history of Turkish communism. Extreme leftists were angered by Ipekçi's publication of it, for Nazim Hikmet remains valuable to communists and their sympathizers as a symbol of something rare in Turkey—a pro-Russian Turk. Zekeriya Sertel made it clear that Nazim Hikmet lost most of his fondness for communism and Russia during his years in exile in Moscow.[9]

One of Ipekçi's most intense preoccupations during the final year of his life was to take serious steps to mitigate Greek–Turkish strains. While viciously competitive party politics in both countries made it difficult for weak governments to act,[10] Ipekçi was convinced that initiative from Greek and Turkish businessmen, professors, journalists and private citizens could bring both peoples together and stop the periodic bouts of posturing and sabre-rattling over the Aegean and Cyprus. He hoped to persuade his own profession—the journalists—to resist the temptation to magnify every misunderstanding and whip up tension whenever a problem arose. He persuaded a group of Greeks to join him in setting up a permanent mechanism for private meetings and exchanges. The very day he was killed he had gone to Ankara to get assurance from both Ecevit and Demirel that they would contain their urge to score points against each other on this issue and quietly support his initiative.

It is hard to see how promoting Greek–Turkish reconciliation could so alarm any forces on the right side of the Turkish political spectrum as to bring them to organize Ipekçi's killing. It is not hard to see how the Soviet Union, which has been encouraging and exploiting Greek–Turkish antagonisms for 20 years would find such activity distasteful, particularly when it was part of Ipekçi's broader vision of a Turkey solidly rededicated to the US, NATO and Europe, putting its economic house in order and dealing firmly with terrorism by enforcing martial law. The same vision anticipated an equally positive role for Greece.

All of Abdi Ipekçi's objectives contradicted the aims of the massively financed Soviet destabilization program in Turkey which was coming close to succeeding by the end of the 1970s.[11] Whether Agca knew whose purposes he was really serving by the time he was selected for the Ipekçi murder—or whether he seriously believed his half-baked claim that by killing him he was serving some abstract aim of purifying society of evil through terrorism—we still do not know. We may have to wait some time to find out. What we now know of the Ipekçi killing is nevertheless worth examining to see what we can learn about how Agca was guided, what he was promised and how all this might relate to the plot to kill the Polish Pope.

The Murder

It is not totally outside the realm of possibility that a group of young men, mostly from Malatya, might get together and decide to kill a major public figure and that they might then organize to carry out the killing in a reasonably efficient manner. Agca tried to assert as much immediately after he was captured in June 1979:

> I am against the present system and I killed Ipekçi because he was a defender of this system. I have no connection with any organization. I killed him just to cause terror . . . I chose Ipekçi because he had no police protection and was the easiest to get.

Glib, but not very convincing, especially in view of the fact that we now know (as Agca's interrogators did not then) that he had already had money deposited in his bank accounts far in excess of any sum a group of young men from Malatya could generate on their own. We still do not know what some of the others might have been paid. Agca eventually retracted this story, was sprung from prison and went on to implement the scheme to kill the Pope. His actions have to be examined in the context of the total pattern they form. To try to interpret the Ipekçi killing as a random isolated act is to concentrate on the least likely explanation of it.

The murder was smoothly accomplished. Either it was well planned or Agca and his friend(s) were lucky. The day he was killed Ipekçi had returned from Ankara on an early evening flight, conferred hurriedly with half a dozen of his reporters and writers in his office and then rushed home to pick up his wife for a dinner engagement. His car had been parked in the street near the *Milliyet* building. Someone must have been watching to see him leave and alert Agca and his companion(s), presumably by telephone. This could have been done from several nearby buildings; someone in the *Milliyet* building itself could have done so. Ipekçi was alone. It was a gloomy winter night. The drive across the Golden Horn and up into the Beyoglu section of the city would have taken at least 20 minutes, perhaps half an hour. As he turned off a busy avenue in Nişantaşi onto the street where he lived (it has since been renamed for him), he was shot through his car window. The time was about 8:30. He died almost instantly, his body riddled with at least seven bullets which left several holes in the vehicle.

As many as eleven cartridge cases were reportedly found in the car and on the pavement at the site of the shooting. No one was standing by as the shooting occurred but several people in the street heard the shots, saw men running and provided testimony afterward that has never been fully reconciled. Agca's gun had eight bullets, he said. But the weapon was never found. Like everything about this incident, there is confusing information on what happened to it. Agca said he went to the Aksaray Gray Wolf Club and gave it to Mehmet Şener, a friend from Malatya. Yavuz Çaylan, Agca's accomplice, said it was wrapped in a piece of cloth and thrown out of the car window after they had cleared the area. No cloth-wrapped gun was ever reported— but that would not be surprising in the conditions that prevailed in Istanbul at that time. When Agca was captured, he said he had stood waiting to shoot Ipekçi as he slowed down to turn while Yavuz Çaylan remained in the driver's seat with the engine running. Directly after the shooting Agca said he leaped into the car and Çaylan sped away. Arrested immediately after Agca was caught, Çaylan pleaded no advance knowledge of Agca's intention to murder Ipekçi. How thoroughly he was interrogated is not clear. He was eventually sentenced to three years' imprisonment.

A Third Man?

Two witnesses said they saw *two* men jump into the right rear door of the red Anadol. Another claimed he saw two men run to the car, but one got into the rear and one into the driver's seat. Still another claimed to have seen a Volkswagen, which has never been otherwise identified, waiting near the site of the shooting. Much of this testimony was given long afterward. No one has tried to reconcile it. In the early stage of the investigation it was not deemed important.

But in the fall of 1979 after Agca had withdrawn his original confession and claimed he had not shot Ipekçi—but knew who did— the issue of a possible third man became pertinent. It has never been laid to rest. A whole body of speculation has developed around another young man from Malatya, Oral Çelik. Less seems to be known of him with certainty than of any other figure connected with Agca. Agca did not mention Çelik in 1979, nor did his name come up as significant during the investigations that were made after Agca's capture. At the time interest was centered on Mehmet Şener. Later it was Ömer Ay. Şener narrowly evaded arrest when Agca was caught and escaped abroad. He eventually turned up in Switzerland where he remains in police custody but the Swiss authorities, mysteriously, have as of this writing still refused to permit his extradition in spite of repeated requests by both Turks and Italians. Ömer Ay was arrested in Germany and after a prolonged legal battle returned to Turkey at the end of 1982—but is said to have had little important information. Leftist journalists have gradually centered on Oral Çelik as a key figure who has been built up into the architect and guide of all of Agca's activities.

In Ugur Mumcu's *Agca Dosyasi*, published in March 1983 in Istanbul, Çelik is dramatized as a senior Gray Wolf who masterminded the plot to kill Ipekçi and who may have been in St Peter's Square at the time of the shooting of the Pope. Agca's failure to mention him either in Turkey or in Rome is seen as evidence of an obligation on Agca's part to protect him. Çelik was allegedly a rightist militant under suspicion of having murdered a leftist schoolteacher in Malatya. He is claimed to have been a close friend of Agca before he left Malatya. He is alleged to have been the organizer of Agca's escape from prison. German ZDF television claimed in a program aired in May 1983 that it had uncovered a new figure who could be the key to explaining the plot against the Pope—Oral Çelik. His whereabouts are unknown. There are few photographs of him.

Oral Çelik may be a key man. The reinvestigation of the Ipekçi murder which got under way in Turkey at the end of 1982 should produce a better basis for judgment than we have now. Perhaps Çelik was the main link between Agca and his ultimate sponsors. Perhaps, disguised as a Gray Wolf, he was actually a Bulgarian or Soviet agent. There is also the possibility that Çelik may turn out to be of little consequence. It is not necessary to postulate a Çelik to explain Agca. What does seem probable is that Agca had contacts with his sponsors that have not yet come to light. Someone gave him guidance, indoctrinated him, promised him money, met with him and reviewed the actions he was going to take.

The case for a third man in the Ipekçi shooting is stronger than the argument that it had to be Oral Çelik.[12] If there was a third man the fact that the murder was carefully planned in advance is further demonstrated; but it has long been evident. The third man issue has legal importance, however, that could eventually make possible Agca's return to Turkey. Italian law prevents extradition of a fugitive, no matter what his crime, if he is under death sentence in his own country. If it could be demonstrated that Agca had not killed Ipekçi and was merely an accessory to the crime, the death sentence which the Istanbul military court passed on him on 28 April 1980 could be commuted to life and he could be returned to Turkey where he could help clarify the background of the Ipekçi assassination and its relationship to the larger terror and destabilization scene in Turkey at the time, including foreign involvement. All this would be possible if it were only the Ipekçi killing that had to be taken into account, but there is a fair probability that Agca also committed two other murders before he left Turkey. Those would also subject him to Turkey's mandatory death penalty for murder.

Capture and Trial

The Ipekçi assassination had a profoundly demoralizing effect on Turkey. It undermined Turks' confidence in themselves. It caused fear to grow that there was no area of Turkish life, no profession, no group of citizens no matter how committed to peace and order and reconciliation who could be left untouched by senseless violence. Rightists did a poor job of defending themselves against insinuations of guilt. Leftists were—characteristically—much more articulate and agile in arguing that only they could protect society from brutality and urged moderates to support them.

It should be noted in passing that no one in Turkey made any religious allegations in connection with the killing. Erbakan's National Salvation Party was not implicated, though it was more anti-Western than Türkeş's party. Agca, when captured, did not even hint that he had had any Islamic motive for killing Ipekçi and made no pretense of being religious. This is worth remembering when we examine the evolution of the plot against the Pope. Religion was a *new* element in Agca's cover story and did not carry it off convincingly in explaining his attack on the Pope.

The Turkish Journalists' Association offered a reward of nearly $100,000 for information leading to the apprehension of Ipekçi's killer. Police arrested Agca at the Marmara Cafe in the Beyazit district of Istanbul on 25 June 1979 on the basis of an alleged anonymous phone call. No one has ever claimed the reward. The Marmara Cafe was known as a Gray Wolf hang-out. It was almost as if the arrest had been staged to substantiate the impression that Ipekçi had been killed by the extreme right, at the connivance of Alparslan Türkeş.

Police and security officials were surprised at how eager Agca was to talk. He confessed readily to the killing, claimed to be a terrorist above ideologies, confided he had considered killing the US, British and Israeli consuls as well as two Turkish businessmen. He claimed to have taken no money, no instructions from anyone. All this parallels his performance in Rome after the shooting of the Pope. He identified Yavuz Çaylan as the driver of the getaway car and told about giving the gun to Mehmet Şener. Çaylan was quickly picked up. Şener somehow got warning that Agca had been caught and did not show up the next day at the teahouse where he worked, where police were ready to arrest him. He abandoned his car on the street and disappeared.

There was a good deal of confusion among the authorities working on the case. The place where Agca claimed to be living was not searched until several days after his capture. His home in Malatya was searched and his mother questioned only on 10 July. He reacted angrily when he heard this—evidence of embarrassment at the predicament into which he had plunged his family. These delays are partly explainable by the fact that Agca's arrest was at first tightly held. Interior Minister Hasan Fehmi Güneş did not even brief Prime Minister Ecevit on the case for several days, though Güneş came to Istanbul to oversee the interrogation.[13] He says he was struck by Agca's zeal to dramatize himself, his sharp mind, his arrogance, and his capacity to obfuscate and confuse his interrogators. Güneş now claims Agca did not appear to him to be either a rightist or a leftist.[14] His personal participation gave Agca a basis for claiming, after his trial started, that Güneş had offered him a deal:

After I was captured, Interior Minister Güneş came to Istanbul to talk to me. His proposal was that if I would say that a high official of the National Action Party had ordered me to kill Ipekçi or if I would claim membership in that party, then Güneş would rescue me.

Güneş specifically denied Agca's allegation in an interview published in the Turkish magazine *Yanki*, 4-10 July 1983, but admitted that Agca had been inadequately interrogated after his capture.[15] With his initial interrogation completed, Agca was presented to the public in a televised press conference on 11 July 1979. He behaved as if he had been born an actor, answered penetrating questions coolly, seemed to be enjoying himself, and insisted

> I was not the servant of any political ideas or ideology. And I will not be. I do not believe that at this time any ideology can bring any different result. I have not joined any party, group or organization with a political purpose. I am a terrorist acting on my own.

The conference attracted wide attention in Turkey and abroad. In spite of his protestations of lack of political sponsorship—and in some quarters because of them—he was labeled a Gray Wolf. Ecevit's government encouraged this conclusion, which had already become an article of faith among leftist extremists, including the left wing of Ecevit's party. As his political position weakened, Ecevit became more dependent upon vocal leftists in his party. Abroad, where Turkish domestic politics were poorly understood, Agca simply went into newspaper files as a Gray Wolf.

Foreign interest in the case waned quickly, though Agca was the subject of almost continual attention in the Turkish press for the next five months.[16] He was moved to Selimiye Prison in Üsküdar in mid-July and investigation and interrogation continued in preparation for his trial. When queried about the large sums of money he had received, he at first refused to give any information and then maintained that he did not know how many bank accounts he had. He gave repeated hints that he expected to be released—or rescued? Much information he gave seemed designed to mislead and confuse the authorities. They became concerned about security and on 25 September moved him to the more isolated Kartal–Maltepe military prison which is located 20 km outside the city on the Asian side on the edge of an industrial area not far from the Sea of Marmara. It was considered the country's highest security facility. But at this period in Turkey police and security forces and even the army itself had been so affected by terrorism and political dissension that no institution could be considered immune to infiltration by foreign agents bent upon undermining the authority of the state.

Escape

When Agca's trial began he was as self-assured as he had been at his press conference three months before. It was puzzling, for he should have been humbled by knowledge that as a confessed murderer his fate was sealed. On 12 October he claimed Interior Minister Güneş had offered him a deal. Güneş was in no position to defend himself, for an affair with singer Aynur Aydan had been exposed in the press and he was caught up in scandal. He had resigned on 5 October. On 14 October mid-term elections took place involving approximately one-third of the country's provinces. Demirel's party came out ahead. The electorate had given Ecevit a strong vote of no confidence. He resigned on 16 October. A Demirel-led government took office on 12 November but did not receive a vote of confidence in parliament until 25 November. The economy was in deep crisis, operating mostly underground. Terrorism had continued to spread in spite of martial law. Neighboring Iran had degenerated further and the personnel of the US Embassy in Tehran would soon be taken hostage. It was not a good time to be holding a major assassination trial involving a mysterious young killer who obviously represented more than he claimed. The court was ill-equipped to cope with the next unexpected turn of events. On 24 October Agca told it that he had not killed Ipekçi but that he knew who did and would reveal the true story at the next session of his trial!

This astonishing development led the court to direct that he again be psychologically assessed. On 5 November he was taken, along with a rightist named Attila Serpil, to the prison hospital for examination. In a sequence of still unexplained events Serpil and Agca succeeded in laying their hands on two pistols and took several prison officials hostage. Since there was no way to escape even if they killed their hostages, they were eventually persuaded to surrender. How the pistols—which ballistic tests allegedly determined had been used in several terrorist killings—came into the prison was never revealed. The suspicion is inescapable that this was an escape scheme that had been arranged from the outside with the help of accessories inside the prison. The signal Agca had given to his sponsors two weeks before when he reversed his confession—get me out or I will really start to talk—was being acted upon.

The next rescue attempt 18 days later was more skilfully conceived. It required more time and money. How many people were involved in it is still unknown. Several soldiers and officers were arrested in the wake of it. A private by the name of Bünyamin Yilmaz was sentenced to 15 years for having taken large bribes to facilitate the escape. Agca slipped out of his dormitory at night, was able to change into a soldier's uniform and made his way—obviously with a high degree of pre-arrangement—through several locked and guarded inner doors to the main exit gate of the prison, where he walked out.

The Turkish military, which administered the prison, was deeply embarrassed. So was Demirel's new government. All the more so the morning of 26 November when the *Milliyet* switchboard received a telephone call:

> This is Mehmet Ali Agca. I have just sent you a statement. Look in the mailbox next to the drugstore across from your building and you will find my statement there.

The statement, written in Agca's own readily recognizable hand, condemned the visit to Turkey of Pope John Paul II—due to arrive in Istanbul the next evening—and threatened to kill him. *Milliyet* publicized it immediately.

There were reports that Agca was subsequently seen at the Marmara Cafe, carrying a machine pistol and accompanied by several friends. A lottery ticket seller, a young man named Ramazan Gündüz, was found murdered a few days later. He was alleged to have been the caller who tipped off the police in June. Somewhat later a student named Haydar Seyrangah was also found murdered. Suspicion was directed at Agca. From this time onward reports of sightings of Agca were always second or third hand. The organization which had arranged his rescue from prison was assumed to have spirited him away. But where? Given the state of political confusion Turkey had fallen into by this time, few Turks cared.

Agca's sponsors had a hardened, seasoned, proven terrorist back in their possession, ready to meet new challenges. His performance in the Ipekçi affair had been first-rate. The support mechanisms serving him had functioned well. He had acquired good rightist credentials—widely accepted as stronger than they in fact were. He had been worth the money invested in him. He thought of himself as free, but he was trapped the way his sponsors wanted him to be. He had justified himself as a terrorist above ideology as if he had come to believe what he was told to say. He would have no alternative but to continue doing what his sponsors wanted him to do. What was that going to be? Did his letter threatening the Pope indicate that he was already being prepared for his ultimate target?

9
THE EVOLUTION OF THE PLOT AGAINST THE POPE

Genesis

When did the plot against the Polish Pope first begin to take form? Certainly not as late as March or April of 1981 and in all likelihood quite early in 1980. It may have been taking shape when Agca wrote his note to *Milliyet* immediately after his escape the night of 23 November 1979. Unless—and until—a defector with knowledge of the innermost workings of the Kremlin appears, we may never know with certainty. More information is bound to develop, but the process may take time.

There was unease in the Kremlin from the moment Cardinal Wojtyla was elected Pope. There must already have been a thick KGB file on him. The papal visit to Poland in June 1979 gave the Kremlin leadership a full measure of the scope of this man's performance as Pope. It shattered any lingering illusions that accommodation with him might be easy. If a *modus vivendi* was going to be possible at all, he had to be intimidated, blocked, neutralized. Early Kremlin thinking may not necessarily have been about killing him, however.

It is pertinent to consider here a point often raised by those who shrink from contemplating the likelihood that Soviet leaders plotted John Paul II's assassination which has already been discussed at greater length in Chapter 5. The Soviets do not assassinate foreigners, it is said; they confine themselves to Soviet citizens or exiles who were citizens. A pope would, therefore, be out of bounds.

It is impossible to demonstrate that such a distinction has ever existed in Soviet practice. In the 1930s the OGPU engineered killings in Western Europe of people who were never Soviet citizens. In the period since World War II there have been numerous cases of disappearance, kidnapping and murder of people who never owed allegiance in any sense to the Soviet Union. Naturally, since Soviet leadership has been preoccupied primarily with tightening its grip on Eastern Europe, most of these people have been East Europeans.

But let us not forget that in Soviet eyes John Paul II *is* an East European. He was a citizen of the Soviet empire. His elevation to the papacy did not confer a new status on him in anything but a technical sense. In the psycho-political mindset of Soviet political leaders he is analogous to the exiled leaders whom Khokhlov and Stashinsky were sent to murder in the 1950s. He is thus a kind of exile who has escaped jurisdiction of the communist imperium. He is only secondarily a pope, certainly not a pope like any predecessor. Thus even if there were a rule against murdering people who do not 'belong' to the Soviet bloc, it would not apply to John Paul II.

There are many clues to how the plot against the Pope may have developed. They fall into three groupings. First, there is what was being said and done by the Soviet Union during this period. Secondly, there is Agca's trail with all its twists and turns *and gaps* that still have to be explained. Finally, there is Poland itself. Chapter 7 has provided an outline of the Polish background. We must now examine certain Polish events in comparison with developments elsewhere. This chapter will review each of these sets of clues in turn and suggest how they fit together.

From Soviet Unease to Acrimony

Despite the suspicion with which the Soviets viewed the election of a Polish Pope in October 1978 they put a good face on their anxiety. Brezhnev sent a congratulatory telegram and John Paul II sent a reply thanking him. Both were printed in *Pravda*. The KGB press agency Novosti, then put the Pope on notice that he would fare best with Moscow if he behaved himself, but the tone was gentle. A long Novosti article issued on 23 October expressed hope that the new Pope would continue the political course followed by his predecessors John XXIII and Paul VI. Their dealings with the Eastern bloc had been characterized by a willingness to compromise and a desire to avoid alarming the Russians. Under them it often appeared that the Vatican was more interested in avoiding antagonizing Moscow than in a vigorous defense of the rights of believers living under communist rule. It is not surprising that Moscow preferred that this policy continue.[1]

A second Novosti article on 9 November 1978 suggested that the Pope could make 'an important contribution to the positive solution of the problems of the struggle for peace, to the national equality and economic development of countries'. These phrases are code-words for supporting Soviet positions in the Third World. Meanwhile Yosif Grigulevich, an academician who specializes in the Catholic Church and enjoys the status of corresponding member of the USSR Academy of Sciences, also displayed a gentle touch in an article in the 27 October issue of *Novoye Vremya*. He discounted the notion that a Polish cardinal had been elected Pope because he would know 'what socialism and communism are and how to combat them'[2] and characterized Wojtyla's elevation as a defeat for conservative Italian cardinals. John Paul II knew how to read communist communications. For all their mildness, these were veiled threats.

For the next few months the new Pope did not get much attention in Soviet media, in contrast to the publicity he received in Poland and the rest of the world. His first major trip abroad, to Mexico at the end of January 1979, went unreported in the USSR. Later some of the positions he took in Puebla against participation by priests in radical social and political movements were denounced.[3] In an article in the Armenian paper *Kommunist* on 14 March 1979, Grigulevich criticized the Pope's utterances in Mexico. It is worth noting how high this part of the world already ranked among Moscow concerns at this time. Was it the same current that was reflected in Agca's reference to El Salvador in his note on shooting the Pope more than two years later?

Reticence in the early months of John Paul II's papacy did not mean that the Kremlin was not watching the Vatican closely. Moscow was not happy with the Pope's decision to increase Radio Vatican broadcasting time in several East European and Soviet languages; nor with his appointment of East Europeans to important positions in the Vatican bureaucracy. Soviet leaders are unlikely to have missed the steps the Pope took in the final weeks of 1978 to improve the Church's relations with Peking. Nothing was said publicly, but Andrei Gromyko may have raised the subject when the Pope granted the Soviet foreign minister a two-hour audience on 24 January 1979. TASS simply said afterward that the furtherance of international détente was discussed. There were many things more specific than international détente worrying Gromyko.

In November 1978 Lithuanian priests organized a 'Catholic Committee for the Defense of the Rights of Believers'. The committee's first act was to send the Pope a letter affirming their unconditional loyalty and asking for his blessing. The KGB had already stepped up its harassment of Catholics in Lithuania, closing churches and turning them into social clubs and atheist museums. In Poland preparations for the papal visit were well advanced. Gromyko was later reported to have expressed the fear that 'it would have the same effect on the masses in Poland as the Ayatollah Khomeini had in Iran.'[4]

If Gromyko's purpose had been to intimidate John Paul II, he failed. In March 1979 the Pope addressed a letter to Cardinal Slipyj, Metropolitan of Kiev exiled since 1963 to the Vatican, in which he encouraged him to begin preparations for marking the 1,000th anniversary of the conversion of Kievan Russia at the end of the 1980s.[5]

Like it or not, the Soviets found no excuse to postpone the papal visit to Poland in June 1979. I have already described its electrifying effect. As he moved around the country, John Paul II referred time and again to the fact that it was not only the people of Poland he was visiting. He talked of 'the brother peoples and the neighboring peoples'. He criticized communism for allowing 'evident privileges for some and discrimination against others'. Peace and social harmony, he said, could be achieved only on the basis of

> respect for the objective rights of the nation, such as the right to existence, the right to freedom . . . No country should ever develop at the expense of another, at the cost of enslavement . . . conquest, outrage, exploitation and death.

He even implicitly rejected the Soviet-controled Warsaw Pact by saying that the validity of alliances depended on whether they led to prosperity for member states.[6]

Soviet media reported cursorily on the Pope's activities in Poland each day he was there. The most detailed account, in *Izvestiya* on 9 June, reported his visit to Auschwitz. He was approvingly cited on the role played by the Russian people in World War II and the death of six million Poles, but his remarks about the sufferings of the Jews were ignored.

After the Pope's Polish trip, an increasingly strident campaign was orchestrated by Soviet media, attacking the Catholic Church and castigating the Pope as an inveterate opponent of socialism. The gloves were off. But there was a distinct difference between the central media, read and analyzed by foreign correspondents in Moscow and followed abroad, and the provincial press, mostly unnoticed outside the Soviet Union. The provincial press became ascerbic on the Pope and disparaged those who admired him. The admirers were numerous. In the Lithuanian city of Klaipeda 149,000 believers signed a petition addressed to Brezhnev and the United Nations demanding the return and reopening of a church confiscated by the communist government. The church had originally been built with state permission with donations of the congregation. When it was finished in 1960 Soviet authorities confiscated it and turned it into a concert hall.

From Soviet Acrimony to Alarm

The Pope's visit to Poland in July 1979 frightened the Kremlin. Strains were growing between church and state in long-quiescent Czechoslovakia and there were disturbing developments elsewhere in Eastern Europe. The Kremlin's options for action in Poland itself were now severely restricted. The communist state was losing its legitimacy and the people were losing their fear of it. Though Soviet citizens had been prevented from crossing the border during the visit, the Pope's influence gave them new courage too.

A conference of secretaries of central committees of communist and 'workers' parties of socialist countries was held in East Berlin during the period 3–5 July 1979, in the immediate aftermath of the triumphal Polish visit. *Problems of Peace and Socialism* reported this meeting shortly afterward but did not reveal that the agenda included the problem of countering the activity of the Catholic Church under the leadership of John Paul II.[7] This came out two years later when Ivan Poluk, a senior official of the Central Committee of the Communist Party of the Ukraine, wrote in an article in *Questions of Scientific Atheism*:

> As was noted at the conference of secretaries of the central committees of communist and workers' parties of socialist countries on international and ideological questions (Berlin, 1979), the policy of the Vatican toward the socialist countries has entered a new phase, which is marked by a sharp increase in the activity of the Roman Catholic Church, by a desire to turn it into a political opposition in the socialist countries.[8]

Poluk, of course, was most concerned about the Ukraine. What he says confirms that even at this relatively early stage the Kremlin was anxious not only about the situation in Poland, but in Moscow's own 'home' territories:

For the present leadership in the Vatican, the Ukraine is an object of particular solicitude. It is trying to use the still considerable active nucleus of the Catholic Church as a basis for extending religious influence over the population of the republic.[9]

What steps were decided upon at the Berlin conference? Poluk does not tell us and no other sources have as yet provided information. The conference may have been a milestone in the development of the plot to kill the Pope. A subject so sensitive as assassination would probably not have been broached at a meeting such as this, but reports to the Kremlin leadership on the fear and frustration that undoubtedly surfaced at this conference could have strengthened the conviction that drastic measures might be required to cope with the Polish Pope.

Kremlin disquiet must have been intensified by the Pope's American trip at the end of September 1979. Stopping briefly in Ireland en route, he arrived in Boston to be met by Rosalynn Carter and then went to New York to address the United Nations. The visit culminated on 6 October with a reception on the north lawn of the White House in Washington. Soviet media gave the Pope's American trip minimal coverage. Polish media broadcast little else. Other Western radios covered it thoroughly so Soviet citizens who wanted to be informed had their choice of Polish or Western stations.

Next came the visit to Turkey at the end of November 1979. It was never mentioned in the Soviet media. It polarized all Soviet worries: the historic seat of the Eastern Church . . . memories of Ss. Cyril and Methodius . . . of Polish–Turkish friendship . . . Truman doctrine . . . the Pope's flaunting of terrorism . . . It was enough to give Brezhnev apoplexy. This was a period when Brezhnev's health was steadily worsening.

Soviet media over the next few months followed a markedly hardened line. Yosif Grigulevich, who had started out by giving John Paul II the benefit of doubt, turned to sarcasm. In an article reviewing the first 18 months of his reign, he commented on the Pope's 'enviable mobility' and noted that 'bourgeois propaganda' was creating a special image for him, endowing him with 'wisdom, courage, fearlessness and energy and presenting him in such varied roles as swimmer, cyclist, skier, singer, author, playwright and poet'. In a guidance article for propagandists he underscored the Pope's conservatism and claimed that some of his actions were 'arousing widespread opposition and vigorous protests in the ranks of the clergy and mass Catholic organizations'.

By the end of the year, Grigulevich had abandoned sarcasm for direct attack. He called the Pope's statements in Africa irrelevant, his visit to France a piece of self-advertising and accused him, in his speech before UNESCO, of having used terms reminiscent of 'the odious effusions of Maoists'. In Brazil, Grigulevich found the Pope 'vague and ambiguous, as usual' and berated him for 'nowhere, never and in no way' criticising American imperialism.[10] Grigulevich was mild compared to provincial propagandists. We will come to them in due course. Let us turn back to Mehmet Ali Agca.

Agca on the Run: Progress Eastward

Ten days short of 18 months passed from the time Agca walked out of Kartal-Maltepe prison in November 1979 to his reappearance in St Peter's Square as a papal assassin in May 1981. The first eight months of this time are much more of a mystery than the latter ten. Much light has been shed on Agca's final ten months on the road to Rome. Very little has been learned about the earlier period.

However, we do know that quite soon after his escape he crossed into Iran which in itself is something of a mystery. Nobody was *going* to Iran at this period, least of all Turkish terrorists. The country was in a state of anarchy, especially the north-eastern region Azerbaijan, where Agca crossed. There is no record of any interest on Agca's part in Iran. He knew no Persian. If he had been an ardent Shi'ite, there might have been some arcane rationale for his going to Iran—though Turkish Shi'ites (*Alevis*) have little affinity for Iran and there is no pattern of frequent contact—but he was not Shi'ite. His background was Sunni. And he was apathetic toward religion. There is no evidence of close ties between Turkish and Iranian terrorists of any kind. Nevertheless Agca made his way eastward across Turkey as winter descended over the Anatolian plateau, reached Erzurum, which in January at 7,000 feet has a Siberian climate, and had himself smuggled into Khomeini's Iran on the night of 1 February 1980. It makes no sense. Unlike some other aspects of the Agca story, there seems little doubt that it happened.

How and when Agca arrived in Erzurum is not clear. One sketch of his trail has him going from Istanbul to Ankara by a car driven by Hasan Hüseyin Şener, a medical student in Istanbul and the brother of his friend Mehmet Şener. He is said to have stayed for a few days in a house in Bahçelievler belonging to a minor official, Mustafa Dikici. From there he reportedly went south-east to the small Cappadocian city of Nevşehir where he stayed with Hamit Gökenç, a former elementary school teacher in Malatya. Gökenç may have given him his passport. With Gökenç and another friend by the name of Mehmet Kurşun (said to be from Akçadag in Malatya province), Agca is then supposed to have returned to Ankara and stayed with Hasan Murat Pala. How long is uncertain. There is a great deal for the investigatory commission the Turkish government set up in December 1982 to clarify.[11]

Another report has Agca spending a month in Erzurum before he was smuggled across the Iranian border. Timur Selçuk, a 30-year-old student at Atatürk University in Erzurum, confessed that Agca had stayed with him one night, threatened him and forced him to find a smuggler to escort him across the border. Money to pay the smuggler is said to have been given to Selçuk by Mehmet Şandir. Şandir is listed as a partner in a trading firm called Tümpaş which includes among several other partners, Musa Serdar Çelebi, the Director of the Turkish Federation in Frankfurt and an important activist in Türkeş's National Action Party.

He was later to emerge as a key man in the activation of the plot to shoot the Pope. If Çelebi's links to Agca, even indirectly, go back to the winter of 1979/80, immediately after the escape from prison, we have good evidence of high-priority handling of Agca at this time through channels which on the surface appeared rightist but which in actuality were being directed from the East. Çelebi was already well linked to the Bulgaria-based Turkish smuggling world.

Çelebi was finally exposed in the fall of 1982 after Agca had given extensive testimony to the Italian authorities. With the Çelebi connection established, the outlines of the support structure that was looking out for Agca began to emerge. But why did this network first deliver Agca to Iran? Surely professional smugglers who had their own penetrations of Turkish customs and police could have whisked him directly across the border into Bulgaria from Istanbul, or got him out of Istanbul by boat?

I can advance only two plausible reasons for Agca's sponsors to send him to Iran: the first would be to build credibility—cover—as a religious fanatic. It is not the kind of credibility that would carry much weight in Turkey or in the Middle East, but it would not have to carry weight there. Agca's Turkish career was over. It would serve its purpose in Europe. Western journalists and government officials

were obsessed with Islamic fundamentalism after Iran fell to
Khomeini. It was a mysterious force that could be used to explain
almost any irrationality. If a plan were already being developed to do
away with the Pope employing a Turk as an assassin, it was desirable
that he appear to be a fanatic Muslim. How to prove his Muslim
devotion? Have him go to an Iran in the throes of an Islamic revolution.

The main problem with this hypothesis is that Agca's subsequent
peregrinations do not reflect it. Perhaps concepts changed. Planning
for assassination need not be a logically consistent process. In fact, it
is very unlikely to be. There are many signs that the organizers of the
plot to kill the Pope adjusted Agca's cover stories as time went by.

What would the other reason for going to Iran be? It is the easiest
route from Turkey to the USSR. By why not go over the border
directly? While the Turkish–Iranian border has always been relatively
porous, easy to cross either legally or illegally, the opposite is true of
the Turkish–Soviet border. The Turkish side is much less heavily
guarded than the Soviet side, but Agca trying to escape would almost
certainly be recognized by Turkish guards if caught. And more would
be lost than Agca—why would an alleged Gray Wolf be fleeing to the
Russians? The whole rationale that had been encouraged to explain
the murder of Ipekçi would collapse if the assassin were found seeking
asylum in the Soviet Union. Then why not a legal crossing with false
documents? Surely the Russians could have produced a high quality
false passport for Agca. But they could not have altered his distinctive
appearance. Even with the best false passport in the world, there
would be high risk of recognition, for Agca's picture had been in
Turkish newspapers for months. Only a trickle of Turks cross into the
Soviet Union—occasional diplomats or other officials; a few businessmen; very occasionally people permitted to visit relatives. They are
carefully checked as they leave. This would not be a feasible route for
Agca either. Agca caught going with a false passport to the Soviet
Union would raise the same basic political questions as if he were
going illicitly with none.

On the other hand, the route through Iran would be relatively safe.
Safe, that is from the dangers of exposure while passing through. In
Iranian Azerbaijan, Kurds and Azeris were resisting control by the
fundamentalists in Tehran who were themselves preoccupied with the
crisis they had provoked by seizing the US Embassy. For a lone
fugitive Turk going to Iran simply to hide, the danger of falling into
difficulty would have been greater than if he had remained in his own

country; but Soviet agents, probably Soviet Azeris, could move about with little fear of Iranian interference. Agca, once in Iranian territory and in the hands of a 'welcome party' that knew its way around, could be brought up to the Soviet border in a day or two.

Is there any evidence that this is what actually happened? Nothing solid. There was a flurry of press reports in the fall of 1981, loosely attributed to Vatican and East European sources, that Agca had spent several weeks in the Soviet Union, receiving training at a KGB camp at Simferopol in the Crimea.[12] He was said, among other things, to have practiced shooting from above his head at a moving target standing in a vehicle and also to have gone through exercises in how to confound interrogators if caught. Some of these reports were combined with lurid accounts of meetings of Warsaw Pact commanders under the chairmanship of Soviet Defense Minister Dimitri Ustinov at the end of 1980 to discuss how to deal with the Polish crisis, including a debate over whether it was necessary to eliminate the Pope. According to some of these accounts, Ustinov's position was that the Pope did not have to be killed, only incapacitated so that he could not perform his functions.

Agca has to know what he did in Iran and where he went next. Since he began to talk to the Italian authorities in 1982 about his activities in Europe, we have reason to expect that he will eventually also reveal a version of his movements after his escape from prison in Turkey. When this will happen is hard to say. He may have revealed something to two Turkish judicial officials who interrogated him for a week in June 1983. If Agca did spend some time in the Soviet Union, all doubt about his sponsorship would be removed. There would also be no credible basis for his claim to be acting above ideologies. No Turk could have illusions about the meaning of movement into the Soviet Union under circumstances such as these.

Still nothing has come to light to support reports that Agca enjoyed hospitality and received training in the USSR. The reports would not be worthy of consideration if other plausible explanations of how Agca spent the months between February and the middle of July 1980 had been advanced. None has. In fact, stories current in 1981 about his coming back to Turkey from Iran on an Indian passport carrying the name of Yoghinder Singh looked increasingly implausible to me after I visited the Turkish–Iranian border in Hakkari province in June 1981. Sizable numbers of Indians and Pakistanis were crossing on buses into Turkey from Iran, it is true. Many were being interned on evidence or suspicion of drug running. Agca, with non-Indian features and no Indian language, would have become immediately suspect among such people. Turkish guards would have had little difficulty establishing that he was not an Indian or Pakistani. On his Istanbul University entrance form he scored his lowest marks in English and had replied to the foreign language question: 'English— very little; studied in school.' This does not imply enough English to be credible as an Indian and he would quickly have been exposed.

There is no firm reason to believe that Agca returned to Turkey after crossing into Iran. There are stories that he went from Iran to Syria or Lebanon to be sheltered and further trained by the PLO and was then sent to Bulgaria from there. Perhaps the Ahmed Jibril faction of the PLO would have taken him over at this time. But there is no more to go on with these stories than with those about the Soviet Union. Agca's travels during the months before he shot the Pope were so extensive and, on the surface, seemingly irrational that almost any tale seems worthy of consideration. Unexpected facts about his movements and contacts may still come to light.

Agca in Bulgaria

Agca may have arrived in Bulgaria as early as the spring of 1980, five months after his escape. He turns up with certainty in the Bulgarian capital in the second week of July. He claimed during his interrogation in Rome to have stayed at half a dozen hotels there. They are not the stopping places of ordinary Turks transiting Bulgaria. At least four of them are in the de luxe category but perhaps Agca was bragging about the Moskva, the Grand Hotel Sofia and the Grand Hotel Balkan. No one has ever been able to check their guest registers. However, there is no doubt about his staying at the Vitosha, Sofia's newest and plushest international hostelry. No one from the West has ever checked its guest registers either, but Agca's claim to have stayed there has been confirmed by the admissions of others. Agca bragged to his Italian interrogators that he never needed money and identified a series of Turkish 'friends' who, he said, had supplied him with close to TL 5 million ($50,000-$70,000 at exchange rates of the time) on the road to Rome. All these Turkish 'friends' were Turkish mafia types—smugglers with Bulgarian connections and habitués of the Vitosha.

Very early Agca admitted meeting two people during his stay at the Vitosha who played a role in his further progress. From a Turk named

Ömer Mersan who had come to Sofia from Munich he ordered a false Turkish passport. Mersan, he said, introduced him to a Bulgarian named Mustafaev.[13]

Mersan worked for a Turkish import-export company in Munich with a Balkan name, the Vardar Corporation. It was one of several with which the notorious smuggler Abuzer Ugurlu and several other well-known Turkish mafia figures are connected. It was deeply involved in weapons and drug trafficking, as well as smuggling of less sensitive contraband such as watches and electric appliances. Agca may have had only a limited idea of the scope of the operations of this company, for the information he gave in Rome in 1981 implicated him more deeply than he might have realized in this conspiratorial web just at the time when the Italian authorities were uncovering information on other Bulgarian-related arms and drug operations. After repeated efforts, the Turkish police had persuaded the Germans to arrest Ugurlu on narcotics charges. He was extradited to Turkey in March 1981, two months before Agca shot the Pope. His trial, which began in 1982, is still not finished as of the summer of 1983—the more his operations are exposed, the more far-reaching they turn out to be.

Mersan, when arrested for interrogation by Munich police after Agca had identified him in May 1981, admitted meeting a Turk named 'Metin' in room 911 of the Vitosha but denied having had anything to do with a passport. He was released. The passport, nevertheless, materialized. If Agca came to Bulgaria with an Indian passport (a mere formality, it can be assumed), he had acquired a more viable identity by the time he departed. Henceforth he was Faruk Özgün. The real Faruk Özgün was a 28-year old textile worker in Nevşehir where Agca had reportedly spent a few days in December 1979 after his escape from prison. The passport was issued on 11 August 1980 and bore Agca's picture. It had not been issued with it. Numbered 136635, it had been altered. So had the next passport in the series, carried by Ömer Ay (implicated in the Ipekçi killing) but issued in the name of Galip Yilmaz. When the real Faruk Özgün was arrested in June 1981, he claimed never to have known Agca but admitted selling his passport to a teacher named Ibrahim Kurt. Kurt, a girlfriend and a policeman, Erhan Ender, who had assisted them, were later convicted, but the network of which they were a part has never been fully explained. It no doubt had ramifications that extended beyond Agca.

Ömer Ay eventually fled Turkey to Germany in March 1981. He was arrested and interrogated at length in Hamburg in the summer of

1982. At the time he was thought to be a major figure in the papal plot and was alleged to have been in St Peter's Square when the Pope was shot. Under interrogation he denied a link to Agca and claimed to be a social democrat politically. He admitted distributing propaganda in Turkey during the period of terrorism. He was finally extradited to Turkey in October 1982. He has since been reported to have had little information and no links to Agca. Like almost all aspects of this web of conspiracy, however, all this remains to be verified.

Agca seems to have received his passport at the end of August 1980. Who delivered it to him is unknown. He has now reportedly admitted meeting the Turkish smuggler Bekir Çelenk in Sofia during his stay at the Vitosha. A major operator like Çelenk would hardly have undertaken a task so mundane as delivering Agca's passport—or would he? For all the care that had been taken to provide Agca a passport with a genuine name that would check out innocently if authorities in countries through which he traveled queried Turkey, there was carelessness about the entry and exit stamps. According to them, Agca would have to have spent a day between the Turkish exit point Kapikule, outside of Edirne, and the Bulgarian border station a few hundred yards away, Kapitan Andreevo. The Turkish exit stamp was dated 30 August and was obviously false. The Bulgarian entry stamp, dated 31 August, may have been genuine. The Bulgarian exit stamp, for Kalatina, a point on the Yugoslav border on the opposite side of the country is also dated 31 August. The aim was obviously to make it appear that Agca had simply traveled across Bulgaria in a day, as hundreds of thousands of Turks do each summer.

Why, in keeping with this minor, imperfectly executed detail, was Agca not instructed if and when caught in Rome, to deny that he had ever done anything but cross Bulgaria by bus or car in a day? Was it because by that time the instruction was considered superfluous because Agca was to be shot as soon as he shot the Pope?

There must have been more for Agca to do in Sofia than while away his time waiting for a passport. Perhaps Mustafaev kept him busy with training and briefing. Mustafaev is unlikely to be his real name, but he may nevertheless have been a Bulgarian of Muslim origin or a Bulgarian Turk.[14] In the total drama of the plot, he appears to have been a bit player rather than a major actor.

Agca in Germany

Agca's route across Yugoslavia and Austria to Germany has not been firmly established but it is probably a standard bus route and there is no reason to assume that he stopped long on the way. Exit and entry stamps are no longer put in passports in most non-communist European countries, a practice which makes smugglers and terrorists difficult to trace. It cannot be excluded that Agca was welcomed by Ömer Mersan in Munich or even by Musa Serdar Çelebi in Frankfurt, but Mersan has denied contact and so did Çelebi. These men and several others like them—apparent rightists identified both with the Türkeş party and with a variety of smuggling interests dependent on Bulgarian connections—provided the milieu within which Agca was sheltered and given the self-assurance to feel at home in Europe.

Agca was new to Europe. He knew no European language. His English was rudimentary. Though plentifully supplied with money, he was still essentially a provincial Turk from a poor background. A Turk who grows up under modern conditions in a middle-class family in Ankara, Istanbul or Izmir feels at home in a European atmosphere. Agca needed to be brazen and quick-witted to adapt so fast and avoid stumbling into embarrassment. He would also have to avoid too much exposure among the enormous concentrations of Turks who inhabit every major German city. These people would be familiar with his face and his history from reading about him the previous year in Turkish newspapers. All the major Turkish dailies distribute same-day editions in Germany. He might even be prone to strut and brag if he developed too many links to local Turkish residents. It is impossible to believe that Agca was simply left on his own in Germany. He needed help and was too valuable a property to his sponsors to be neglected. He was tagged for important terrorist tasks.

In September 1980 Turkish intelligence headquarters in Ankara began getting reports of Agca's presence in Germany. When the reports had enough details, they were flashed by the Turkish Foreign Ministry to the Turkish Embassy in Bonn which took them to the German Foreign Office with the request for a priority investigation. Turkish security had been sending alerts to Interpol ever since the previous spring, but these carried the number of the passport Agca had obtained in Malatya before he killed Abdi Ipekçi. Turkish authorities knew nothing of the new passport in the name of Faruk Özgün. Nobody seems to have paid much attention to Interpol notices anyway.

The first Turkish note to the Germans on Agca was dated 3 October 1980 and reported he had been seen in Frankfurt. The next, sent on 6 November, reported Agca in Berlin; so did a note sent 11 December. Meanwhile the Turkish Embassy advised the German Foreign Office that Mehmet Şener, another suspect in the Ipekçi killing, had been seen in Hamburg. A note sent 29 December reported Agca had been seen at Bad Würzach in Baden-Württemberg but how long before it is not clear. Other evidence, as we shall soon see, makes it highly probable that Agca had left Germany a month before and had not returned. Each note eventually received a routine reply—the German Justice Ministry informed the Turkish Embassy that no evidence of Agca's presence had been found when police checked out the reports. It is not surprising. These bureaucratic actions, performed routinely, took weeks. Agca was constantly on the move.

After he was captured in Rome, evidence was found that Agca had gone at least twice to Switzerland in the early fall of 1980 where he stayed at the Hotel Ruetli in Zurich 9-12 September and spent the period 27-31 October in the Hotel Krone in Lucerne. He must have gone to meet someone. Perhaps he was being considered, or used, for other activities during this period.

Back in Germany, a mysterious murder took place in the town of Kempten in Bavaria on 25 November 1980. The victim was Necati Uygur, a grocer who had served as a member of the South German Executive Committee of Türkeş's party. Before he died in a hospital of multiple bullet wounds, Uygur recounted that his assailant had shouted at him in Turkish as he fled, 'Do you know Agca?'

Tunisian Interlude

The Uygur murder arouses suspicion that something had gone wrong in the Türkeş-oriented support structure in Germany. Had Uygur learned more about Agca than he was supposed to know and threatened exposure? Agca fled Germany immediately and, as far as we can tell, never returned.

By the end of November he was in Tunis, having arrived by air from Italy. He told his interrogators in Rome that he went to Tunis after a telephone call from Ömer Mersan who told him Mustafaev wanted to meet him there. Someone must have helped him make these spur-of-the-moment arrangements. Tunisian security officials have confirmed that Agca stayed first at the Hotel du Lac in Tunis and then moved to the Hotel Continental in Hamamet, a nearby resort. He volunteered in Rome that he met Mustafaev at the Hotel du Lac where the latter outlined a scheme for killing Tunisian President Bourgiba and Maltese Prime Minister Mintoff at a meeting which had not yet been publicly announced but did take place on 12 December. Agca said he turned down this mission because security was likely to be too heavy. After this, as far as we know, Mustafaev dropped out of Agca's peripatetic life.

What did Agca do in Hamamet for the better part of two weeks? No information has come to light, but Libya is not far away to the east. Suspicion of a Libyan side-trip arises naturally. Could Mustafaev have been acting on behalf of Qaddafy when he proposed the Bourgiba–Mintoff double assassination? Or is the whole business a tale of Agca's designed to divert attention from something else? When he was first interrogated in Rome, Agca denied having spent time in Germany but claimed to have visited Britain, Belgium and France. No evidence of visits to these countries has ever been found. Such claims were almost certainly part of initial diversionary maneuvers. He never tried to reaffirm them later. He must have been making them to divert attention from Germany—where some things had gone right and some things may have gone wrong but where he initially wanted to obscure his connections. But the links to Germany could not remain hidden. They were too extensive and Agca's diversionary tales were too inept. About the Tunis side-trip we are less sure.

Agca returned to Italy via ferry from Tunis to Palermo on 13 December 1980. He avoided flying whenever he could—no doubt on the advice of his sponsors—for there was always the danger that he could fall into some sort of embarrassment in the course of the complex security checks that have become routine in air travel in recent years. He stayed overnight at the Hotel Liguria in Palermo and then headed north by train. Whether he stopped in Rome is unknown. If he did, it would have been his first visit to the city where five months later he would become world-famous.

Musa Serdar Celebi

He was next in Milan, where Musa Serdar Çelebi came from Frankfurt to meet him on 15 December. All this was unknown until Agca began talking to the Italian authorities in the summer of 1982. He claimed that the Milan meeting was their first. The killing of Uygur in Kempten and Agca's refusal to go along with Mustafaev's proposal in Tunis may have caused alarm among his sponsors. If Çelebi was as much of a key man in this whole undertaking as now seems likely, he may have felt compelled—or been instructed—to talk personally to Agca to get things back on the track. Agca claimed that Çelebi gave him DM 1,000 (about $500 at that time) in Milan and they talked about the work of Çelebi's Turkish Federation.

The Turkish Federation was founded in 1978 to serve as a co-ordinating body for cultural, religious and welfare organizations set up by Turks in Germany. The rationale made sense. Ostensibly non-political, the group was regarded as an extended arm of Türkeş's National Action Party. But it may have been intended to serve purposes quite beyond even those which might be on the party's own hidden agenda. What has come to light of Çelebi's activities and revelation of his connections with major Turkish mafia figures, like Bekir Çelenk and Abuzer Ugurlu who enjoyed special status in Bulgaria, provokes speculation that Çelebi's Turkish Federation may have been designed from the beginning to serve Soviet clandestine needs of many kinds in Germany and Europe.

Çelebi is a more conventionally successful young man than most of those we have encountered in contact with Agca. He was born in 1952 into a respectable family in Dörtyol near Iskenderun. He was a good boy scout and a good student who attended high school in Iskenderun and then took an engineering degree at Istanbul's Technical University, the best of its kind in Turkey. He married a young woman with a law degree. After working briefly as a junior official in the Agriculture Ministry he joined the Customs Ministry in 1976. Temptations he was unable to resist there are probably the origin of his links with the smuggling world. He also became involved in National Action Party politics. What work brought him to Germany is not clear— perhaps it was mafia operations—but he seems soon to have been putting most of his energy into the Turkish Federation and a series of business ventures used by Turkish smugglers as fronts. His mother and father, interviewed in January 1983, confirmed his rightist political associations and said that he had not returned to Turkey because he had been sought as an accessory in the Türkeş trial.[15] In 1981 he started a Turkish-language magazine in Germany called *Yeni Hedef* (*New Goal*), sympathetic to Türkeş.[16]

Because Çelebi was a well-known, articulate Türkeş supporter, he was sought out by the press immediately after the shooting in Rome in 1981 and gave interviews to TV and newspaper reporters. He denied ever having met Agca and condemned his attack on the Pope un-equivocally. When asked to characterize Agca politically, he used almost the same terms Agca had applied to himself: a terrorist above ideology. There the matter rested until Çelebi was arrested in Frankfurt on 3 November 1982.

It was impressive, after long months of poor co-ordination between various countries' security services and judicial authorities and minimal exertions on the part of some of them to probe seriously, to see the Germans cleverly interrogating Çelebi after his arrest. First denying knowing Agca at all, he backtracked and acknowledged going to Milan to meet a Turk named 'Murat' who needed financial help. He learned only after Agca's shooting of the Pope, he claimed, that 'Murat' was really Mehmet Ali Agca. This limp story broke down in the face of the information with which the Germans next confronted Çelebi. Agca claimed it was Çelebi who had come to Zurich on 3 March 1981 to tell him that Bekir Çelenk would pay him DM 3 million (nearly $1.5 million at that time) for killing the Pope and assure him sanctuary in Bulgaria. Çelebi denied relaying this offer, but the Germans had found a tape of an intercepted telephone conversation from Agca in Majorca to Çelebi in Frankfurt in late April 1981: 'I have received the money,' Agca said, 'I will now go to Rome and finish the job.' Çelebi's extradition to Italy as a prime accessory in the case was arranged during December 1982. He arrived in Rome on 14 January 1983. In all likelihood the Italians have succeeded in learning a good deal more from him. The Zurich meeting in March 1981 may not have been the first time the attack against the Pope was discussed between Agca and Çelebi.

Bulgarian Connection in Rome

Nevertheless, it appears that the plan to shoot the Pope had not yet taken final form—or was not yet the highest priority—at the turn of the year 1980/1. Another assassination was of more immediate interest to the Kremlin: Lech Walesa. Walesa, with his ten million-strong Solidarity labor federation behind him, had become a formidable power in Poland. The Polish government recognized Solidarity in the Gdansk Agreement of 31 August 1980. The Soviets stepped up their military maneuvering. During the final year of the Carter Administration warnings to the Soviets of the dire consequences—both political and economic—of sending troops into Poland had been sounded almost weekly by one key figure in Washington or another. The sanctions that had been applied following the Soviet invasion of Afghanistan left the Soviet leadership no reason to assume that the United States was bluffing. Brezhnev's hands were tied and Poland was behaving more and more like an independent country with Solidarity and the Church holding the real power and the communist party largely an illusion. The 'poison' was spreading into the Baltic and the Ukraine.[17]

Agca made his way back to Rome. There he was no longer on his own but in direct contact with Bulgarian intelligence officers. According to his statements to the Italian authorities in the summer of 1982 Agca met with three Bulgarians at the Hotel Archimede in early January 1981 to discuss the assassination of Walesa when he came to visit the Pope two weeks later. The talk was of blowing up Walesa's car it seems. Agca had had no experience (but may have had some training) in this type of operation. His skill was close range shooting. Agca does not know what happened. The operation never came off. Walesa had his historic meeting with John Paul II on 18 January followed by lunch. Security for the visit was co-ordinated by Luigi Scricciolo, the head of the Foreign Department of the Italian socialist labor federation, who a year later would be arrested and eventually confess that he had been a Bulgarian agent since 1976 . . .

A plot to kill Walesa would hardly have been discussed by the Bulgarians with Agca unless it had been well advanced and thought to be urgent. Why was it called off? We will not know until Scricciolo tells publicly all he knows. Scricciolo was at the height of his usefulness to his communist employers during the winter of 1980/1. His prestige among them must have been high. He may have understood the dynamics of Solidarity in Poland better than the Kremlin did. It is likely to have been obvious to him that figures such as Cardinal Wyszynski and Pope John Paul II were more pivotal figures in Poland—and less replaceable than Walesa. Some officers of the KGB must also have understood Solidarity well enough to realize that the killing of Walesa might as easily have set Poland aflame as cowed it. Walesa had extraordinary charisma, but he also had a strong organization under him. Another leader would have filled Walesa's shoes. Solidarity's strength in depth has been demonstrated retrospectively by its ability to maintain itself as an underground organization since the crackdown of December 1981.

Agca's movements over the next six weeks are not fully known. The Bulgarians must have continued frequent contact with him. He moved into the Pensione Isa in the Via Cicerone on 19 January 1981, alternating between this hotel and the Archimede on most of the rest of his Rome visits. He had a close call in early February. He was recognized by a Turk in the fashionable Biffi Cafe in Milan. The Turk notified the Italian police, but by the time they appeared Agca was gone and the incident simply became another in a long list of reported sightings Turkish intelligence had accumulated in which other governments showed little interest. Agca stayed overnight at the Hotel Anker in Aarau, Switzerland on 6 February. Then he met with Çelebi in Zürich on 3 March. From this time onward his movements take on a pattern that in itself tends to confirm activation of the plot to shoot the Pope as a high priority.

Since Agca was already in direct touch with the Bulgarians in Rome, why did the money offer for killing the Pope come through Çelebi on behalf of Çelenk? The likeliest explanation is that the Bulgarian connection in Rome was subsidiary. The Bulgarians there were neither the architects nor the prime contractors for Agca's activities. They were journeymen with the task of seeing that plans drawn up and approved elsewhere were executed efficiently. Control rested in Sofia or Moscow. The architects remained in Moscow. They were pressing the men in Rome to get on with the job. Something had to be done about this Polish Pope.

Impatience and Rancor

The best evidence we have of the way thinking was developing in the USSR is the increasingly vicious tone of the provincial press. The longest and most derogatory attack on the Polish Pope up to that time appeared in the Belorussian journal *Polymya* in March 1981. It is likely to have been written no later than the previous month. Thirty pages of accusations were hurled against him, allegedly based on testimony of eye-witnesses. The Pope was called a 'split personality' who was really a 'militant anti-communist' and a 'cunning and dangerous ideological enemy'. He was accused of having both known and acquiesced in an alleged Nazi–Vatican scheme to exterminate the Polish people, including the clergy, during World War II. This 'malicious, lowly, perfidious and backward toady of the American militarists' was orchestrating a struggle against socialism in the interest of his 'overseas accomplices' and his 'new boss in the White House'. He was then attacked for having called a synod of Ukrainian Catholic bishops the year before. This same synod was the subject of two major articles, which also came out in March 1981, in the organ of the Central Committee of the Communist Party of the Ukraine, *Radyanska Ukraina*. One of them criticized the Pope for 'having found warm words' for the 'coven of political corpses'—bishops— who had collaborated with the German occupiers.[18]

These were strong words. Unnoticed in the West at the time, articles such as these constituted a clear declaration of war against the Pope. Few epithets rank higher on the Soviet scale of political vituperation than Nazi collaborator.

Vitriolic outbursts like these were absent from the Soviet central press. The Kremlin gave the impression of ignoring the Pope at the international level. Repeated military moves along Poland's borders persisted, but the Reagan Administration continued without change the Carter Administration's stance on intervention in Poland and frequent warnings of the consequences of invasion were sounded from Washington and West European capitals.

The Cardinal's Illness

The evidence we have—the aborted plot against Walesa, the direct involvement of the Bulgarians with Agca in Rome, the Çelenk 'offer' of DM 3 million relayed by Çelebi to Agca in early March, the accusations of Nazi collaboration in the Soviet provincial press—is enough to justify a hypothesis that the KGB had been given the go-ahead on the plan to kill the Polish Pope some time in the winter of 1980/1. Timing apparently remained open. An unexpected turn of events in Poland soon gave a distinct urgency to the scheme.

Cardinal Wyszynski, 'Uncrowned King of Poland' (as a banner on his coffin at the end of May proclaimed), fell ill in early March 1981. Though 79, he had up until this time been extraordinarily vigorous for his age, continually on the move supervising the affairs of the Polish Church. Suspicion of cancer arose in mid-March. Though suffering fatigue and strain, the cardinal kept to a full schedule. Shortly after his last meeting with General Jaruzelski on 26 March, his doctors, who had been making tests for two weeks, found serious evidence of cancer. A conclusive diagnosis of rapidly advancing cancer was made on 13 April. The facts about the cardinal's condition were at first tightly held, but it must be assumed that the Soviets would have learned no later than mid-March that something was awry. It is inconceivable that the KGB would not have had agents in his entourage and listening devices in his residence. There would have been no higher priority in Poland. The cardinal was given only a few weeks, at best, to live. As early as 31 March he told his entourage that he did not expect to be able to participate in a meeting of the Polish episcopate scheduled for 7 June. He wrote in his diary the next day, 'This is the beginning of the "via dolorosa" '. A few Polish exiles in the West with close links to the Vatican and to Warsaw learned in early April that the cardinal's days were numbered.

Wyszynski's private secretary, Father Bronislaw Piasecki, kept a day-by-day chronicle of his last weeks which was published in Rome in 1982.[19] Read in conjunction with what we know Agca was doing during this time, this moving document suggests the assassin's movements, probably quite unbeknownst to him, were directly related to the rapid decline of the cardinal in Warsaw. Wyszynski had frustrated Soviet designs in Poland for more than 30 years. It was now certain he would pass from the scene. If the Polish Pope could be eliminated simultaneously, two of the pillars of Polish nationalism would be removed. Solidarity by itself would be a manageable problem.

Wyszynski said mass for the last time on 30 April. His condition was now widely known. Though failing rapidly physically, he maintained his full mental capacity. He wrote a remarkable letter to Polish Nobel laureate, Czeslaw Milosz, on 3 May. On this day, celebrated as Poland's real national holiday, he had a 20-minute telephone conversation with the Pope in which the two discussed their hopes for the Church in the East. A conversation such as this was almost certainly intercepted by the KGB as, no doubt, were all communications, telephonic or otherwise, between the Polish episcopate and the Vatican. The Vatican was kept informed daily of Wyszynski's condition during this entire period.

Wyszynski developed serious heart trouble on 9 May. There was a possibility he might succumb at any moment. The Pope had his personal secretary, Father Stanislaw Dziwisz, fly from Rome to Warsaw two days later, on 11 May, to see the dying cardinal.

Agca on the Move

After his meeting with Çelebi in Zurich on 3 March, Agca's trail dims for two or three weeks. We next find him taking care of the most basic requirement for shooting the Pope—the gun. He claimed when captured after the attack to have obtained it in Sofia from a Syrian whose name he said he had forgotten. If he actually did receive it in Sofia in 1980, it seems more likely that a Turk from Germany such as Ömer Mersan or a Bulgarian such as Mustafaev gave it to him. No Syrian connection with the gun has been found, but its pedigree has been well established. Produced in the Fabrique Nationale of Herstal, Belgium, the 9 mm Browning semi-automatic pistol 76C23953 was first sold to a dealer in Neuchatel, Switzerland who sold it to a Zürich dealer, Wilhelm Glaser. Glaser sold it to an Austrian, Horst Grillmaier, living in Krems on the Danube north-west of Vienna, on 9 July 1980. Grillmaier, when arrested by the Austrian police in May 1981, claimed to have sold the gun to one Otto Pintner, living near Salzburg—when, exactly, was not clear. Grillmaier, like Ömer Mersan, was released and was said to have disappeared.

Whether Pintner was simply an alibi or a link in a chain that passed the weapon to Agca has not been established, but a good deal has been learned about Grillmaier. Italian intelligence had him on its records as a former Nazi with suspicious East European connections and large income from unknown sources. There was evidence in the files of several European security services that he had supplied weapons to international terrorists. Further investigation revealed that he had links to Turkish smugglers, notably Abuzer Ugurlu and Bekir Çelenk, spoke Turkish and traveled frequently to Eastern Europe as well as the Middle East. But nothing that came up was regarded by Austrian police as sufficient cause even for further investigation of Grillmaier until the night of 11 January 1983.

That night guards manning the Austrian post at Kleinhaugsdorf on the Czechoslovak border noticed that a vehicle coming across had simply been waved through on the Czech side. This was unusual. They stopped it for a search. It had papers confirming that it carried 15,000 rounds of ammunition being imported into Austria. The search uncovered more than the ammunition: 308 pistols and seven Draganov—late model Soviet—sniper rifles with night sights. These were consigned to Horst Grillmaier. The pistols were consigned to another weapons dealer named Leopold Willert. The driver was a Czechoslovak citizen named Peter Bardon, a man who had been living 'privately' in Austria but making frequent trips to Czechoslovakia. He was arrested. In the next few days so were Grillmaier, Willert and six other people. It was a bad time for Grillmaier to come to international notice again, for the Bulgarian connection was being publicized everywhere. Italy requested his extradition to testify about the gun that had gone to Agca. As of this writing the case is still under investigation in Austria.

Like several other aspects of Agca's rightist connections, Grill-maier looks as if he might have been selected as the gun supplier to enhance the impression that the papal plot had been hatched among rightists in Turkey. For the Bulgarians, supplying Agca with a gun should have been the least difficult part of the whole undertaking. Why not give him one that had been brought in through the diplomatic pouch—and one whose provenance was less traceable than the one he used? Those who devised the plot chose a more complicated—and in the end less plausible—scheme. The idea was apparently for Agca to have a gun that had 'Nazi credentials'.

If Agca had actually received his gun in Sofia in 1980, he would have had to carry it with him to Germany where, it is true, he might have used it to murder Uygur in Kempten. But he could not have carried it to Tunis by air. If it had been in his possession at that time, it had to be given to someone for safekeeping. Perhaps it *was* left in Switzerland or Austria. This would explain Agca's travels during late March which seem to have included a visit to Austrian Vorarlberg and culminated in delivery of his gun to Ömer Bagçi, a 36-year-old Turk working in Olten, Switzerland, in early April. Agca did not want to be encumbered by the weapon during the next phase of his travels.

He was back in Rome, staying at the Hotel Archimede, 5-7 April, no doubt in touch with the Bulgarian team in Rome who had been told to expedite the plot. On 8 April he left Rome by train for Perugia where he checked in at the Hotel Posta as Faruk Özgün. The next day he enrolled at the University for Foreigners, paying the $210 fee, getting documentation as a student. He attended a single class on 10 April in beginning Italian and was never seen there again.

From Perugia he returned to Rome where he stayed at the Hotel Torino the night of 12 April, telephoning a Turk named Hasan Taşkin in Sarstedt-Hildesheim in Germany. This was not the first time he had telephoned this man who, along with his brother Behlül, was linked to both Turkish rightist political circles and smuggling interests—the familiar combination. It was found that Agca had booked similar calls at several other hotels where he had stayed. Taşkin was interrogated by German police after the shooting of the Pope and, like Grillmaier and Mersan, immediately released on his insistence that he did not know Agca. The relationship remains to be explained but it is likely to be of more than incidental importance.

Agca is next reported in the Austrian province of Vorarlberg in mid-April. On 19 April he stayed overnight at a sailor's hotel in Genoa and spent several hours at another hotel with a prostitute named Georgina who made disparaging comments about his performance when interviewed later by a journalist. He then went back to Milan and booked a two-week Italian holiday tour to Majorca at the Condor Travel Agency.

The tour group consisted of Italian couples. They were put up at the Hotel Flamboyan. He associated little with other members of the party, who seldom saw him. A whole series of entertaining tales has been published in newspapers in Turkey and Europe about Agca's time in Majorca. They feature a Hungarian beauty, an American woman with a yacht and possible meetings with Bekir Çelenk who is alleged to have been visiting the neighboring island of Minorca during this period in his Panamanian-registered yacht, on vacation from England. Bekir Çelenk was living in England at this time, operating out of a firm called Oscar Maritime Shipping Company, in London.[20] What we do know Agca did in Majorca was make two highly significant telephone calls. The first, to Çelebi in Frankfurt has already been described. Then he called Ömer Bagçi in Switzerland and told him to have his gun at the Milan railway station by 9 May. From whom had he received the money? Where was it? Did Çelenk bring it on his yacht? Agca may have told Judge Martella, but the judge has not yet released any information.

Agca flew back to Milan with the tour party on 9 May, immediately picked up his gun from Bagçi and took the train to Rome. There his Bulgarian friends had made reservations for him at the familiar Pensione Isa.

Bulgarian Big Brothers

During the first year after Agca's shooting of the Pope, even those who were convinced of the likelihood of an East European connection had no expectation of finding that Agca had been personally guided during the days preceding the shooting by East European agents in Rome. There was no need to postulate such paternalism. It would be poor intelligence practice. Why could not Agca simply have returned to Rome, with which he was now familiar, gone to St Peter's Square and shot the Pope?

Was there fear that with the money paid, he would go off without doing the job? Was there apprehension that he might get stage fright when the appointed hour neared and back out? Unlike the Ipekçi murder on a dark winter night, this one would have to be in broad daylight in the midst of thousands of people. Escape could not be assured. These must be the reasons why the three Bulgarian officials had been meeting with Agca in Rome since December or January. He did not know them by true name. To him Sergei Antonov, who sometimes wore a beard, was Bayramiç, Ayvazov, the Embassy cashier, was Kolev and Kolev, who worked in the Embassy's military office, called himself Petrov. Agca had been taken to Antonov's apartment at Via Pola 29 and Ayvazov's at Via Galiani 36. It was Agca's impression that the senior member of the team was Ayvazov (not Antonov), whose cashier duties at the Bulgarian Embassy may have been pro forma, just as Antonov's work as chief of the Balkanair office seems to have demanded little of his time and even less of the technical knowledge usually possessed by career airline representatives. What language did they speak? Probably Turkish. It is widely understood in Bulgaria.

The Bulgarian big brothers were in a hurry. Someone was pressing them. Antonov and Ayvazov went with Agca to St Peter's Square on both 11 and 12 May to examine its layout and establish the best approach for the shooting. Some of them—either the Bulgarians or Agca—must have attended the Pope's Wednesday audiences during the preceding weeks. 11 and 12 May are the same days Father Dziwisz, the Pope's personal secretary, flew to Warsaw and returned after giving the Pope's message to the dying Wyszynski. He was back on the 13th and at the Pope's side in St Peter's Square when Agca shot him.

On May 13 Antonov and Ayvazov picked Agca up in the Piazza della Repubblica at 3 p.m. in a blue Alfa Romeo. They stopped off at Ayvazov's apartment to pick up a gun and an overnight bag in which he also had a grenade—to cause diversionary panic, if necessary, Ayvazov told Agca. Antonov then drove into the Via della Conciliazione, the broad avenue that leads directly west to St Peter's Square, and parked the car in front of the Canadian Embassy to the Holy See. Agca seems to have thought he might make it back to this car for his escape—but it is difficult to believe that this was the Bulgarian plan. Antonov and Ayvazov walked with Agca to the Square. Photographs taken at the time show a man with a close resemblance to Antonov near the assassin at the time of the shooting.

What about the stories that have multiplied ever since about men seen running away—'Mediterranean types' rumored to be Turks— Mehmet Şener, Ömer Ay, Oral Çelik? Aren't they more likely to be Ayvazov? Was there perhaps another Bulgarian in the square too, arriving separately? We find no trace of another Turk in Rome during these final days before the plot reached its climax and what we now know of the Bulgarian involvement leaves little room for a Turk. There is no indication that Agca had a Turkish partner in any of his travels preceding the shooting.

When Agca was caught he had several notes on him on scraps of paper. They reflect the same sense of urgency we detect in the rest of what we know of these last days before the shooting: '13 May, Wednesday, appearance in the square. 17 May, Sunday, perhaps appearance on the balcony. 20 May, Wednesday, Square, *without fail.*'

These were the dates of the appearance of the Pope scheduled for the next week. If something went wrong the first Wednesday, it was imperative that the job be done the next one. Why? Wyszynski was dying. He might not even live that long. Other jottings in the notes referred to hair dye (it was found in his room in the Pensione Isa—if he had escaped he must have intended to return there before fleeing Rome), round trips to Florence or Naples, money, clothes and shoulder bag. Another said, 'If necessary, wear a cross' and, finally, 'Important tear up postcards.' He had; those of St Peter's Square were found in the wastebasket of his room at the Pensione Isa.

Agca seems to have planned on escape. The Bulgarians' intentions are less clear. Ayvazov did not use his grenade. Having it with him in a bag would in itself have been sufficient reason for him to flee the square forthwith when it became apparent that Antonov (if that was his mission) was not going to be able to shoot Agca. Antonov must then have fled too. Perhaps both are amonblurry figures that have turned up in tourists' photographs.

Another piece of paper found on Agca contained five telephone numbers, all Bulgarian offices or apartments in Rome. Unlike the notes described above, this one was not publicized. No Italian official made reference to it in briefings of journalists during the next few days. For all practical purposes it disappeared. I discussed in Chapter 1 how significant it was for the future development of the investigation of the plot that this information not be revealed prematurely— whether the initial suppression of it had been by accident or design, the result was the same.

Though Agca hoped to escape, he had also been promised to be rescued if caught. This promise is unlikely to have rested only on the word of the Bulgarian big brothers who helped directly in Rome. It must have been made to Agca by Çelebi and perhaps by Celenk. Agca knew that the network in which they operated spread far and wide. He had good reason to feel confident that they could deliver on their promise. He had already been rescued from prison in Turkey by another branch of the same international network. He obviously took pride in the loyalty he felt to his sponsors. This accounts for his behavior after his capture, exactly parallel to his behavior in Istanbul in the summer of 1979. It took a long time for his confidence in their promises to erode.

Warsaw

In the Polish capital, in spite of the precarious condition of his heart, Wyszynski's entourage gave the news of the attack on the Pope to the dying cardinal. When told he remained silent for a long time and then seemed to shrink into the bed. Finally he commented, 'I was always afraid that this would happen.'

The chronicle of his last days does not reveal whether he expressed suspicion of East European instigation, but it is probable, for everyone else in Poland did. On 22 May the Polish bishops gathered around his bed. Of the Pope he commented to them, 'We do not need to tell each other about the strange synchronization of our lives, particularly in the last years, until this very moment.' In spite of the blow the Pope had suffered, Wyszynski remained optimistic about the church. He told the bishops, 'The East is open to the Church in Poland. The whole East can be conquered.'

Three days later the gravely wounded Pope in his hospital at the Gemelli Clinic talked to the dying cardinal by phone. The men in the Kremlin, reading the transcript of the call which the KGB probably prepared for them, must have felt doubly frustrated. Shooting the Pope had not solved their problem in Poland. And the survival of the Pope would compensate for the loss of Wyszynski in that tough, indomitable country.

10
ACTIONS AND REACTIONS

'The Tracks Lead to Washington'

I described in Chapter 1 how quickly, long before any Western leader had publicly expressed even a hint of suspicion that the Kremlin was behind the shooting in St Peter's Square, the Soviets rushed to lay blame for the deed on the United States. While most of the Western press went on giving the Soviets the benefit of the doubt, the Soviet press unleashed a massive campaign of insinuation, distortion and blatant lying to try to deflect suspicion from the Kremlin. These actions were a continuation of a longstanding Soviet campaign to blame the West for the terrorism that was designed to undermine it. This campaign reached extravagant heights in the same period that the Pope was being vilified in the Soviet provincial press and the plot to assassinate him went into its final phase.[1] It is possible that some of these diatribes were designed to deflect reactions the Kremlin leadership had to expect in the wake of what was then envisioned as the successful assassination of John Paul II. Of course, only the most senior leaders in Moscow and a small group within the KGB would have been aware of such a plan.

Even if Agca had been killed on the spot, some suspicion of Soviet complicity might have arisen. His rightist cover was probably developed in expectation that he would be killed immediately—or later, if he escaped. He would have been much more convincing as a dead Gray Wolf than he was alive. Even if he had been killed, Poles in Poland would have almost certainly suspected the Kremlin. Until a defector appears who can tell us, we are unlikely to know what Kremlin planning really was and what, if anything, was done to pre-empt the adverse reactions that came in the wake of the attack.

Disappointment in the Kremlin must have been intense in Moscow when Judge Santiapichi announced his verdict on Agca's trial on 25 September 1981. The case would not be closed. Investigation would continue. During the year that followed, central Soviet media continued to follow their established line unchanged: the US did it. In the

Soviet provincial press, attacks against both the Vatican and the Pope increased. But there were long periods when Moscow stayed silent. Encouraged as the Kremlin must have been by the passivity and occasional gullibility of parts of the Western press, they could not relax. Some media organizations were going to pursue it. The story would not die.

When the September 1982 *Reader's Digest* appeared, Moscow launched a campaign of vilification against Claire Sterling, the author of the article on the plot. When NBC's White Paper was aired on 21 September 1982, TASS termed it a 'foul, anti-Soviet sensation invented by the CIA'. When NBC broadcast an update of the same program with important new information in January 1983, Moscow threatened reprisals, but took none.

There was little inventiveness, no humor, in Soviet counterthrusts. These were not humorous times. Brezhnev was dying. Andropov was maneuvering to improve his chances for the succession. General Jaruzelski's 'coup' in Warsaw on 13 December 1981 exposed the ideological bankruptcy of the Soviet position there. The effort the Kremlin was putting into encouraging the peace movement and intimidating Western Europe produced meager results. When the arrest of Sergei Antonov in November 1982 exposed a Bulgarian connection that had already been visible—but for the most part not seen—the KGB must have been temporarily thrown into consternation. Why had the Bulgarians not taken the elementary precaution of rotating their intelligence team in Rome? What kind of advice had Ambassador Tolubeev been giving to Zhivkov? Why were not the KGB officers overseeing the Bulgarian KDS alert to the danger?

Ayvazov had to leave Italy in unseemly haste invoking diplomatic immunity. Sparse Soviet media comment in early December treated Antonov's arrest as a Bulgarian problem. Moscow fumbled for a couple of weeks. There must have been hope that the Antonov case could be ignored. Surely a bargain of some sort could be struck with the Italians. Somebody could be bribed or frightened or both . . . It was a futile hope. The widespread listening to Western radio in the USSR in recent years has made it far more difficult than it used to be for Soviet media to avoid giving at least minimal attention to important news stories. By mid-December the Soviets had decided that bluffing it out would not work. So the word went out to strike back. There was, none the less, nothing new to strike back with. So the response was the same as in the summer of 1981—with accusations multiplied, rhetoric intensified, language more shrill. The titles of articles from late 1982 into the first weeks of 1983 demonstrate the frenzy which gripped Soviet propagandists—here is a random selection that appeared in the central press between 14 December and 1 April; there were dozens of others:

'Absurd Affirmations', *Pravda*, 14 December 1982.

'The Tracks Lead to Washington', *Izvestia*, 26 December 1982.

'The "Antonov Affair"', or the Attempt to Prove the Impossible', *Literaturnaya Gazeta*, 29 December 1982.

'Slander Record', *Izvestia*, 30 December 1982.

'Who's Behind It?—The Origin of a Falsification', *Pravda*, 30 December 1982.

'The Tracks Lead to Langley—on the Role of the American Intelligence Services in the Slanderous Campaign against the Bulgarian People's Republic and the USSR', *Pravda*, 5 January 1983.

'Portrait of a Terrorist—How Agca was Made a Leftist', *Literaturnaya Gazeta*, 19 January 1983.

'The Gray Wolf, the Red Hat and Henry Kissinger's Earmuffs', *Literaturnaya Gazeta*, 26 January 1983.

'The Slanderers are not Quieting Down', *Izvestia*, 18 March 1983.

'A Red Cap for the Gray Wolf', *Izvestia*, 25 March 1983.

These articles and others like them were variations on the same themes: the hullabaloo about the Bulgarian connection was a Western tactic to divert attention from plans for aggression against Eastern Europe. Everyone knows that CIA masterminds international terrorism—it is hopeless to try to put the blame on the USSR. The suggestion that anyone in a socialist society could have anything to do with terrorism runs counter to Soviet policy and ideology. The Soviets argued that Agca was trained by Americans in Turkey who supported Türkeş's Gray Wolves. Soviet propaganda claimed Agca invented the Bulgarian connection when he was visited and propositioned by Italian intelligence agents after his conviction.

Nowhere in these accusatory, self-righteous outpourings was there admission of the fact that Agca had spent at least several weeks in Bulgaria in the summer of 1981, no reference to Palestinian training, no reference to the mystery of where Agca went after he escaped to Iran. These are very delicate subjects for the Russians. The conclusion of a Radio Liberty researcher who analyzed a large volume of this material in January 1983 sums it up well:

> Soviet media coverage of this major story, while relatively copious, has been denunciatory rather than investigatory . . . It has had as its goal not the elucidation of the case but only the repudiation of what Moscow calls a dirty campaign of lies and insinuations directed against the Soviet Union and its allies.[2]

Many of the biggest names in the Soviet propaganda hierarchy were drawn into the damage-limiting effort. They did not distinguish themselves at this thankless task. Leonid Zamyatin, chief of the Central Committee's International Information Department, described revelations of the Bulgarian connection as 'an evil-minded campaign that has not a grain nor an iota of truth'. It was all a scheme, he maintained, to discredit Bulgaria and the USSR among Catholics. Georgi Arbatov, director of the Institute for the Study of the USA and Canada of the USSR Academy of Sciences, could only claim that 'the US had invented the Bulgarian connection as an explanation for the attempted assassination of the Pope' because 'the Reagan Administration was frustrated at the speedy, smooth change of leadership in Moscow after the death of Brezhnev and wanted to cause the Soviet Union difficulty'. Pretty thin gruel from a Soviet figure who is supposed to understand how America works.

Meanwhile Kremlin frustration had resulted in a major press attack on the Pope himself. On 30 December 1982 TASS publicized a Communist Party Central Committee issuance which called the Pope a rigid anti-communist whose church was carrying on subversion in Poland and elsewhere in Eastern Europe:

> Unlike his predecessors, the present head of the Catholic Church . . . has taken a much more conservative position vis-a-vis the socialist world . . . The notorious Solidarity, which came to symbolize the crisis provoked by the anti-socialist forces on instructions from overseas, was born not in the wave of disorders that

swept the country in the summer of 1980, but in the Catholic Church. Poland is not only the object of the Vatican's subversive activity. It sends 'specialists' in catholic propaganda to other socialist countries of Eastern Europe.

Calling the Pope 'the former Archbishop of Krakow', TASS accused him of using 'the language of Christian prayers' to disguise his political aims.

The article could be interpreted as a veiled argument that the Pope had invited assassination. The Pope had done nothing to provoke this verbal assault. The Vatican had remained silent during the arrest of Antonov and exposure of the Bulgarian connection. The Vatican press office issued a terse response the same day that said the Soviet attack

. . . contrasts with the reality of the facts and the situation that are well known to all, on which world public opinion has pronounced a judgement that can hardly be contradicted. It contradicts also the evaluation made by Soviet sources, including Soviet officials, who have recognized on various occasions the high skill and untiring work of Pope John Paul II for peace and a just solution of the grave problems that threaten humanity.

The Vatican clearly had the better of the argument. It was even supported by the Italian Communist Party paper *Unita* on 31 December 1982. This direct, unprovoked attack on the Pope in language hitherto used only in the Soviet provincial press added to the growing impression even among charitable skeptics in the West that the Kremlin leadership was behind the plot.[3]

Bulgarian Burlesque

Bulgaria's media paid less attention to the plot against the Pope than those of any other East European country until Sergei Antonov's arrest. Then they had to become engaged. Bulgarian counteractions heightened the impression of culpability; Ayvazov had fled Rome and Bekir Çelenk, who was in London when Antonov was arrested, rushed back to be 'taken into custody' in Sofia and ostentatiously imprisoned on 9 December. He was subsequently released to live in the Hotel Moskva, less luxurious than the Vitosha. In face of repeated Turkish and Italian requests for his extradition, Çelenk was released 'for lack of evidence' early in 1983. He did not leave Bulgaria. The Bulgarians arrested two Italian tourists in a transparent move to secure hostages for trading. Ambassador Tolubeev and his Bulgarian charges must have spent a few sleepless nights before the unprecedented press conference which was held in Sofia on 17 December 1982. It featured Kolev and Ayvazov, Antonov's wife, Rositsa, and Bekir Çelenk. Çelenk's protestations of innocence were even less convincing than the alibis of the others.

The press was not permitted to talk to the suspects privately, but a Turkish reporter found an opportunity to interview Rositsa Antonova before the press conference.[4] The interview revealed several interesting points which Bulgarian propaganda has since attempted to obscure or deny. Married 13 years, she said she had been living separately from her husband since 1977. Even when she had gone to Italy for a year to study art (she was completing a degree in esthetics at Sofia University, she said) she had seen very little of him 'because of the demands of his profession'. During the previous year she had seen him only in the course of a brief trip to Italy. In all she had spent only a year in Italy since 1977—'I came back because there were no good educational opportunities for our 12 year old daughter in Italy'. She went on to give a dreary picture of her life in Italy: 'Not many people came to our house there. Because my husband's work kept him so busy, we didn't often go to entertainment places. I went to museums on my own.'

Some would say that the picture Rositsa Antonova painted of her husband would represent a typical intelligence operative; in this interview she made no specific mention of his airline duties. The interview did not establish the exact dates of her stay in Rome, but it seems to put in doubt all the detailed argumentation the Bulgarians later made about her alleged presence—or absence—during meetings with Agca in the spring of 1981. Who could say whether a woman who brought in tea at one of these meetings was Rositsa Antonova? Might she not have been a Bulgarian embassy secretary?

The Bulgarian defense effort has had three main features: (1) Repeated protests of innocence coupled with violent accusations of frame-up—always in the last analysis by the United States. The tactic is the same as Moscow's and creates the same counterproductive impression. (2) Elaborate argumentation on fine points designed in part to obscure the fact that most of the information Agca provided the Italians fits together logically and information supplied by Scricciolo supported identification of the Bulgarians and their pattern of operation. Bulgarian sophistry extended to allegations of misrepresentation of Ayvazov's address because the street name, Galiani, was spelled with two l's rather than one! (3) Amusing attempts to turn known and hard-to-deny facts in the opposite direction. For example, the Bulgarians could not deny Agca's stay in Bulgaria—they insist they could not be expected to identify him among hundreds of thousands of Turks who cross Bulgaria every year. They ignore the fact that almost none of these Turks stays in the Vitosha or Sofia's other de luxe hotels and that Bulgarian security keeps track of those who do. The Bulgarians claim Scricciolo was in fact a Western agent since he contacted known Polish dissidents on visits to Poland, passed money from Western labor unions to Solidarity and attended a meeting in the US Embassy in Rome. One of the most contrived of these arguments is the claim that Agca had to have been abetted by NATO because he traveled through seven (sic) countries before the shooting in Rome.[5]

The flood of material the Bulgarian news agency put out in December, January and February 1983 heightened the impression of confusion in Sofia. Many of the Bulgarians participating in these denial efforts were probably sincere in doing so, since only a very limited circle in Bulgaria would have had knowledge of an operation so sensitive as killing the Pope. On the other hand, large numbers of Bulgarians have to know of the extent to which Bulgaria has tolerated and exploited Turkish and other Middle Eastern smugglers and aided subversive operations in many other countries. These Bulgarians must have their own doubts about their officials' loud protestations of innocence. Others must have seen the illogic and internal contradictions in most of the Bulgarian claims.

Defectors are bound, sooner or later, to give us a clearer picture of what Bulgarians really think about their government's efforts to absolve itself of complicity. There have been some curious moves in the shadows, leading to rumors that Moscow might eventually sacrifice Zhivkov and let blame for the plot rest on the Bulgarians.[6] KGB chief Chebrikov made a visit to Sofia in late May 1983. The transfer of Soviet Ambassador Tolubeev from Sofia to another assignment was announced in June 1983.

The official press in Poland has repeated much of the Soviet and Bulgarian invective on the shooting of the Pope. One gets the impression this is done for the most part with tongue in cheek. The Polish population, well informed by Western radio broadcasts, has plenty of information to make up its own mind. Poles have doubtlessly enjoyed the discomfort Moscow's and Sofia's vituperation reveals.

Disinformation and Misinformation

Disinformation on the papal plot—deliberately concocted documents or stories with no apparent origin except the East—began to appear in the fall of 1981. It reflected familiar KGB techniques. The aim was to reinforce the allegations that Agca was a committed rightist fanatic. In late October 1981 the Munich tabloid *Bildzeitung* featured a story claiming German police had discovered that Agca had stayed for six months in a hotel in Ottobrunn, near Munich, while being trained by a German neo-Nazi group. When? Not specified. No dates. No real facts. No German police official could be found to verify it. Though *Milliyet* gave the story headlines on 24 October 1981, it evaporated quickly. Too many specifics had already been established about Agca's travels and connections by that time to give the tale a semblance of seriousness.

Another item of disinformation that appeared the same month has had a longer life. It is a letter allegedly written from Agca to Alparslan Türkeş from Munich. It lacks a date. No original of the letter has ever appeared. Photocopies of it 'were sent by unknown persons to certain individuals and organizations'.[7] This is a common Soviet technique. Absence of a date is understandable for a forgery, much less likely with a genuine letter. Genuine Agca letters have invariably been dated. The forgers did not want the 'authenticity' of their work called further into doubt by use of a date that would later prove untenable. In fact, Agca is not firmly known to have spent time in Munich at all. The content of the letter is its most dubious feature. It consists merely of a string of National Action Party slogans, using language that is not characteristic of Agca. The letter would be forgotten except for the attention Turkish journalist, Ugur Mumcu, has continued to give it. He wrote a column on it in January 1983 and dramatizes it as genuine in his book *Agca Dosyasi*. This is not surprising, perhaps, in view of the credence Mumcu has in the past given to Soviet forgeries.[8]

Unconvincing as the Agca letter to Türkeş looks, not much would be proved if it were genuine. By the time it appeared, evidence was already accumulating that Agca had been sheltered in a network camouflaged to look rightist though ultimately serving Soviet purposes. Proof of the nature of the network materialized when Musa

Serdar Çelebi's key role became evident in the fall of 1982.

During the winter of 1981/2 when new facts about the plot against the Pope were coming out slowly, misinformation and disinformation spread. Some was designed to prove that Agca had, after all, acted out of deeply anti-Christian motivation. Malatya, so a widely circulated story went, suffered severely at the time of the Crusades and intense anti-Christian sentiment had survived there ever since. So it was natural for Agca to attack the Pope . . . If one bothers to read half a page of Malatya's history in a tourist guidebook, this tale is seen to be fantasy. So many armies have fought in what is today southeastern Turkey since the time of the Crusades that memory of alleged Crusader atrocities would long since have been obliterated. Modern Malatya came into existence only in the mid-nineteenth century when the old city, several miles to the west, was the scene of fighting between the Ottoman armies and the rebellious Egyptian leader, Mehmet Ali. There are other problems with the story too. The Agca family ancestors came from a region well to the north of Malatya with roots extending up to Kayseri. Agca's mother and father only moved to Malatya in 1965.[9]

Another tale which developed in the months following the shooting dramatizes former CIA agent Frank Terpil as Agca's trainer in Libya. The story has been repeated over and over again in many variations and even, occasionally, taken up by serious media outlets in the US and Europe.[10] The story can be embroidered to substantiate a CIA link only if those who use it ignore the vigorous prosecution by American authorities of the entire group of men with former intelligence connections who served Qaddafy. Tales of Terpil and Agca cannot be useful to the Russians except for diversion—in the end they focus attention on Soviet links to Qaddafy and Palestinian terrorism. Agca may have had a Libyan connection, but nothing has yet come to light to substantiate it.

Soviet disinformation specialists have not had an easy time fabricating material that would divert attention from mounting evidence of East European instigation of the plot against the Pope, but they have not stopped trying. An example of a variation on familiar themes came to light in the spring of 1983. It seems first to have appeared in the Madrid weekly *El Tiempo* in early March. It was a forgery of an alleged 1978 'top secret' memorandum from Zbigniew Brzezinski to President Carter purporting to outline a plan for destabilizing Poland. Curiously, the Warsaw paper *Zycie Warszawy* reprinted the forgery on 13 March 1983 under a Washington dateline. The 'memorandum' implies that the election of Wojtyla as Pope was an intrinsic part of the destabilization scheme. The forgery may reflect an authentic KGB analysis from late 1978 attributing the Polish Pope's election to a successful conspiracy Brzezinski purportedly mounted through Cardinal Krol of Philadelphia and West German Catholic leaders. This forgery seems to have been designed more for effect inside the Soviet empire than in the West. Among other things, it may have been seen as potentially useful in prosecuting Solidarity leaders.[11]

Disinformation is a way of life for the Soviet leadership, simply one aspect of the 'active measures' that are always being used to further Soviet purposes and confuse the non-communist world.

The process continued during the summer of 1983. In early July, two forged cables allegedly sent from the US Embassy in Rome in August and December of 1982 suddenly appeared in left-wing publications in Europe. Their purpose was to demonstrate that the 'Bulgarian Connection' was deliberately fabricated by the US and implemented by cooperative Italians. The US State Department commented on 15 July 1983: 'The two documents are clearly intended to discredit the US as well as the Italian magistracy that is investigating the possible involvement of Bulgarian agents in the papal assassina-

Difficult as it may be to produce convincingly, there is bound to be more disinformation as the story of the plot against the Polish Pope continues to unfold.

The mysterious kidnapping of Emanuela Orlandi, the 15-year-old daughter of a Vatican official, on 22 June 1983, has the marks of yet another Soviet–Bulgarian instigated attempt to depict Agca as backed by Islamic fundamentalists. The abduction was carried out by unknown persons claiming to be Turks and 'identified' in early August 1983 as the 'Anti-Christian Turkish Liberation Army' allegedly seeking Agca's release. No organisation such as this has ever been identified in Turkey and the name is implausible. The kidnapping produced a quite contrary result when Agca, brought to Rome for interrogation about the incident on 8 July, made his impromptu declaration to journalists that he knew he was working for the KGB and had been trained in Syria and elsewhere by Soviet agents.

Governmental Reactions

The Italian government and the Vatican were both accused in 1981 of not pursuing the plot vigorously enough, or minimizing the investigation, of trying to hush up the whole affair and seek a compromise with the Kremlin. There may have been both Italian and Vatican officials who leaned toward overcaution, but they did not carry the day. The officials who made the decisions that set the course for continuing investigation had a clear idea of what their responsibilities were. They showed foresight, moral fortitude and political discretion—a good sense of balance. They understood that steady, purposeful, determined action was more important than mere words or political posturing.

There has been greater contentiousness about the pursuit of the plot in Washington than in Rome, though there is no need for the United States government, in spite of Soviet efforts to implicate it, to play a primary role in current investigations in Italy, Turkey, or elsewhere in Europe. Nevertheless, as leader of the West, the American government is expected by its own people, by its allies and by world public opinion, to play a role in assessing a plot so momentous in its implications as an attempt to kill the Pope. It is as important for Western defense that American intelligence specialists analyze the Soviet commitment to terrorism and destabilization and the mechanisms for executing such operations as it is that they study the characteristics of Soviet nuclear warheads and missiles and estimate Soviet leaders' intentions of using them.

A Subdued Pope?

The reactions of the Pope and the Vatican to the plot are of more than academic interest. Was John Paul II intimidated by the attack? Has his influence been reduced as a result? Are the voices of caution in the Vatican louder now and more listened to? Has his health been impaired permanently? Has the Kremlin, after all, even though its scheme was botched, gained from it?

I have never thought so. I do not think so now. The Pope's second visit to his homeland in June 1983 was not the action of a subdued man. It was General Jaruzelski who was visibly demoralized. The Pope was careful to avoid confrontation and hollow rhetoric before he was shot. He has avoided needlessly pushing the Kremlin into corners since. But he knows that his position was strengthened by the attack, not weakened. And it will be further strengthened if a Bulgarian/KGB/Kremlin connection is confirmed so decisively that even those who wish to believe otherwise or forget the episode will be compelled to recognize its significance.

The Pope was severely wounded. Initial medical treatment was not as effective as had been hoped. A second, dangerous operation was needed in August 1981 to set him firmly on the road to recovery. Had he not led a vigorous, outdoor life and been in prime health for a man of his age, the balance would probably have been tipped the other way in the summer of 1981. The long-term effect of his wounds is impossible to estimate, but there is little evidence, two years later, of serious after-effects. The Pope did not surrender control of the Vatican establishment during the long weeks of convalescence. He forgave Agca and has regularly had parcels of Turkish delicacies sent to him in his prison cell. As soon as his energy began to return, he resumed the same kind of schedule he had followed before.

One of the first foreign church leaders the Pope received when he again became active was the Ethiopian Orthodox Patriarch, Abuna Tekla-Haymanot, who came to visit him at Castel Gandolfo on 18 October 1981. The Ethiopian Orthodox Church, strong in its ancient traditions and never subordinate to Rome, has experienced an extra-ordinary burst of vigor since a Moscow-supported communist-style regime was established after deposition of Haile Selassie in 1974.[12] Ethiopian communist leaders have had to accommodate to the church but the relationship is uneasy. The men in the Kremlin could take little comfort when they learned of the Pope's meeting with the Ethiopian patriarch, as unprecedented in modern church history as the Pope's historic pilgrimage to Turkey to visit the Patriarch of Constantinople less than two years before. To the Ethiopian the Pope gave the same message:

> This meeting of ours is part of a much wider spiritual movement—that common search among all Christians for growth together toward full unity.

John Paul II has continued his strong interest in Catholics in the Soviet Union, sending messages to Ukrainians and Lithuanians, receiving delegations of their bishops in the Vatican. His appointment of Latvian Cardinal Vaivods as the first cardinal in the Soviet Union is not evidence of a desire to placate the Kremlin. It was the Kremlin leaders who made the concession of permitting Vaivods to go to Rome to receive his hat.

The Pope's and Cardinal Wyszynski's vision of the church conquering the East is more alive than ever before. So is the Pope's determination to play an active role in furtherance of freedom and human rights in the entire world. He has continued to travel abroad several times each year. His visit in March 1983 to insurgency-ridden Central America, one of the Kremlin's prime targets for destabilization and anti-American agitation, underscored his boldness and self-confidence.[13]

Boldness is coupled with compassion and a remarkable capacity to forgive, if not to forget. These qualities were demonstrated in the Pope's reception of a delegation from Bulgaria in the Vatican on 26 May 1983. It was made up of both Catholic and Orthodox church representatives as well as government officials, including a member of the staff of the same Bulgarian Embassy in Rome out of which the plan for the Pope's assassination was implemented. This visit occurred in the immediate aftermath of KGB Chief Chebrikov's unusual 4-day visit to Sofia in the third week of May. The Bulgarian visit was an implicit recognition of both the Pope's strength and his own Commitment to exploit it with political skill and magnanimity.

The Polish Pope—this Slav—is never foolhardy. His emotions are always under control. He knows his strength. As long as he lives, he is unlikely ever to be subdued.

CONCLUSION

Historical, inferential, circumstantial and solid factual evidence all point in the same direction to explain the plot against John Paul II—toward Moscow. The probability that the Kremlin leadership and the KGB were the architects of the plot to kill John Paul II is far greater in 1983 than it seemed in 1981. It is likely to be even greater in 1984 and 1985.

The Bulgarians were the prime contractors for the undertaking. It is extremely unlikely that they were the initiators. Subcontractors included a motley mixture of seemingly disparate elements: Turkish mafia tycoons, petty smugglers, profit-seekers, corrupted and deceived political rightists, probably a few misguided leftists as well. The whole cast of characters who aided Mehmet Ali Agca on his way to Rome has not yet been identified. How he was selected, trained and prepared remains to be clarified too. But the general outlines are clear. They are unlikely to change radically. The gaps in the picture will begin to fit together when Agca tells all he knows.

It is possible—likely perhaps—that Agca's initial recruitment was of the false flag type. But it is improbable that he could have remained ignorant of his true sponsors for very long after his rescue from prison in November 1979. No sane Turk could be involved with Bulgarians in planning the killing of Lech Walesa and John Paul II and not realize he was serving Soviet Russian interests, interests deeply inimical to the West and to Turkey itself as most Turks see them.

Agca will probably be able to tell us relatively little about the larger framework of the plot, but it should be possible to deduce a good deal from what he knows—when the scheme was first broached to him, how it was rationalized, what pressures his sponsors reflected, what worries they might have had, what they said they expected to gain from it.

To fill in the rest of the story we will need other sources. It may be many years before they all appear. Defectors from Bulgaria will eventually provide some information. Defectors from the Soviet Union will have much more. Most defectors are likely to have only second- and third-hand knowledge. With luck, defectors with first-hand experience of the development of the plot may appear.

Judge Martella, the investigating Italian official, has already learned much more than has been made public from talking with Agca, interrogation of Çelebi, Bagçi and others. The possibility that Antonov might decide to confess should not be ruled out. Information from the other cases that are still under investigation in Italy—the web of relationships around Luigi Scricciolo and the massive drug and arms smuggling ring—is bound to help explain some aspects of the plot against the Pope and all the East European linkages it entails. Information from all these sources will be brought to bear when Antonov, Çelebi and others are brought to trial. But, contrary to popular expectations, the trial of Sergei Antonov is not going to be the final step in the denouement of the plot.

Several Turkish trials are in progress. Confessions may emerge out of these trials too. And evidence which Turkish investigators are gathering on Agca's background will provide new insights into the way Soviet 'international' terrorism has been organized and supported. Who were Agca's sponsors in Turkey? Who put money into his bank accounts? Who indoctrinated him in the nihilist notion of terrorism as an end in itself, a means of purifying society? Where was he trained? Where *did* he go from Iran and why did he go there in the first place?

The Russians are as far from developing a credible countertheory that would explain the plot against the Pope as they were when Novosti put out its first dispatch insinuating American responsibility on 27 May 1981. The Bulgarians go on undercutting themselves by the pettiness and contrived nature of their argumentation. Both Moscow and Sofia have failed the sizable constituency in the West which would be predisposed to accept some plausible alibi. But what could the alibi be? As time passes and more evidence accumulates, it is increasingly difficult to devise one.

So Moscow and those beholden to it fall back on vituperation and disinformation. Both ploys are time-worn. The message John Paul II brings to the world is eternally fresh. 'Marxism is no more convincing than any other excuse for tyranny', *The Economist* recently observed (19 March 1983). No excuse for tyranny is convincing for long. Against the Polish Pope's pleas for freedom, human rights and social reconciliation, Marxism as preached from Moscow has little force. Vituperation is equally unpersuasive as an argument for innocence. Moscow's and Sofia's diatribes stand as an indictment of themselves.

CHRONOLOGY

An Agca Chronology 1958-1982

With references to Papal and Polish developments.

1958 9 January—Born in Güzelyurt, Malatya province. Family soon moved to nearby Hekimhan where Mehmet Ali began elementary school.

1960 Sister Fatma born.

1963 Brother Adnan born.

1965 Family moved to Malatya and settled in Yeşiltepe district.

1966 Father, Ahmet Agca, died.

1968-76 Helped mother, Müzeyyen Agca, eke out living. Worked on construction sites during the summers. Developed great interest in reading. Wrote poetry from age of 10 or 11. Wrote novel at age of 13. Gained reputation as excellent student.

1973 Completed Yeşiltepe junior high school. Planning to be teacher, entered Mustafa Kemal Teacher-Training High School in Malatya.

1976 Completed teacher-training high school with high grades. Claims to have avoided involvement in student clashes and politics. Took nationwide university entrance examinations in spring and qualified for University of Ankara. Entered History and Geography Faculty of that university in fall, staying at Beşevler student dormitory.

1977 Spring—Traveled to Syria and Lebanon with Sedat Sirri Kadem? Met by Teslim Töre who arranged training at PLO camp south of Beirut? Returned to Turkey.

1 May—Bloody May Day rally in Taksim Square, Istanbul, dramatizes rapid growth of terrorism in Turkey.

Summer—Agca returned to work in Malatya?

Fall—Agca returned to University of Ankara.

13 December—Bank account opened for Agca at Beyazit branch of Türkiye İş Bankasi in Istanbul with deposit equivalent of $1,600. Bank deposits continue during following year.

1978 6 January—Ecevit returned to power as Prime Minister.

Winter—Agca attending University of Ankara?

Spring—Agca took nationwide university entrance examination for second time and qualified for economics at University of Istanbul.

196

Summer—Agca said by mother to have returned to Malatya to work. Further terrorist training at home or abroad?

9 October—Agca obtained certificates of draft deferral and good police record from authorities in Malatya.

October—Entered University of Istanbul, registering for solid list of courses in economics and related subjects. No evidence of attendance at class.

16 October—Cardinal Wojtyla elected Pope John Paul II in Rome.

24-26 December—Violent rioting in Kahramanmaraş—worst outbreak of terrorism in Turkey to date.

29 December—Equivalent of $8,000 deposited into Agca's account in Gebze branch of Yapi-Kredi Bankasi, capping year in which more than $16,000 had been deposited in Agca's bank accounts. Agca claimed to have traveled from Istanbul to Malatya on this date.

1979 4 January—In Malatya, Agca withdrew same sum from local Yapi-Kredi Bankasi account.

10-12 January—Agca deposited appoximately $4,000 in Ziraat Bankasi branch in Malatya.

20 January—Agca issued passport in Malatya. Presumably soon returned to Istanbul.

24 January—In Rome, Soviet Foreign Minister Gromyko had two-hour audience with Pope.

1 February—*Milliyet* editor-in-chief, Abdi Ipekçi, assassinated.

February—Agca spent mid-term vacation with family in Malatya, then returned to Istanbul.

2-10 June—Pope made historic visit to Poland.

25 June—Agca arrested in Marmara Cafe, Istanbul, and confessed to Ipekçi assassination.

3-5 July—Secretaries of Eastern bloc communist parties met in Berlin to discuss 'ideological questions'.

11 July—Agca presented to press in Istanbul on completion of first phase of interrogation. Afterwards moved to Selimiye Prison in Üsküdar.

25 September—Agca transferred from Selimiye to Kartal-Maltepe prison as trial about to begin.

1-7 October—Pope John Paul II visited United States.

5 October—Turkish Interior Minister Hasan Fehmi Güneş resigned.

12 October—On second day of trial, Agca claimed Güneş had offered him deal—leniency in return for declaration of rightist sponsorship—during interrogation.

16 October—Ecevit's government fell.

24 October—Agca retracted his confession. Claimed he did not murder Ipekçi but knew who did. About same time told mother, during prison visit, he was scapegoat for others.

5 November—Agca attempted escape during course of psychiatric examination.

12 November—Demirel government took office; received vote of confidence in parliament on 25 November.

23 November—Agca escaped from Kartal-Maltepe during night dressed in soldier's uniform.

26 November—Agca telephoned *Milliyet* to call attention to his note attacking Pope's imminent visit.

27 November-1 December—Papal visit to Turkey.

December—Agca involved in killing of Ramazan Gündüz and Haydar Seyrangah allegedly in revenge for tipping off police? Traveled to Ankara, Nevşehir and back to Ankara?

1980   January—Agca arrived in Erzerum.

24 January—Far-reaching economic reforms decreed in Turkey. Terrorism worsening.

1 February—Agca smuggled over border into Iran.

11-15 February—Eighth Congress of Polish Workers' Party tried to gain control over worsening political and economic situation; prime minister replaced.

Winter/Spring—Agca in Iran? In Soviet Union? Further PLO training? To Bulgaria?

28 April—Agca sentenced to death *in absentia* in Istanbul.

9 July—The gun Agca used in shooting the Pope sold to Horst Grillmaier in Krems, Austria.

11 July—Agca met Ömer Mersan at Vitosha Hotel in Sofia.

July/August—Agca in Sofia, met Mustafaev; met Bekir Çelenk? Intense labor unrest in Poland.

11 August—Agca's false passport issued in Nevşehir in name of Faruk Özgün.

28 August—Agca death sentence confirmed by Turkish court of appeal.

30 August—Agca passport stamped for exit from Turkey.

31 August—Agca passport stamped for entry into Bulgaria and exit into Yugoslavia. Agca departed from Bulgaria this date? Lech Walesa's Solidarity officially recognized by Polish government in Gdansk Agreement.

Early September—Agca arrived in Germany?

5 September—Kania replaced Gierek as First Secretary of Polish Party.

9-12 September—Agca stayed in Hotel Ruetli, Zurich, Switzerland.

12 September—Military leadership assumed control of government in Turkey and took immediate steps to bring terrorism to halt.

3 October—Turkish Embassy in Bonn sent note to German Foreign Office reporting Agca seen in Frankfurt; arrest and extradition requested.

Mid-October—Pope sent apostolic blessing to congress of Polish and Ukrainian historians meeting in Munich.

27-31 October—Agca stayed in Hotel Krone in Lucerne, Switzerland.

6 November—Turkish Embassy in Bonn sent Germans second note reporting Agca seen in Berlin. Request for arrest and extradition repeated.

25 November—Necati Uygur murdered in Kempten, Germany—Agca implicated?

30 November—Agca flew to Tunis from Italy. Met Mustafaev who allegedly proposed assassination of Bourgiba and Mintoff at meeting scheduled for 12 December. Agca refused. Went to resort of Hamamet and stayed until 13 December. Did he visit Libya during this time?

11 December—Third Turkish Embassy note to Germans reported sighting of Agca in Berlin at some previous date.

13 December—Agca returned by ferry from Tunis to Palermo. Stayed overnight at Hotel Liguria in Palermo.

15 December—Agca met Musa Serdar Çelebi in Milan.

Late December—Agca in Rome. In contact with Bulgarians there?

Entire year—Pope John Paul II continued vigorous leadership of papacy in Rome and visited nine foreign countries in the course of the year.

1981 Early January—Agca met Bulgarians at Hotel Archimede in Rome. Assassination of Lech Walesa discussed.

18 January—Walesa visited Pope in Vatican. Assassination attempt not implemented.

19 January—Agca moved into Pensione Isa in Rome, remaining until end of the month?

4 February—Agca recognized by a Turk in the Biffi Cafe in Milan; had escaped by time police arrived.

6 February—Agca stayed overnight at Hotel Anker, Aarau, Switzerland.

9 February—Jaruzelski appointed prime minister in Warsaw as Solidarity continued to gain strength.

3 March—Agca met Musa Serdar Çelebi in Zurich. Çelebi relayed offer from Bekir Çelenk of DM 3 million for killing Pope.

March—Belorossian journal *Polymya* called Pope 'cunning and dangerous ideological enemy', 'malicious, lowly, perfidious and backward toady of the American militarists'. Pope was also sharply attacked in the Ukrainian communist press.

Early March—79-year-old Cardinal Wyszynski fell ill in Warsaw. By mid-month there was suspicion of cancer.

26 March—Wyszynski's last meeting with Jaruzelski.

31 March—Wyszynski confided in his diary that he did not expect to live long. Knowledge of his illness now widespread.

3 April—Agca entered Switzerland at Diepoldsau, arriving from Austria. En route to give his gun to Ömer Bagçi in Olten?

5-7 April—Agca back in Rome at Hotel Archimede. In contact with Bulgarians.

8 April—Agca left Rome by train for Perugia.

9 April—Agca enrolled in University for Foreigners in Perugia, obtaining student documentation.

10 April—Attended single class at University.

11 or 12 April—Returned to Rome; stayed at Hotel Torino night of 12 April. Telephoned Hasan Taşkin at Sarstedt-Hildesheim in Germany.

Mid-April—traveled again to Austria?

13 April—Wyszynski diagnosed as having incurable cancer and given very little time to live.

19 April—Agca booked 2-week holiday trip to Majorca in Milan.

25 April—Agca departed by air to Majorca with Italian tour party.

25 April-8 May—Agca in Majorca, little seen by other members of the tour group. Telephoned Çelebi in Frankfurt informing him, 'I have received the money promised. I will now go to Rome to finish the job.' Telephoned Bagçi in Olten, Switzerland and asked him to come to Milan with gun on 9 May. Met with Bekir Çelenk on Minorca? Met mysterious Hungarian woman?

30 April—Wyszynski said mass for last time in Warsaw.

3 May—Polish national holiday. Wyszynski sent message to Czeslaw Milosz and had telephone conversation with Pope.

Early May—Turkish Embassy in Rome informed Italian Foreign Ministry Agca sighted in Italy, requested arrest and extradition.

9 May—Wyszynski developed serious heart condition; end feared near. Agca returned to Milan and picked up gun from Bagçi. Took train to Rome and put up at Pensione Isa where caller had already reserved room for him.

11-12 May—Antonov and Ayvazov accompanied Agca on both days on reconnaissance visits to St Peter's Square. Father Stanislaw Dziwisz, papal secretary, flew to Warsaw to see dying cardinal and returned to Rome next day.

13 May—Agca picked up by Bulgarians at 3 p.m. and driven, with stop at Ayvazov's apartment to pick up gun and overnight bag with grenade, to parking place in front of Canadian Embassy to the Holy See on Via Conciliazione. They walked to Square. Agca shot Pope at 5:21 p.m. and was immediately apprehended.

14 May—Pope's would-be assassin firmly identified as Mehmet Ali Agca, escaped assassin of Abdi Ipekçi. Intensive interrogation in Rome began.

25 May—Last telephone conversation between gravely wounded Pope and dying Cardinal Wyszynski in Warsaw.

27 May—Soviet press agency Novosti issued long dispatch on papal assassination insinuating American guilt.

28 May—Wyszynski died in early morning hours.

20 July—Agca trial began in Rome.

22 July—Trial completed; Agca sentenced to life imprisonment.

23 July—Agca rejected right of appeal.

25 September—Judge Santiapichi delivered 50-page verdict declaring Agca's attack on Pope to have been the result of a conspiracy. Case to remain open.

October—Judge Ilario Martella selected to continue investigation.

6 October—Anwar Sadat assassinated in Cairo.

18 October—Continued political ferment in Poland resulted in ouster of Kania from First Secretaryship and his replacement by Jaruzelski.

13 December—'Military coup' in Poland.

17 December—US General James Dozier kidnapped in Verona.

1982   28 January—Dozier rescued.

February—Luigi Scricciolo arrested.

May—Agca began to talk to Martella.

July—Scricciolo confessed to activities as Bulgarian agent.

23 September—Agca wrote letter to Cardinal Casaroli expressing fear of being killed.

3 November—Musa Serdar Çelebi arrested in Frankfurt.

25 November—Sergei Ivanov Antonov arrested in Rome. Revelations about 'Bulgarian Connection' filled world press for several weeks.

Late December—Turkish government ordered complete reinvestigation of Ipekçi killing.

NOTES

Chapter 1

1. *Nauka i Religia*, 9, 1981, pp. 57-8.
2. *Soviet Covert Action (The Forgery Offensive)*, Hearings of the Committee on Oversight of the Permanent Select Committee on Intelligence, House of Representatives, 96th Congress, 2nd Session, 6, 19 February 1980, Washington, DC, 1980, pp. 66-7.
3. 'U.S. Protests Soviet Innuendo on Shooting of Pope', *New York Times*, 27 August 1981.
4. For example, Ernst Genri, *Protiv Terrorizma* ('Against Terrorism'), Moscow (Novosti), approved for printing, 23 October 1981.
5. *Milliyet* (Istanbul), 24 May 1981.

Chapter 2

1. I had been asked by the *Reader's Digest* to do an initial assessment of the attack on the Pope a few days after it occurred and visited Turkey during June 1981. I delivered my first report to the *Digest* in early September and was then asked to undertake a more extensive investigation. The first priority, I felt, was to get a deeper understanding of Agca's background. The *Digest* arranged for me to meet with Claire Sterling in Rome, enroute to Turkey, and I delivered a copy of my first *Digest* report to her on 20 September 1981. I arrived in Turkey again on 30 September.
2. Kemal Karpat, *The Gecekondu*, Cambridge, 1976, provides basic data on the psychology of the inhabitants of what are often incorrectly termed 'slum' areas. This work refutes almost all the facile generalizations about such areas being sloughs of despond and breeding grounds of political irrationality that were repeated by many commentators who reported on Agca's background in the wake of his attack on the Pope. *Gecekondu* dwellers, Karpat's surveys demonstrate, have a higher rate of participation in the political process than the national average and tend to vote most frequently for middle-of-the-road politicians.
3. I was skeptical at the time and thought Müzeyyen Agca was nursing a comforting illusion. I am less sure now. After his trial got under way in the fall of 1979, Agca withdrew his earlier confession to the Ipekçi murder and claimed that while he had not committed it, he knew who did. This was interpreted later as a signal to his sponsors to speed up his rescue or he would talk. The issue had not been resolved when he escaped and the court, in the face of no contrary evidence, concluded that he had been the murderer and sentenced him to death in absentia in April 1980. The issue of accomplices was left open. Subsequently the view that he may not have been the sole or even the primary killer has gained advocates in Turkey. This problem will

be discussed further in Chapter 8.

4.Turkish high-school students in the provinces prided themselves on neat dress and good grooming after the military took over and restored order in the schools.

Section Two

1. Karl Marx, *The Eastern Question, Letters Written 1853-56 Dealing with the Events of the Crimean War*, edited by Eleanor Marx Aveling and Edward Aveling, London, 1897. (These selections originally appeared in the *New York Tribune*, for which Marx was a correspondent during this period.)

Chapter 3

1. Lord Kinross (Patrick Balfour), *Ataturk, Rebirth of a Nation*, London, 1964, p. 504.

2. Evangelos Averoff-Tossizza, *By Fire and Axe, the Communist Party and the Civil War in Greece, 1944-49*, New Rochelle, NY, 1978.

3. John Barron, *KGB, the Secret Work of Soviet Secret Agents*, New York, 1974, pp. 29-57.

4. For analysis of these and other strains in the Turkish–American relationship see George S. Harris, *Troubled Alliance*, Washington, DC/Stanford, Calif., 1972.

5. Jacob M. Landau, *Radical Politics in Modern Turkey*, Leiden, 1974.

6. Margaret Krahenbuhl, *Political Kidnappings in Turkey, 1971–1972*, Rand Corporation Report R-2105-DOS/ARPA, Santa Monica, Calif., July 1977.

7. The Turkish government issued a comprehensive White Book prepared by a ministerial commission, *Türkiye Gerçekleri ve Terörizm*, Ankara, 1973.

8. Paul B. Henze, 'Turkey, the Alliance and the Middle East', Working Paper 36, International Security Series, Woodrow Wilson Center for Scholars, Smithsonian Institution, Washington, DC, December 1981, analyzes the political background of these events.

9. The forged field manual is described and reproduced in part in *Soviet Covert Action (The Forgery Offensive)*, Hearings before the Subcommittee on Oversight of the Permanent Select Committee on Intelligence, House of Representatives, 96th Congress, 2nd Session, 6, 19 February 1980, US Government Printing Office, Washington, DC, 1980.

10. Erbakan had won 48 seats in parliament in 1973; by 1977 his party was down to 24. Türkeş's seats rose from 3 to 16 during the same interval.

11. *12 September in Turkey, Before and After*, issued by the General Secretariat of the National Security Council, Ankara, July 1982 (Turkish edition issued in 1981), pp. 56-9.

12. Aydin Yalçin, 'Terrorism in Turkey', a statement to the Subcommittee on Security and Terrorism of the Senate Judiciary Committee, US Congress, 25 June 1981, Washington, DC.

13. Leftist journalist Ugur Mumcu has produced the most comprehensive study of Bulgarian-backed arms smuggling that has appeared to date: *Silah Kaçakçiligi ve Terör*, Istanbul, 1982. Its political conclusions have to be taken with reserve, for the author avoids all implication of Soviet backing of Bulgarian activities and attempts to make a case for involvement of NATO governments in abetting arms traffic and destabilization—essentially the same line that Soviet disinformation, from the Tunçkanat 'documents' of the 1960s through the forged US Army Field Manual of

the 1970s, has tried to sell.

14. Statistics and related data are from the 1982 Turkish government publication, *Türkiye'deki Anarşi ve Terörün Gelişmesi, Sonuçlari ve Güvenlik Küvvetleri ile Önlenmesi*, Ankara, 1982. The statistics are provided partially in a briefer English-language edition of the same publication, *Anarchy and Terrorism in Turkey*, Ankara, 1982.

15. Kenneth MacKenzie, *Turkey in Transition*, Ankara, 1981.

16. Turkish government publication, *Türkiye'deki Anarşi ve Terörün Gelişmesi, Sonuçlari ve Güvenlik Küvvetleri ile Önlenmesi*.

17. Ibid.

18. Ibid.

Chapter 4

1. 'Terrorists' Weakness', *New York Times*, 3 April 1982.

2. *Die Welt* (Hamburg), 24 January 1981. On 23 January 1981 *Le Figaro* (Paris) reported similar remarks by Pertini in an interview with one of its correspondents, though in this instance the President was not quoted as having mentioned the Soviet Union by name.

3. Vittorfranco S. Pisano, *The Structure and Dynamics of Italian Terrorism*, International Association of Chiefs of Police, Gaithersburg, Md, 1980. Includes extensive chronology and bibliography.

4. A recent example is analyzed by Kevin Devlin in 'The Mystery of the Fake *Rinascita'*, RFE/RL Background Report RAD/71, Munich, 5 April 1983. See also, by the same author, 'Moscow's Men at Work in the PCI', RFE/RL Background Report RAD/51, 23 February 1982 and 'Soviet Letter to PCI on Poland', RFE/RL Background Report RAD/72, 23 March 1982.

5. Rizzoli Editore, *Rapporte sul terrorismo*, Milan, 1981.

6. Claire Sterling, *The Terror Network*, New York, 1981, p. 289.

7. Walter Tobagi who worked for *Corriere della Sera* as cited by John Phillips, 'Philosopher of Violence whose Theories were put to the Test' in (London) *Times Higher Education Supplement*, 18 June 1982.

8. Phillips, ibid.

9. Claire Sterling, 'Italy's Terrorists—Life and Death in a Violent Generation', *Encounter* (London), July 1981.

10. 'Dimensionen des italienischen Terrorismus', *Neue Zürcher Zeitung*, 5 January 1982.

11. Kevin Devlin, 'The PCI and its "Afghans" ', RFE/RL Background Report RAD/113, Munich, 23 April 1981.

12. Barbagli and Corbetta, *Il Mulino*, Bologna, November-December 1978.

13. Kevin Devlin, 'Pro-Soviet Challenge Fades in PCI Congress Debates', RFE/RL Background Report RAD/43, Munich, 25 February 1983.

14. 'Moro, i 55 giorni che sconvolsero l'Italia', *Il Giornale* (Milan), 9 April 1982.

15. Extensive coverage in: *Il Giornale* (Milan) and *La Stampa* (Turin), March-June 1982. 'Halbzeit im Romer Moro Prozess', *Neue Zurcher Zeitung*, 25/26 July 1982.

16. Sue Ellen Moran, 'An Italian Red Brigadist Talks to the Authorities: the Peci Revelations', Rand Corporation Report WD-1385-AF, Santa Monica, Calif., January 1982.

17. 'Italian Guerrillas from Left, Right said to Co-operate', *Washington Post*, 5 July 1981.

18. 'Il "puzzle" bulgaro riconstruito in 18 mesi', *Il Giornale* (Milan), 21 December

1982. 'La lunga metamorfosi di Scricciolo prima "perseguitato", poi pentito', *La Stampa* (Turin), 10 December 1982.

19. 'Organizzati da Scalzone e dal suo gruppo . . . ', *Il Giornale*, 31 August 1982. ' "Pista bulgara" anche a Trento . . . ', *Il Giornale*, 23 December 1982. 'Un br pentito al processo Moro "Aiuti dai servizi segreti Urss" ', *La Stampa*, 21 May 1982.

20. 'Ora Scricciolo accusa i bulgari . . . ', *Il Giornale*, 9 December 1982. 'La Polonia, confessa Scricciolo obiettivo del complotto di Sofia', *La Stampa*, 11 December 1982.

21. 'Un "atto d'accusa" contro Scricciolo i suoi rapporti politici da Varsavia', *Il Giornale*, 13 December 1982.

22. *New York Times*, 23 March 1983.

Chapter 5

1. Crane Brinton as cited in Alexander Dallin and George Breslauer, *Political Terror in Communist Systems*, Stanford, Calif., 1970, p. 23.

2. Tibor Szamuely, *The Russian Tradition*, London, 1974, Chapter 18, 'Discipline and Terrorism', pp. 335-68.

3. Karl Marx, *The Eastern Question, Letters Written 1853-1856 dealing with the Events of the Crimean War*, edited by Eleanor Marx Aveling and Edward Aveling, London, 1897, p. 78.

4. Ibid., p. 4.

5. Ibid., p. 2.

6. *Neue Rheinische Zeitung*, 5 November 1848, as cited in Albert Parry, *Terrorism from Robespierre to Arafat*, New York, 1976, p. 71.

7. Parry, ibid., pp. 131-45.

8. Ibid., p. 131.

9. Ibid., p. 137.

10. Betram Wolfe, *An Ideology in Power—Reflections on the Russian Revolution*, New York, 1969, p. 173.

11. Alexander Solzhenitsyn, *The Gulag Archipelago*, I-II, Harper & Row, New York, 1973, Chapter 2, 'The History of our Sewage Disposal System', pp. 24-92.

12. The best account, which originated as *samizdat*, is Aleksandr Nekrich, *The Punished Peoples*, New York, 1978.

13. Outstanding examples include: Grigory S. Agabekov, *OGPU, The Russian Secret Terror*, New York, 1931; W.G. Krivitsky, *In Stalin's Secret Service*, New York, 1939; Jan Valtin, *Out of the Night*, New York, 1940.

14. For example, David J. Dallin, *Soviet Espionage*, New Haven, Conn., 1955; John Barron, *KGB, The Secret Work of Soviet Secret Agents*, New York, 1974; John Barron, *KGB Today, The Hidden Hand*, New York, 1983.

15. Ladislav Bittman, *The Deception Game*, Syracuse, NY, 1972, pp. 142-3.

16. Claire Sterling, *The Terror Network*, New York, 1981, pp. 290-2.

17. These developments are dealt with in the books of Barron and Sterling already cited and documented in detail in *Soviet Covert Action (The Forgery Offensive)*, a report of Hearings before the Subcommittee on Oversight of the Permanent Select Committee on Intelligence, House of Representatives, 96th Congress, 2nd Session, Washington, DC, 1980; also in *Soviet Active Measures*, Hearings before the Permanent Select Committee on Intelligence, House of Representatives, 97th Congress, 2nd Session, Washington, DC, 1982. Also 'The Soviet Forgery War', *Wall Street Journal*, 13 July 1982.

18. Herbert Romerstein, *Soviet Support for International Terrorism*, Washington,

DC, 1981.

19. Sterling, *The Terror Network*, p. 17.

20. The 1982-3 controversy about 'Yellow Rain' demonstrates all these tendencies; see Robert L. Bartley and William P. Kucewicz, ' "Yellow Rain" and the Future of Arms Agreements', *Foreign Affairs*, Spring 1983; Stephen J. Solarz, 'Yellow Rain—Beyond a Reasonable Doubt', *Wall Street Journal*, 22 June 1983.

21. David J. Dallin and Boris I. Nicolaevsky, *Forced Labor in the Soviet Union*, New Haven, Conn., 1947.

22. Robert Conquest, *The Great Terror, Stalin's Purge of the Thirties*, New York, 1968.

23. Solzhenitsyn, *The Gulag Archipelago*. The writing of this monumental work in seven parts in Russian was completed in 1967 in the Soviet Union.

24. Barron, *KGB*, pp. 306-31.

25. Walter Krivitsky, *In Stalin's Secret Service*, New York, 1939.

26. Nikolai Khokhlov, *In the Name of Conscience*, New York, 1959.

27. Barron, *KGB*, p. 318.

28. Ibid., p. 318.

29. Ibid., p. 319.

30. 'Arafat Says PLO Aids Foreign Guerrilla Units', *Wall Street Journal*, 14 January 1982; 'Die Palästinensische Befreiungsorganisation', *Neue Zürcher Zeitung*, 22, 23 August 1982.

31. Ernst Halperin, 'Moskau und der internationale Terrorismus', *Neue Zürcher Zeitung*, 8 January 1982.

Chapter 6

1. *Rabotnichesko Delo*, 28 May 1962, as cited in James F. Brown, *Bulgaria under Communist Rule*, New York/London, 1970, p. 129.

2. Hugh Seton-Watson, *The Imperialist Revolutionaries*, Stanford, Calif., 1978, pp. 104-6; Brown, ibid., pp. 297-9.

3. James A. Field Jr., *America and the Mediterranean World*, Princeton, NJ, 1969, p. 362.

4. S. Radeff, *Stroitelite na Suvremenna Bulgaria*, vol. I, Sofia, 1973, p. 731 as cited in Stephen Constant (ine Daneff), *Foxy Ferdinand, Tsar of Bulgaria*, New York/London, 1980, p. 30.

5. L.A. Dellin (ed.), *Bulgaria*, Praeger, New York, 1957, p. 118, as cited in Constant, *Foxy Ferdinand*, p. 329.

6. Interview in *Die Weltwoche* (Zurich), 9 February 1983.

7. Ladislav Bittman, *The Deception Game*, Syracuse, NY, 1972, pp. 146-7.

8. This and subsequent references to specific Bulgarian actions, unless otherwise noted, are from Radio Free Europe Research Report Bulgaria/6, 'International Terrorism and "the Bulgarian Connection" ', Munich, 24 March 1982.

9. Interview in *Die Weltwoche* (Zurich), 9 February 1983.

10. Interview in *Le Quotidien* (Paris), 24 January 1983.

11. Nicaraguan Bares Plan to Discredit Foes', *Washington Post*, 19 June 1983.

12. FBIS, Cairo MENA in Arabic, 6 December 1978.

13. FBIS, Sofia BTA in English, 6 December 1978.

14. FBIS, Cairo Voice of the Arabs in Arabic, 6 December 1978.

15. *Literaturen Front*, 16 February, 1967, as cited in Brown, *Bulgaria under Communist Rule*, p. 260.

16. The Markov case is recounted in detail by Kyril Panoff, 'Murder on Waterloo Bridge', *Encounter* (London), November 1979.

17. In its plot to murder one of its defected writers, Virgil Tanase, in France in 1982, the Romanian regime (which may not benefit from such close KGB support as Bulgaria does) employed the ancient method of having an agent surreptitiously drop poison in a drink. The abortion of this scheme and the French DST's exposure of it, after the Romanians had awarded the would-be assassin a decoration, constitute one of the most dramatic propaganda successes any Western intelligence service has had against a communist country in recent years. 'Romanian Writer Describes French Foiling of Plot to Kill Him', *Washington Post*, 1 September 1982; 'Histoire d'une Mystification', *Le Monde*, 1 September 1982.

18. Ugur Mumcu, *Silah Kaçakçiligi ve Terör*, Istanbul, 1981/2 (six printings to date).

19. Statement to author in a personal interview in Ankara, 27 January 1983.

20. 'KINTEX Şirketi' in Mumcu, *Silah Kaçakçiligi ve Terör*, pp. 191-213.

21. 'The Current Situation', *Briefing* (Ankara), 27 December 1982, pp. 15-17.

Chapter 7

1. M.K. Dziewanowski, *Poland in the 20th Century*, New York, 1977, pp. 26-7.

2. Hugh Seton-Watson, *Nations and States*, Boulder, Colo., 1977, pp. 120-31.

3. Dziewanowski, *Poland in the 20th Century*, p. 82.

4. Vojtech Mastny, *Russia's Road to the Cold War*, New York, 1979, p. 26.

5. Janusz K. Zawodny, *Death in the Forest*, South Bend, Indiana, 1962, p. 24.

6. Mastny, *Russia's Road to the Cold War*, pp. 23-35.

7. *Hearings of the Select Committee on the Katyn Forest Massacre*, House of Representatives, 82nd Congress, 1st and 2nd Sessions, 1951-2, Part 4, Washington, DC, 1952, p. 777, as cited in Zawodny, *Death in the Forest*, p. 157.

8. 'The Poles Know Well of Soviet Guilt', *Washington Times*, 19 April 1983.

9. Zawodny, *Death in the Forest*, p. 182.

10. Ibid., p. 183.

11. Sarah Meiklejohn Terry, *Poland's Place in Europe*, Princeton, NJ, 1983, pp. 342-3.

12. Bruce Page, David Leitch and Philip Knightley, *The Philby Conspiracy*, New York, 1981; Introduction by John Le Carré, pp. 6-7.

13. Jan Nowak provides a vivid, brief first-hand account of the Warsaw Uprising in *Courier from Warsaw*, Detroit, 1982, pp. 343-88. There are many others.

14. Michael Charlton, 'On the Origins of the Cold War—I, The Spectre of Yalta', *Encounter* (London), June 1983, pp. 7-28.

15. The figures are from an official Polish publication issued in 1960 as cited in Dziewanowski, *Poland in the 20th Century*, p. 143.

16. Francis X. Murphy, *The Papacy Today*, New York, 1981, pp. 181-2.

17. Leopold Unger, 'The People versus the Party', *Wilson Quarterly*, Spring 1983, pp. 50-68.

18. Cited in Jan Nowak, 'The Church in Poland', *Problems of Communism*, January-February 1982, pp. 1-16.

19. Among the best recent collections of timely material on Poland's problems are two special issues of the London journal *Survey* devoted exclusively to Poland, Nos. 109, 110, Fall 1979/Winter 1980. See also the special section on Poland in the *Wilson Quarterly*, Spring 1983, pp. 48-87.

20. Nowak, 'The Church in Poland', p. 12.

21. Ibid., p. 11.

22. 'Attack on the Pope: New Link to the Bulgarians', *New York Times*, 23 March 1983.

23. Murphy, *The Papacy Today*, p. 183.

24. Ibid., p. 179.

25. 'The Polish Population of the USSR: Partial Results of the 1979 Soviet Census', RFE/RL Research Report RL 125/80, Munich, 27 March 1980.

26. 'The Twelfth Report of the Lithuanian *Chronicle* on Catholics in the USSR', RFE/RL Research Report RL 124/83, Munich, 21 March 1983; 'Lithuanians Retain their Share of Population in the Lithuanian SSR', RFE/RL Research Report RL 118/80, 25 March 1980; Alex Alexiev, 'The Kremlin and the Pope', Rand Corporation Report P-6855, Santa Monica, Calif., March 1983.

27. 'Cardinal Julijans Vaivods and the Catholic Church in Latvia', RFE/RL Research Report RL 72/83, Munich, 8 February 1983; Alexiev, 'The Kremlin and the Pope', p. 7.

28. Roman Szporluk, 'The Ukraine and the Ukrainians' in *Handbook of Major Soviet Nationalities*, New York/London, 1975, pp. 21-48.

29. 'The Ukraine and Ukrainians in the USSR' RFE/RL Research Report RL 100/80, Munich, 11 March 1980; 'The Ukraine and Ukrainians in the USSR: Additional Data from the Soviet Census of 1979', RFE/RL Research Report RL 339/80, Munich, 23 September 1980.

30. Wladislaw Bukowinski, *Wspomienia z Kazachstanu*, Biblioteka Spotkan, Paris, 1979.

31. The quotation is from the journal *Voprosy Nauchnovo Ateizma* (*Questions of Scientific Atheism*) as cited in 'Increasing Activity of the Ukrainian Catholic Church in the Western Ukraine', RFE/RL Research Report RL 119/83, Munich, 16 March 1983.

32. Citied in RFE/RL Research Report RL 119/83 as noted in preceding footnote. See also RFE/RL Report RL 220/83, 'Group Formed to Defend Catholics Rights in the Ukraine', Munich, 6 June 1983.

33. N.O. Safronova, *Uniats'ka Tserkva i fashizm*, Lvov, 1981, as cited in RFE/RL Research Report RL 119/83 as noted in footnote 31.

34. B.Ya. Ramm in an article in *Questions of Scientific Atheism* as cited in RFE/RL Research Report RL 119/83 as noted above.

35. Ibid., in an article by P.K. Kurochkin.

36. 'Poland: "I will be a Milder Hangman" ', *Wall Street Journal*, 31 December 1981.

Chapter 8

1. For example, in Ugur Mumcu, *Agca Dosyasi*, Istanbul, 1983.

2. 'S. Sirri Kadem' in Ugur Mumcu, *Terörsüz Özgürlük*, Istanbul, 1982, pp. 81-4. The other organizations Agca listed in addition to Teslim Töre's THKO, were *Emegin Birligi, Akincilar, Ülkücüler, Halkin Kurtuluşu* and *THKP-C*.

3. 'Unutulan Adresler' in Mumcu, *Terörsüz Özgürlük*.

4. 'The Plot to Murder the Pope', *Reader's Digest*, September 1982.

5. This is a strong argument against the notion that Agca might merely have been hired by smugglers to kill Abdi Ipekçi to deter him from pursuing investigative reporting on their activities. The idea that Turkish smugglers could have had any interest of their own in assassinating the Pope is hard to rationalize under any circumstances. Some commentators who wish to avoid recognizing the implications of the Bulgarian/Soviet connection have nevertheless tried to advance it.

6. This discovery came long after Agca had escaped. The failure of the investigators and the court to follow through on the issue of his bank accounts is only one of many aspects of Agca's background that were not probed in the confusion of 1979. The

reopened investigation that began in December 1982 may shed further light on these questions.

7. This process began in June 1983 when two Turkish officers were permitted to come to Rome to talk extensively to Agca.

8. Mumcu, *Agca Dosyasi*, esp. pp. 51-7, 88-92, 135-9.

9. Columnist Hasan Pulur in *Hürriyet*, 21 July 1983, provides firsthand recollection of the publishing of the Sertel memoirs. He served as intermediary between Ipekçi and Sertel in negotiating for them. As the series began to appear, *Milliyet* was flooded with protest letters demanding cessation of publication. These letters echoed attacks in the Soviet-sponsored broadcasting stations *Bizim Radyo* and 'The Voice of the Turkish Communist Party'. On checking the letters, *Milliyet* found all the names and addresses unverifiable and apparently false. Subsequently the expulsion of Sertel from the Turkish Writers' Federation was announced in the leftist press. The executive committee of the Federation had engineered the expulsion without the knowledge of the Federation's president, playwright Aziz Nesin. Nesin resigned in protest and the expulsion was reversed. Leftist writer Kemal Sülker subsequently published a 242-page book attempting to refute Sertel's recollections: *Nazim Hikmet'in Sahte Dostlari* (Istanbul, 1979). It attacks Ipekçi and *Milliyet* as representatives of the 'rightist press'. This sequence of events demonstrates how deeply the Sertel memoirs angered Moscow. It provides further evidence that Ipekçi was not antagonizing the right in Turkey during this period.

10. The background of these issues is dealt with at length in Paul B. Henze, 'Turkey, the Alliance and the Middle East', Smithsonian Wilson Center, International Security Series Working Paper 36, Washington, DC, December 1981.

11. Paul B. Henze, *Goal: Destabilization—Soviet Agitational Propaganda, Instability and Terrorism in NATO South*, EAISR Reprint Series RS-13-1, Marina del Rey, Calif., December 1981. Also Paul B. Henze, 'The Long Effort to Destabilize Turkey', *Wall Street Journal*, 7 October 1981.

12. Ugur Mumcu, who likes to cite file numbers and excerpts from numbered police reports as well as eye-witness statements, provides none to support his repeated contentions in *Agca Dosyasi* that Oral Çelik was the evil genius who managed Agca's terrorist career. Unless Mumcu has information which he regards as too sensitive to divulge, his case rests largely on his own contrivance.

13. When Güneş did brief Ecevit, he had to fly to Antalya where Ecevit was holding talks with visiting Bulgarian Prime Minister Zhivkov. If the Bulgarians were involved with Agca in Turkey at this stage, this is indeed an ironic coincidence.

14. Hasan Fehmi Güneş's statements in 1979 were much less equivocal. He encouraged the characterization of Agca as a Gray Wolf. He gave similar judgements in 1981 in the immediate wake of the shooting in Rome. He first expressed the view that Agca was neither rightist nor leftist to Claire Sterling in late 1981. She cites him specifically in her *Reader's Digest* article of September 1982.

15. To the question 'Why was the interrogation not extended?' Güneş in this same *Yanki* interview gave an intriguingly equivocal answer: 'I cannot at present tell you why it was not extended. I know, but I cannot say. Because of the responsibility I carried at that time I will ask you not to go into this issue.'

16. This fact alone negates the Bulgarian claim that it would have been impossible for the Bulgarian authorities to have known who Agca was when he arrived in Bulgaria in July 1980. His name had become a household word in Turkey. His picture was printed thousands of times in Turkish newspapers. Bulgarians could not have been unaware of his identity no matter what name he had on his passport. As we shall see in Chapter 9, there is good evidence that he was received in Bulgaria with full knowledge of his identity and background.

Chapter 9

1. The characterizations are from Alex Alexiev, 'The Kremlin and the Pope', Rand Corporation Report P-6855, April 1983, on which I have drawn extensively, with permission of the author, for this section. A condensed version of this study appeared in the *Wall Street Journal*, 30 March 1983.

2. Both Novosti dispatches on the Pope are cited from the RFE/RL Report RL 414/81, 'How the Pope is Faring in the Soviet Media', Munich, 19 October 1981.

3. Ibid. There has been a great deal of misunderstanding of this issue. John Paul II's attitude toward it is based on intimate experience with organizations such as 'PAX' in Poland and 'Pacem in Terris' in Czechoslovakia which were set up with the aim of drawing priests and laymen away from the discipline of the church and into communist-directed political and social activity—i.e. activity in support of the totalitarian regime. The church in Eastern Europe, therefore, and nowhere more successfully than in Poland, has opposed this kind of politicization of the priesthood. The new Pope disappointed social activists in the church in Latin America by disapproving of their activities which, for the most part, have been directed *against* established authority rather than undertaken in support of it. They are also, in some countries, working closely with protest and rebel movements which enjoy the sympathy and material support of Havana and Moscow. Some of the 'progressive' critics of the Pope's stance find themselves in the dilemma of supporting Moscow's exploitation of such movements in the church in Latin America for its own political purposes while being lukewarm or even chilly toward his concern with using the force of the church to advance genuine freedom in Eastern Europe and the USSR. Cf. Francis X. Murphy, *The Papacy Today*, New York, 1981, pp. 186-94.

4. *Soviet Analyst*, 28 June 1979, as cited in Alexiev, 'The Kremlin and the Pope'.

5. RFE/RL Report RL 119.83, 'Increasing Activity of the Ukrainian Catholic Church in the Western Ukraine', Munich, 16 March 1983.

6. Alexiev, 'The Kremlin and the Pope', pp. 3-4.

7. *Problemy Mira i Sotsializma* 9/1979, pp. 54-5.

8. I.V. Poluk, 'O praktike raboty po protivodeistsviyu katolicheskoi i uniatskoi propagandy,' *Voprosy Nauchnovo Ateizma*, 28, 1981, pp. 202-3.

9. Ibid., pp. 202-3.

10. References for these and previous citations are in RFE/RL Report RL 414/81 as cited in note 2 above.

11. Most of this information on Agca's movements in Turkey before escaping into Iran is included in Ugur Mumcu's *Agca Dosyasi*, Istanbul, 1983.

12. *New York Post*, 4 September 1981; *Hürriyet* (Istanbul), 30 September 1981.

13. This name has been very confusingly reported, first coming out as 'Mustafa Eof'; the name could also be Mustafayeff; other variations are possible.

14. Well over 10 per cent of the Bulgarian population of nine million is Turkish; in addition, there is a sizable group of native Slavic Muslims called Pomaks. Some knowledge of Turkish is not uncommon in Bulgaria among non-Muslims.

15. *Yeni Düşünce* (Istanbul), 28 January 1983, pp. 16-18.

16. Çelebi apparently learned in the summer of 1981 that I was doing research on the papal plot. I received a parcel of Türkeş-oriented publications including *Yen Hedef* in the mail in the late summer. More than a year later I noted the return address on the envelope: 'M. Serdar Çelebi, Gutleutstrasse 173, 6 Frankfurt/M. 1, W. Germany'.

17. 'Soviets Say 1981 Polish Crisis Spurred Dissent in Estonia', *Washington Post*, 20 April 1983.

18. Alexiev, 'The Kremlin and the Pope'; RFE/RL Research Report 414/81, 19 October 1981.

19. Bronislaw Piasecki, *Ostatnie Dni Primasa Tysiaclecia*, Rome, 1982.

20. Ugur Mumcu's two articles on Agca in Majorca published in *Cumhuriyet* (Istanbul), 22, 23 February 1983, include most of the tales that have developed about his activities there.

Chapter 10

1. *Literaturnaya Gazeta* of 11 March 1981 contains an especially virulent example.

2. RFE/RL Research Report RL 33/83, 'Soviet Media Reaction to the Possible "Bulgarian Connection" ', Munich, 17 January 1983.

3. The *New York Times* reporter Henry Kamm was in error when he asserted in a dispatch datelined Rome, 30 December 1982, that 'the Soviet Union has not in many years directed strong public criticism against a pope'. Vilification in the provincial press, which had been going on for a long time, was as official—and probably more indicative of basic Soviet positions—as statements issued by TASS in Moscow.

4. *Hürriyet* (Istanbul), 17 December 1982.

5. The only NATO countries through which Agca is known to have traveled, in addition to Turkey, where he started, are Germany and Italy. Spain, at the time Agca was in Majorca, had not yet joined NATO.

6. Zhivkov got a boost from a surprising source, the plush international business magazine *Leaders* in its first quarterly issue of 1983—which featured Zhivkov on the cover and devoted its lead story to 'The most successful and most stable of all the Eastern European Nations'—Bulgaria. Little is known about the sources of support for *Leaders*; an effort to determine the origin of the story was reported in *The Washington Times*, 23 March 1983.

7. Ugur Mumcu, *Agca Dosyasi*, Istanbul, 1983, p. 107.

8. In a book Mumcu published recently—*Suçlular ve Güçlüler*, Istanbul, 1982—he repeats analysis he wrote during the 1970s based on forgeries without any reference to the fact that the documents cited have been exposed as fabrications.

9. Agca was not the first young man from Malatya to shoot a prominent Turkish journalist. The internationally well-known editor of the then prestigious Istanbul daily *Vatan*, Ahmed Emin Yalman, was shot in Malatya in November 1952, but survived. His assailant, Hüseyin Üzmez, the son of a poor working woman, was a gifted high school student who had been recruited by a group of plotters who purportedly acted out of religious-nationalist sentiments. He was tried in 1953, along with 14 accomplices, and sentenced to 20 years of imprisonment. Yalman, who had been educated in the United States and had close American friends, was himself convinced that the Russians had been behind the assassination attempt; see his *Turkey in My Time*, Norman, Okla. 1956, pp. 252-61. Ugur Mumcu in 1982 interviewed Üzmez, now living in Ankara, who claimed to have had a conversation on a visit back to Malatya 'a year and a half or so' before the assassination of Abdi Ipekçi with a group of boys in the courtyard of a mosque. One of them who asked Üzmez whether he was sorry he had shot Yalman, Üzmez—according to Mumcu—believed might have been Agca. How he made this identification is not clear and lack of dates makes it impossible to determine whether Agca is likely to have been in Malatya at that time. The setting for the meeting—the courtyard of a mosque—sounds conveniently contrived to give the impression of Islamic orientation. Mumcu devotes ten pages of *Agca Dosyasi* (pp. 114-24) to deductions from this conversation. He concludes that Agca was probably planning, out of rightist motivation, to kill Ipekçi at this time, but both the reasoning and the motivation behind the plan are unclear. Only Agca can tell us whether he was aware of Üzmez's deed (which is now seldom recalled in Turkey) and whether he ever talked to him.

10. As a headline story in *Hürriyet* (Istanbul), 1 October 1982; by Ugur Mumcu; also by ABC in the US.

11. Rowland Evans and Robert Novak, 'With a Forged Memo, the Soviets Counterattack', *Washington Post*, 30 March 1983.

12. 'Religion Remains Heart of Revolutionary Ethiopia', *New York Times*, 25 June 1983.

13. According to a defected Nicaraguan specialist in covert operations who worked closely with Soviet and Cuban advisers, harassment of the Pope during his visit to Managua was a high priority communist objective. 'Nicaraguan Bares Plan to Discredit Foes', *Washington Post*, 19 June 1983.

INDEX